The Invention of the Americas

The Invention of the Americas

Eclipse of "the Other"

and the Myth of Modernity

ENRIQUE DUSSEL

Translated by Michael D. Barber

CONTINUUM • NEW YORK

1995
The Continuum Publishing Company
370 Lexington Avenue
New York, NY 10017

Printed in the United States of America

Library of Congress Cataloging-in-Publication Data

Dussel, Enrique D.
  [1492. English]
  The invention of the Americas: eclipse of "the other" and the myth of
modernity / Enrique Dussel ; translated by Michael D. Barber.
      p. cm.
  Includes bibliographical references and index.
  ISBN 0-8264-0796-X (acid-free)
    1. America—Discovery and exploration—Spanish. 2. Indians—First
contact with Europeans. 3. Columbus, Christopher—Influence.
  I. Title
E123.D8913   1995
970.01'6—dc20   94-47964
                                                                    CIP

Contents

Translator's Acknowledgments   7

Preface   9

PART ONE
From the European Ego: The Covering Over • 15

Chapter 1: Eurocentrism   19

Chapter 2: From the Invention to the Discovery
of the New World   27

Chapter 3: From the Conquest to the Colonization
of the Life-World   37

Chapter 4 : The Spiritual Conquest: Toward the Encounter
between Two Worlds?   49

PART TWO
Transition: The Copernican Revolution
of the Hermeneutic Key • 59

Chapter 5: Critique of the Myth of Modernity   63

Chapter 6: Amerindia in a Non-Eurocentric Vision
of World History   73

PART THREE
From the Invasion to the Dis-covery of the Other • 91

Chapter 7: From the Parousia of the Gods to the
Invasion   95
Chapter 8: From the Resistance to the End of the World
and the Sixth Sun   106

Epilogue: The Multiple Visages of the One People and
the Sixth Sun   119

Appendix 1: Diverse Meanings of the Terms *Europe,*
The Occident, Modernity, Late Capitalism   133
Appendix 2: Two Paradigms of Modernity   136
Appendix 3: From the Discovery of the Atlantic to 1502   141
Appendix 4: Map of the Fourth Asiatic Peninsula
of Henry Martellus (Florence 1489)   142

Notes   145
Chronology   211
Index   214

Translator's Acknowledgments

The translator would like to thank Enrique Dussel, and Justus George Lawler of Continuum for his continued interest in this project. Thanks are due also to Mrs. Virginia Duckworth for editing assistance and Mr. Ollie L. Roundtree for technical assistance.

I have translated the German texts (e.g., from Kant, Hegel, Marx) on the basis of Dussel's Spanish translations of those texts, since he frequently utilizes ellipses to omit several pages and since other English translations of these texts would not adequately convey Dussel's own reasons for combining such texts in a single quotation.

Preface

As Richard Bernstein has shown so well in *The New Constellation*,[1] we face a new historical moment and a new constellation of philosophical problems and questions. In this book, I consider a constellation which European or United States thinkers often neglect and which involves far more than what Ihab Hassan has called an "ideological commitment to *minorities* in politics, sex, and language."[2] I focus on the *immense majority* of humanity, the seventy-five per cent of the world situated in the southern hemisphere, the excolonial world. These exploited, excluded, and poor peoples, whom Fanon termed the "wretched of the earth," consume less than fifteen per cent of the planet's income. Their history of oppression began five hundred years ago.

This history of world domination originates with modernity, which thinkers such as Charles Taylor,[3] Stephen Toulmin,[4] or Jürgen Habermas[5] consider as exclusively a European occurrence, having nothing to do with the so-called Third World. The expositions of these thinkers explain modernity by referring *only to classical European and North American authors and events*. My undertaking here differs from theirs, since I argue that while modernity is undoubtedly a European occurrence, it also originates in a dialetical relation with non-Europe. Modernity appears when Europe organizes the initial world-system and places itself at the center of world history over against a periphery equally constitutive of modernity. The forgetting of the periphery, which took place from the end of the fifteenth, Hispanic–Lusitanian century to the beginning of the seventeenth century, has led great thinkers of the center to commit the Eurocentric fallacy in understanding modernity. Because of a partial, regional, and *provincial* grasp of modernity, the postmodern critique and Habermas's defense of modernity are equally unilateral and partially false. The traditional Eurocentric thesis, flourishing in the United States, modernity's culmination, is that modernity expanded to the barbarian cultures of the South undoubtedly in need of modernization. One can only explain this new-sounding but age-old thesis by returning to medieval Europe to discover the motives which produced modernity and permitted its dissemination.[6] Max Weber first posed the question of world history Eurocentrically:

> Which chain of circumstances has resulted in the fact that *on Western soil*[7] and only there cultural phenomena have been produced which, as we[8] represent it, show signs of evolutionary advance and universal validity?[9]

Europe possessed, according to this paradigm, exceptional internal characteristics which permitted it to surpass all other cultures in rationality. This thesis, which adopts a Eurocentric (as opposed to world) paradigm, reigns not only in Europe and the United States, but also among intellectuals in the peripheral world. The pseudo-scientific periodization of history into Antiquity, the Middle (preparatory) Ages, and finally the Modern (European) Age is an ideological construct which deforms world history. One must break with this reductionist horizon to open to a world and planetary perspective— and there is an ethical obligation toward other cultures to do so.

Chronology reflects geopolitics. According to the Eurocentric paradigm, modern subjectivity especially developed between the times of the Italian Renaissance and the Reformation and of the Enlightenment in Germany and the French Revolution. Everything occurred in Europe.

I wish to present a new, world-encompassing paradigm that conceives modernity as the culture incorporating Amerindia[10] and managing a world-system,[11] which does not exist as an independent, self-producing, or self-referential entity, but as a part, as the center, of that system. Modernity is a world phenomenon, commencing with the *simultaneous* constitution of Spain with reference to its periphery, Amerindia, including the Caribbean, Mexico, and Peru. *At the same time*, Europe, with diachronic precedents in Renaissance Italy and Portugal, proceeds to establish itself as the center managing a growing periphery. The center gradually shifts from Spain to Holland and then to England and France even as the periphery grows in the sixteenth century in Amerindia and Brazil, on the African coasts of the slave trade, and in Poland;[12] in the seventeenth century in Latin America, North America, Caribbean, coastal Africa, and Eastern Europe;[13] and in the Ottoman Empire, Russia, some Indian kingdoms, Southeast Asia, and continental Africa up until the mid-nineteenth century.[14] When one conceives modernity as part of center-periphery system instead of an independent European phenomenon, the meanings of modernity, its origin, development, present crisis, and its postmodern antithesis change.

Furthermore, Europe's centrality reflects no internal superiority accumulated in the Middle Ages, but it is the outcome of its discovery, conquest, colonization, and integration of Amerindia—all of which give it an advantage over the Arab world, India, and China. Modernity is the result, not the cause, of this occurrence. Later, the managerial position of Europe permits it to think of itself as the reflexive consciousness of world history and to exult in its values, inventions, discoveries, technology, and political institutions as its exclusive achievement. But these achievements result from the *displacement* of an ancient interregional system born between Egypt and Mesopotamia and found later in India and China. In Europe itself, a series of displacements occur from Renaissance Italy to Portugal to Spain to Flanders and England. Even capitalism is the fruit, not the cause, of Europe's world extension and its centrality in the world- system. Europe hegemonizes the human experience of forty-five hundred years of political, economic, technological, cultural relations within the Asian-African-Mediterranean interregional system. Never the center and during most of its history the periphery, Europe rises to ascendency when it finds itself blocked on the east by Islam and embarks upon the Atlantic in a history that began in Genoa (Italy). Following Portugal's initiative, Spain then moves westward and transforms Amerindia into its periphery without any challenge, in part because China never sought an eastward passage to Europe.

In this book, I will seek the origin of the "myth of modernity," which justifies European violence and is distinct from modernity's rational, emancipative concept. Postmoderns, such as Lyotard, Vattimo, and Rorty,[15] criticize modern rationality as an instrument of terror, but I criticize it for concealing its own irrational myth. I endeavor to overcome modernity through "transmodernity, a project of the future"—which could serve as an alternate title of this book.

The birthdate of modernity[16] is 1492, even though its gestation, like that of the fetus, required a period of intrauterine growth. Whereas modernity gestated in the free, creative medieval European cities, it came to birth in Europe's confrontation with the Other. By controlling, conquering, and violating the Other, Europe defined itself as discoverer, conquistador, and colonizer of an alterity likewise constitutive of modernity. Europe never discovered (*des-cubierto*) this Other as Other but covered over (*encubierto*) the Other as part of the Same: i.e., Europe. Modernity dawned in 1492 and with it the myth of a special kind of sacrificial violence which eventually eclipsed whatever was non-European.

Since I originally delivered these lectures in Frankfurt, I should like to recall the great thinkers of this city, such as Hegel, who lived his adolescence here, and the Frankfurt School, which bears the city's name.[17] By reflecting on historical events, I hope to clarify the possibility of an intercultural philosophical dialogue, such as I have already initiated with Karl-Otto Apel. Although according to Montaigne or Rorty diverse cultures or life-worlds are incommunicable and incommensurable, I want to develop a philosophy of dialogue as part of a philosophy of liberation of the oppressed, the excommunicated, the excluded, the Other. It will be necessary to analyze the historical, hermeneutic conditions of the possibility of intercultural communication. I will strive to spell out these conditions by means of the philosophy of liberation, which starts from alterity, from the one "compelled" into dialogue[18] or excluded from it (the dominated and exploited culture), and from concrete and historical events. The philosophy of liberation begins by affirming alterity, but it also recognizes negative aspects such as the concrete, empirical impossibility of the excluded or dominated one ever being able to intervene *effectively* in dialogue. This inability applies not only to argumentation but even to Rorty's "conversation," since Rorty himself, who denies the possibility of the rational dialogue I desire, fails to take seriously the asymmetric situation of the excluded Other.[19]

I write this preface in Seville as I edit the lectures. This was the land of the Moors, Muslims until that tragic January 6, 1492, when the Catholic kings occupied Granada, handed over by Boabdil, who was the last sultan to tread upon European soil. At this terminal moment of the Middle Ages, a pressured man rushed among the camps of the barbaric Christians, who were far inferior to the subtlety, education, and customs of the ancient caliphate of Córdoba. This man endeavored to sell his ideas to the kings who were involved in their own buying and selling in the *Capitulaciones de Santa Fe*. This man, the last daring navigator of the western Mediterranean hemmed in by Islam, wanted to set out for India via the ocean, the secondary sea, the Atlantic. Just as the Christians occupied Malaga and cut off the heads of Andalusian Muslims in 1487, the same would happen to the "Indians," the inhabitants and victims of the newly discovered continent.[20] The conquest meant broken alliances and treaties, the elimination of the vanquished elites, endless tortures, demands that one betray one's religion and culture under pain of death or expulsion, land seizures, and the distribution of inhabitants among the Christian captains of the conquest. After centuries of experimentation in Andalusia, this victimizing and sacrificial violence parading as innocence began its long destructive path.

Next to the Guadalquivir River in Seville stands the Tower of Gold, which reminds one of the century of "gold," the coast "of the pearls," the "gold" coast (in Panama), the "rich" coast (*Costa Rica*), the rich port (*Puerto Rico*), "Argentina" (from *argentum*, silver).[21] By this tower passed "much of the gold extracted from here, which goes to the kingdoms of Europe and which is more valuable because of the blood of Indians in whose skins it is wrapped as it journeys to Europe."[22] By this tower passed Indian riches en route to Flanders and the wealth of Africa en route to India and China. This is the tower . . . where a new god began to be idolatrously adored . . . a god demanding victims for its violence and continuing these demands to this day.

One ought to remember the theme of this book every October 12 in years to come. What should be one's ethical and rational option in the face of this landmark event, rendered banal by propaganda, superficial disputes, and political, ecclesial, and financial interests?

I WOULD LIKE finally to thank the Johann Wolfgang Goethe University of Frankfurt for having invited me to deliver these lectures from October to December 1992.[23] Also I am grateful to Vanderbilt University, where I taught during the autumn semester in 1991. Especially, I am indebted to the philosophy department of the UAM/Iztapalapa and to the National System of Investigations (Mexico), both of which have enabled me to do this research.

PART ONE

From the European Ego:
The Covering Over

I n this first part, I will take up the European perspective and develop it as completely as possible. Since I have only limited space, this can hardly be an exhaustive study. My themes are for that reason abstract figures (*Gestalten*) in the process that constituted modern subjectivity and culminated in Descartes's expression of the *cogito* in 1636.[1] Spain and Portugal (though I concentrate on the former) at the end of the fifteenth century formed only a segment of the feudal world, or perhaps better, they were Renaissance nations and thus part of the first step toward modernity. Before the rest of Europe, they subjected the Other to conquest and to the dominion of the *center* over the *periphery*. Europe then established itself as the "center" of the world (in the planetary sense) and brought forth modernity and its myth.

It is necessary to include Spain in this originative process, since at the end of the fifteenth century it was the only European power with the capacity for external territorial conquest, as it had already shown in the conquest of Granada. At the same time, Latin America also rediscovered its own *place* in the history of modernity as the *first periphery* of modern Europe. From the very beginning, Latin America endured the effects of global modernization later to be felt in Africa and Asia. Although South America was already known—as mapmaker Henricus Martellus showed in Rome in 1489—only Spain, thanks to King Ferdinand of Aragon's political skill and Columbus's daring, tried formally and publicly to set forth upon the Atlantic to reach India. This adventure was not merely anecdotal or historiographic; it was the birth of *modern subjectivity*.

CHAPTER
1

Eurocentrism

> Universal history goes from East to West. Europe
> is absolutely the end of universal history. . . . Uni-
> versal history is the discipline of the indomitable
> natural will directed toward universality and sub-
> jective liberty.
>
> —Hegel, *Philosophy of Universal History*

A myth lies hidden in the emancipatory concept of modernity that I am going to develop in the course of this book. But first I will discuss a subtle, masked component that subtends much philosophical reflection and many European and North American theoretical assumptions. Eurocentrism and its concomitant component, the developmentalist fallacy, are at issue here.[1] First, consider what Kant in 1784 writes in "Answering the Question: What Is Enlightenment?":

> Enlightenment (*Aufklärung*) is the exit[2] of humanity by itself from a state of culpable immaturity (*verschuldeten Unmün-digkeit*). . . . Laziness and cowardliness are the causes which

bind the great part of humanity in this frivolous state of immaturity.[3]

For Kant, immature culture is culpable and its ethos lazy and cowardly. Today one needs to ask Kant: Ought one to consider an African in Africa or a slave in the United States in the eighteenth century to be culpably immature? What about an indigenous person in Mexico or a Latin American mestizo at a later period?

In the *Vorlesungen über die Philosophie der Weltgeschichte*, Hegel portrays world history (*Weltgeschichte*) as the self-realization of God, as a theodicy[4] of reason and of liberty (*Freiheit*), and as a process of Enlightenment (*Aufklärung*):

> Universal history represents . . . the *development* of the consciousness which Spirit has of its liberty and the evolving realization that history is established through such consciousness. The *development* implies a *series of phases*, a series of determinations of liberty, which are born from its concept, that is, from the naturalness of liberty becoming conscious of itself. . . . This necessity or necessary series of pure abstract determinations of the concept are studied in Logic.[5]

In Hegelian ontology, the concept of development (*Entwicklung*) plays a central role. This concept determines the movement of the concept (*Begriff*) until it culminates in the idea—that is, as it moves from indeterminate being to the absolute knowledge in the *Logic*. Development (*Entwicklung*) unfolds according to a linear dialectic; although originarily an ontological category, today it is primarily considered as a sociological[6] one with implications for world history. Furthermore, this development has a direction:

> Universal history goes from East to West. Europe is absolutely the *end of universal history*. Asia is the beginning.[7]

But this alleged East-West movement clearly precludes Latin America and Africa from world history and characterizes Asia as essentially confined to a state of immaturity and childhood (*Kindheit*)[8]:

> The world is divided into the Old World and the New World, and the latter derives from the fact that America . . . was not

known until recently *for the Europeans*. But this division is not
purely external, but *essential* since this world is new not only
relatively but also absolutely. It is new with respect to *all its
own physical and political characteristics.* . . . The chain of
islands extending between South America and Asia appears
immature and recently formed. . . . Similarly, New Holland
gives the appearance of geographical youthfulness since if one
departs the English possessions toward the wilderness one
finds enormous rivers which still have not carved out their river
beds. . . . Regarding America, especially Mexico or Peru, and
its degree of civilization, our information indicates that its culture expires the moment the Spirit draws near (*sowie der Geist
sich ihr näherte*). . . . The inferiority of these individuals in
every respect is entirely evident.[9]

The immaturity (*Umreife*) marking America is total and physical;
even the vegetables and the animals are more primitive, brutal, monstrous, or simply more weak or degenerate.[10] For this reason:

In what refers to its elements, America's formation is not yet
finished. . . . [Latin] America is, as a result, the land of the
future, which will reveal its historical importance. . . . As the
land of the future, America does not interest us, and besides
the philosopher makes no prophecies.[11]

Latin America, for all that, remains outside world history, as
does Africa. Although there is a trinity (Europe, Asia, and Africa),
nevertheless Africa is always set to the side:

The three parts of the world[12] maintain, then, among themselves an essential relation and they constitute a totality
(*Totalität*). . . . The Mediterranean Sea unites these three parts
of the world, and that fact converts it into the center (*Mit-
telpunkt*) of all universal history. . . . The Mediterranean is the
axis of universal history.[13]

There is thus the concept of the center of history. But of the
three parts which constitute the totality (here Latin America is
simply excluded[14]), two of them will remain inferior. Regarding
Africa, Hegel wrote some pages worth reading, although one
must take them with a grain of salt because they culminate in a
superficial, fantastic, racist ideology. They betray an infinite sense

of superiority, which exposes the state of mind of Europe at the beginning of the nineteenth century:

> Africa is in general a closed land, and it maintains this fundamental character.[15] It is characteristic of the blacks that their consciousness has not yet even arrived at the intuition of any objectivity, as for example, of God or the law, in which humanity relates to the world and intuits its essence. . . . He [the black person] is a human being in the rough.[16]

These are among the most insulting pages in the philosophical analysis of world history. After this, Hegel concludes:

> This mode of being of the Africans explains the fact that it is extraordinarily easy to make them fanatics. The Reign of the Spirit is among them so poor and the Spirit in itself so intense (*das Reich des Geistes ist dort so arm and doch der Geist in sich so intensiv*), that a representation that is inculcated in them suffices to impel them not to respect anything and to destroy everything. . . . Africa . . . does not properly have a history. For this reason, we abandon Africa, we will mention it *no more*. It is not part of the historical world; it does not present movement or historical development. . . . What we understand properly of Africa is something isolated and lacking in history, submerged completely in the natural spirit, and mentionable only as the threshold of universal history.[17]

European pride, the Hegelian unmeasuredness that Kierkegaard ironizes so effectively, shows itself in this paradigmatic text. In addition, Asia plays a purely introductory, infantile role in the development of world history. Since world history moves from East to West, Hegel first set aside Latin America, which is not situated in the East of the extreme Orient, but in the "East" of the Atlantic, and then Africa, the barbarian South, immature, cannibalistic, and bestial:

> Asia is the part of the world where the beginning is verified as such . . . But Europe is absolutely the center and the end (*das Zentrum und das Ende*)[18] of the ancient world and the Occident; Asia is the absolute Orient.[19]

But in Asia, the Spirit is in its infancy, and despotism permits only that one person (the emperor) be free. Asia serves as the dawn,

but in no way as the culmination of world history. Europe functions as the beginning and end of history, even though there are
diverse Europes. For instance, in southern Europe, "the land of the
South of the Pyrenees,"[20] the south of France, and Italy, the Spirit
dwelt in antiquity, when the north of Europe was still uncultivated
(*unkultiviert*). But the South "does not have a nucleus (*Kern*)
stamped in itself,"[21] and for that reason its destiny lies in northern
Europe. There are even two Norths: the east (Poland and Russia),
which is relatively negligible since always in relation with Asia; and
that which is important, the western part of the north of Europe:

> Germany, France, Denmark, the Scandinavian countries are
> the heart of Europe (*das Herz Europas*).[22]

Here Hegel becomes emotional. One can hear in his words the
timbre of Wagner's trumpets. He writes:

> The Germanic Spirit (*germanische Geist*) is the Spirit of the
> New World (*neuen Welt*),[23] whose end is the realization of the
> absolute truth, as the infinite self-determination of liberty that
> has for its content its proper absolute form. The principle of
> the German Empire ought to accommodate the Christian reli-
> gion. The destiny of the Germanic peoples is that of serving as
> the bearer of the Christian principle.[24]

Hegel, expressing a thesis exactly contrary to that which I want
to prove, writes on the German peoples:

> The ideal superior signification is that of Spirit, which returns
> into itself from out of the dullness of consciousness. The con-
> sciousness of its own self-justification arises and mediates the
> reestablishment of Christian liberty. The Christian principle
> has passed through the formidable discipline of culture; and
> the Reformation also gives it its exterior boundary, *along
> with the discovery of America*. . . . The principle of the free
> Spirit has made itself here the flag of the world, and from it
> universal principles of reason have developed. . . . Custom
> and tradition are no longer of value; distinct rights need to be
> founded on rational principles. Thus the liberty of the Spirit is
> being realized.[25]

That is to say, for Hegel, modern Christian Europe has nothing to learn from other worlds or other cultures. It possesses its own principle in itself, and is its full realization:

> The principle has been fulfilled, and therefore the End of Days has arrived: the idea of Christianity has reached its full realization.[26]

The three stages of the German world portray the development of this one Spirit through the kingdoms of the Father, the Son, and the Holy Spirit.[27] The Germanic empire is the kingdom of the totality, in which we see previous epochs repeat themselves,[28] such as the first epoch, the Germanic migrations in the time of the Roman Empire, and the second epoch, the feudal Middle Ages. Everything concludes with three final events: the Renaissance of letters and arts, the discovery of America, and the passage toward India around the Cape of Good Hope to the south of Africa. These three events end the terrible night of the Middle Ages, but do not yet constitute the new age. The third age, modernity, begins with the Lutheran Reformation, a German event, which reaches its fulfillment in the Enlightenment and the French Revolution. Modernity thus attains its culmination in the same terms that Hegel used to describe the English:

> The English were determined to convert themselves into the missionaries of civilization for all the world (*Missionarien der Zivilisation in der ganzen Welt*).[29]

Before this Europe of the North (as today before the United States), no one could pretend to have any rights, as Hegel expresses it in his *Encylopedia*:

> Because history is the configuration of the Spirit in the form of event,[30] the people which receives the Spirit as its natural principle . . . is the one that dominates in that epoch of world history. . . . Against the absolute right of that people who actually are the carriers of the world Spirit, the spirit of other peoples *has no other right (rechtlos)*.[31]

This people (Germany and England especially for Hegel), possesses an absolute right[32] because it is the "bearer" (*Träger*) of the Spirit in this moment of its development (*Entwicklungsstufe*).

Before this people every *other people* have no rights (*rechtlos*). This is the best definition not only of Eurocentrism, but of the sacralization of the imperial power of the North and of the center over the South, the periphery, the old colonial, dependent world. I believe that no commentaries are needed since the texts bespeak a frightful cruelty, an unmeasured cynicism, which is transformed into the very development of the enlightened reason of the *Aufklärung*.

Besides, and this has passed unperceived by many commentaries on Hegel—and even by Marx—the contradictory *civil society* overcomes itself as *state,* thanks to the constitution of colonies that absorb the mentioned contradiction:

> By a dialectic which is appropriate for surpassing itself, in the first place, such a society is driven to look *beyond* itself to new consumers. Therefore it seeks its means of subsistence among other peoples which are inferior to it with respect to the resources which it has in excess, such as those of industry.[33] This expansion of relations also makes possible that colonization to which, under systematic or sporadic form, a fully established civil soceity is impelled. Colonization permits it that one part of its population, located on the new territory, returns to the principle of family property and, at the same time, procures for itself a new possibility and field of labor.[34]

The periphery of Europe thus serves as the free space to enable the poor, the fruit of capitalism, to become proprietary capitalists in the colonies.[35]

Jürgen Habermas treats the same theme in his work *Der philosophische Diskurs der Moderne*[36] when he writes:

> The key historical events for the implantation of the principle of subjectivity are the *Reformation*, the *Enlightenment*, and the *French Revolution.*[37]

I wish to disprove Habermas and Hegel, for whom the discovery of America is not a determinant of modernity.[38] The experience not only of discovery, but especially of the conquest, is *essential* to the constitution of the modern ego, not only as a subjectivity, but as subjectivity that takes itself to be the center or end of history.

On the other hand, it is evident that Hegel as well as Habermas exclude Spain and with it Latin America from the originary definition of modernity. Hegel writes:

> Here one meets the lands of Morocco, Fas (not Fez), Algeria, Tunis, Tripoli. One can say that this part does not properly belong to Africa, but more to Spain, with which it forms a common basin. De Pradt says for this reason that when one is in Spain one is already in Africa. This part of the world . . . forms a niche which is limited to sharing the destiny of the great ones, a destiny which is decided in other parts. It is not called upon to acquire its own proper figure.[39]

If Spain is outside modernity, so much the more is Latin America. My hypothesis, to the contrary, is that Latin America, since 1492, is a constitutive moment of modernity, and Spain and Portugal are part of its originary moment. They make up the *other face* (*te-ixtli* in Aztec), the alterity, essential to modernity. The European ego or subjectivity, immature and peripheral to the Muslim world, continues to develop. Finally, it surfaces in the person of Hernán Cortés presiding over the conquest of Mexico, the first place where this ego effects its prototypical development by setting itself up as lord-of-the-world and will-to-power. This interpretation will permit a new definition, a new *world* vision of modernity, which will uncover not only its emancipatory concept, but also the victimizing and destructive myth of a Europeanism based on Eurocentrism and the developmentalist fallacy. The myth of modernity now takes on another meaning than it did for Horkheimer and Adorno,[40] or than it does for postmoderns such as Lyotard, Rorty, or Vattimo.

Unlike the postmoderns, I will not criticize reason as such; but I do accept their critique of reason as dominating, victimizing, and violent. I will not deny universalist rationalism its rational nucleus, but I do oppose the irrational element of its sacrificial myth. I do not then deny reason, only the irrationality of the violence of the modern myth. I do not deny reason, but rather postmodern irrationality. I affirm the reason of the Other as a step toward a transmodern *worldhood*.

CHAPTER
2

From the Invention to the Discovery of the New World

> When and how does America appear in historical consciousness? This question—whose response obviously presupposes the reconstruction of a process which I am going to call the ontological American process—constitutes the fundamental question of this work.
>
> —E. O'Gorman, *La invención de América*[1]

I will distinguish conceptually among *invention, discovery, conquest,* and *colonization.* These are figures (*Gestalten*) that contain spatially and diachronically distinct theoretical contents. They refer to different existential experiences that merit separate analyses.

THE "INVENTION" OF THE "ASIATIC BEING" OF THE NEW WORLD

We owe to Edmundo O'Gorman the proposal of this first figure (*Gestalt*): the "invention of America."[2] In a philosophical-historical analysis, undertaken in a Heideggerian style, this great Mexican historian describes the ontological experience as lived by Christopher Columbus and as documented by texts handed down to us. This reconstructive adventure will lead us to the conclusion that Columbus *did not discover America* in a strictly ontological sense, according to O'Gorman's vocabulary.

The starting point of the analysis is obvious, and for that reason never sufficiently taken into account. The *world* (*Welt*),[3] or the *world of everyday life* (*Lebenswelt*),[4] of Christopher Columbus was that of an expert navigator of the Mediterranean (the *mare nostrum* of the Romans), whose waters touched Europe,[5] Africa, and Asia[6]—Europe was not yet the "center."[7] Since 1476 Columbus had had extensive experience of the Atlantic—where he had been attacked by pirates and shipwrecked.[8] Because his world was filled with Renaissance fantasy, in spite of its distance from the medieval period, Columbus on his third voyage thought that the delta the Orinoco was the opening of one of the rivers of the earthly paradise.[9] This imaginative world would have pertained to a merchant from Venice, Amalfi, or Naples, from the Florence of the Medici, the Rome of Pius II, or Columbus's native Genoa.[10] In Columbus's world, the Christian Italo-Iberian world faced the Muslim world of North Africa and the Turks.

In the same year, 1492, in which the *Capitulaciones de Santa Fe*[11] were signed on April 17 at Granada, as it fell to the last European Crusade,[12] Columbus, on August 3, set sail. He had only one purpose in mind: to arrive at India by traveling westward. That such a journey would be feasible had been an accepted thesis from the time of Aristotle or Ptolemy to that of Toscanelli.[13] Heinrich Hammer's 1489 map suggested this possibility also.[14] The first explorer to complete this journey would acquire nautical knowledge, amass gold, win honor, and expand the Christian faith—purposes that could coexist without contradiction in that *Weltanschauung*.

Although Columbus was one of the last merchants of the occidental Mediterranean, he was at the same time the first modern man. Previous discoveries via the North Atlantic,[15] such as the one that landed in Helluland ("land of desolation") under Leif Ericson in 992, had no historical impact. Ericson's Vikings failed to integrate their findings in an irreversible manner either into the European *Lebenswelt* or into the economy or history of their own people. Columbus's crossing of the equatorial Atlantic, on the other hand, took on an entirely different significance.[16] The Portuguese never attempted such a venture, even though they had occupied Ceuta in Africa (1415), constructed the first caravels (1441), initiated the African slave trade, and journeyed as far as Guinea[17] and the Cape of Good Hope (1487)[18] trying to reach India and its riches. The Portuguese roved the seas, but they saw only what was already known. Thus, they *discovered* Africa, even though it already held a geographic, historical, and theological place in the Renaissance *Weltanschauung*. One cannot understand Columbus's undertaking in the same terms.

Columbus departed the Canary Islands September 8 and arrived at an island in the western Atlantic on October 12, 1492. The papal bull of 1493, *Inter caetera*, described this location in an objective manner: "islands and lands" situated in the "western parts of the Oceanic Sea, toward the Indies."[19] What Columbus actually saw and what he wanted to see were two different things. He categorically affirmed in his diary that he had landed in Asia:

> The information that I have given to your Highnesses about the lands of *India*, about a leader called Great Kan[20] (which means in our Romance language "king of kings"), and about the repeated requests by him and his ancestors that Rome send teachers of our holy faith.[21] . . . Your Highnesses, as Catholics and Christians, the chief lovers of the holy Christian faith . . . and enemies of the sect of Mohammed[22] . . . have thought to send me, Christopher Columbus, to these *parts of India* to see[23] these leaders and their peoples and lands and, above all [to understand] how we might convert them to our holy faith.[24]

A hermeneutic reconstruction of Columbus's mind would indicate that he thought he had discovered Asia just as he had anticipated. For him the islands, the plants, the animals, the "Indians" (from "India") only confirmed this belief.[25] Columbus writes, according to las Casas:

> At two hours after midnight [October 12], land appeared . . . a little island of the Lucayos that the Indians called Guanahaní. Then they [Columbus's men] saw nude people, people very poor in every respect. They walked about completely nude just as their mothers had given birth to them.[26] Moreover, in order not to lose time, I wish to go find the island of Cipango.[27]

On this basis, O'Gorman's original proposal makes sense:

> But if this is so, one can conclude that the ontological significance of the voyage of 1492 consists in the fact that for the first time someone from the Occidental culture,[28] such as Columbus, attributed a generic meaning to what he found. Columbus conferred on a geographical being (the _Dasein_ of some lands) the specific sense that it belonged to Asia. He endowed this land with _Asiatic being_ (_Seingebung_) because of his own a priori and unconditional presuppositions.[29]

Upon returning, Columbus declared that he had arrived in Asia on March 15, 1493. In his opinion, he had explored the islands just off the Asian continent. Columbus believed these islands lay near Cipango (Japan) but in front of the fourth great peninsula (present day Indochina and Malaysia) on which the Golden Chersonesus (Malacca) was located and on whose other side the ocean turned into the _Sinus Magnus_.[30] In his second voyage,[31] in 1493, Columbus sought to prove that he had explored Asia. Traversing Cuba toward the east, Columbus supposed it to be the Asian continent, the fourth great peninsula, not distant from the Golden Chersonesus. Turning south, he believed that Mangi (China) was not far to the north[32] and that soon he would be heading toward India. However, he could not prove these hypotheses.

After returning to Europe in 1496, Columbus recognized that further exploration was needed. He was convinced that a large continental mass loomed south of the islands,[33] and its discovery would have confirmed his interpretation that he had reached Asia.[34] Thus, in his third voyage he decidedly departed toward the south, seeking to circumnavigate the fourth peninsula. Taking North America for China, he expected that its peninsula, extending south, would eventually open upon Asia, even though he would have actually been reconnoitering South America. Columbus skirted the island of

Trinidad and wandered the sweet waters of the delta of Orinoco, the tributary of a river larger than the Nile or any European river. Columbus imagined that he had reached Asia east of the Chersonesus, but he was unable to return to Spain with conclusive evidence about this passage to India.

In his final (fourth) voyage, from 1502 to 1504, he moved inland,[35] crossed Honduras (part of China in Columbus's view), and followed the coast toward Panama where he received information from Indians (Asiatics) that there was a great sea on the other side of the isthmus. Columbus was overjoyed since he held it for certain that this was the *Sinus Magnus* and that he was near the Ganges River, in fact, only ten days from it.[36] On his return trip from Jamaica, he wrote the kings on July 7, 1503, explaining how the Asian peninsula extended toward the south.

Columbus died in 1506 assured that he had discovered the route toward Asia; he lived and died with this certainty. The Catholic kings, however, betrayed him, abandoning him to his poor and solitary fate, as they had betrayed Boabdil and Granada's Muslim and Jewish people. Because of the expulsion of these people—among other causes—Spain forfeited the future possibility of its own bourgeois revolution.

These European Renaissance explorers invented the Asiatic being of the American continent. Although Columbus officially opened Europe's door to Asia via the west, his invention left the three parts of the world—Europe, Africa, and Asia—intact, like the holy Trinity:

> [Columbus's] hypothesis depended on a priori convictions . . . .
> The fact that South America and the fourth peninsula were
> completely different geographical entities in no way under-
> mined his belief that these northern hemisphere lands were
> Asian. . . . His hypothesis never escaped the *previous* image
> conditioning it. As a result, when he ran across land in an
> unexpected site, he was incapable of an *empirical, revelatory*
> insight into what that land really might have been.[37]

This invention of America as Asia transformed the Atlantic into a commercial center between Europe and the continent to its west.[38] The Mediterranean was then experiencing agony, since it had hoped that its own deterioriation would have been halted after Lepanto in 1571. But the Turks and the Muslims and the entire *mare nostrum* were on the verge of becoming poorer due to gold and silver inflation resulting from the riches pouring in from peripheral Latin America.

Columbus thus initiated modernity. He is the first to leave Europe with official authorization, since, unlike earlier voyages, his was in no way clandestine. Because of his departure from Latin anti-Muslim Europe,[39] the idea that the Occident was the center of history was inaugurated and came to pervade the European life world.[40] Europe even projected its presumed centrality upon its own origins. Hence, Europeans thought either that Adam and Eve were Europeans[41] or that their story portrayed the original myth of Europe to the exclusion of other cultures.

According to O'Gorman's completely Eurocentric thesis,[42] the *invention* of America meant that "America was invented in the image and likeness of Europe since America could not *actualize*[43] in itself any other *form*[44] of becoming human [than the European]."[45] In contrast, I mean by *invention* Columbus's construing of the islands he encountered as Asian. The Asiatic being of these islands existed only in the aesthetic and contemplative fantasy of the great navigators of the Mediterranean. As a result, the Other, the American Indian, disappeared. This Indian was not discovered as Other, but subsumed under categories of the Same. This Indian was known beforehand as Asiatic and reknown in the face-to-face encounter and so denied as Other, or *covered over* (*en-cubierto*).

THE "DISCOVERY" OF THE "NEW WORLD"

Discovery constitutes a new figure after *invention*, one that involves further aesthetic, contemplative experience as well as the explorative, scientific adventure of coming to know *the new*. Because of *discovery*, or the resistance of stubborn experience to a whole new tradition, Europe was led to revoke the long-standing representation of Europe[46] as one of only *three* parts of the earth. However, with the discovery of fourth part (America), provincial and renascent Europe continued to interpret itself as modern Europe, the center of the world. A European definition of modernity, such as

Habermas's, overlooks how *European* modernity constitutes all other cultures as its *periphery*. Instead, I will pursue a world definition of modernity which will neither negate Europe's Other nor oblige it to imitate Europe's path of *modernization* as if that path were the only one.[47] I will trace this distinction between modernity as a legitimate concept and as a false myth back to 1502.

Discovery consists in a person–nature relationship, comprised of poetic, technical, and premodern commercial-mercantilist dimensions.[48] In fifteenth-century Latin Europe, Portugal took the lead in the search for the end of the earth (*finis terrae*) because of its commercially advantageous location on the Atlantic and near tropical Africa.[49] Amerigo Vespucci, another Italian navigator like Columbus, but under Portuguese auspices, left Lisbon in May 1501 for India. His intention, the same one held on an anterior failed voyage, was to pass beneath the fourth peninsula and cross the *Sinus Magnus*.

> Since my intention was to see if I could follow a cape of land which Ptolemy names the Cape of Catigara,[50] which is near the Sinus Magnus.[51]

In search of the strait to India, Vespucci reached the coasts of Brazil.[52] Convinced that he would eventually find the Asiatic *Sinus Magnus*, he navigated southward along territory which the Portuguese controlled from east African outposts.[53] As Vespucci progressed along what he thought was the southern fourth peninsula, his enterprise gradually grew more difficult than expected and ran counter to his presuppositions. The land extensions were greater, the inhabitants stranger, and all his a priori knowledge faltered, even though this knowledge had stood unshaken throughout the eras of Greeks, Arabs, and Latins until the time of Martellus. Vespucci advanced along the coast of South America as far as what he took to be the Jordan River, but in September 1502 he had to return to Lisbon without finding the *Sinus Magnus* or the passage toward India. Slowly Vespucci was transformed into a *discoverer*. In a revealing letter, he discussed his increasing consciousness that he had discovered a new world—not China, but something else. In that letter, addressed to Lorenzo de Medici,[54]

Vespucci indicated *for the first time in the history of Europe* that the continental[55] mass to the east and south of the *Sinus Magnus* discovered by Columbus and mistakenly assumed to be an unknown part of Asia[56] was actually Europe's southern antipode, "a fourth part of the earth."[57] In addition, very primitive and nude human beings inhabited this land. From 1502 until his *Mundus Novus* in 1503 or 1504, Vespucci deepened his awareness of what was happening. It took years to revise a thousand-year-old *Weltanschauung*.

The concrete ego of Amerigo Vespucci accomplished the passage from the Middle Ages to the modern age. Vespucci completed what Columbus, the first modern, had begun. A new world, unknown before, emerged before Europe's eyes. Europe, in turn, opened itself to the new world! Europe's status altered from being a *particularity placed in brackets (citada)*[58] by the Muslim world to being a new *discovering universality*. The modern ego thus took its first step in a diachronic self-constitution that later passed from the *ego cogito* to the practical will to power. O'Gorman writes with great precision:

> When Vespucci speaks of a *world* he refers to the old notion of ecumene, of a portion of the Earth fit for human habitation. If he licitly designates the recently explored countries as a *new world*, it is because he intends to announce the effective finding of one of these *other* ecumenes.[59]

Matthias Ringmann and Martin Waldseemüller use the expression *discovery* in their *Cosmographiae Introductio* in 1507. They depict the "Fourth Part of the Earth" on their map and call it "America" in honor of Amerigo Vespucci, its *discoverer*.[60] In line with O'Gorman's ontology, such a discovery merely recognizes a material or potency upon which Europe could invent its own *image and likeness*. For O'Gorman, America is not discovered as something *distinct* or *Other* which resists subsumption. Rather America serves only as matter upon which *the Same* projects itself; America submits to a "covering over" (*encubrimiento*). Such a Eurocentric thesis is part of a historico-cultural act of domination, however much O'Gorman's intentions may have opposed such domination.

Habermas, whose Eurocentrism resembles O'Gorman's, suggests an intra-European definition of modernity which commences with the Renaissance and the Reformation and culminates in the *Aufklärung*. Latin America, Africa, or Asia have *no importance* for the philosopher from Frankfurt! In this self-centered, Eurocentric definition, Habermas identifies European particularity with world universality. O'Gorman, in spite of his cognizance of domination, denies America by defining it as matter, potency, and nonbeing. Habermas dismisses the relevance of the discovery of Latin America and thereby denies its historical reality, just as Hegel did.

The dis-covering took place historically and empirically from 1502 to 1507. This discovering confirmed the existence of continental lands inhabited by human beings to the west of the Atlantic and previously unknown to Europe. This discovering demanded that Europeans comprehend history more expansively, as a world/planetary happening (*weltliche Ereignis*).

This discovery process terminated in 1520 when Sebastián Elcano, surviving the expedition of Fernando de Magellan, arrived in Seville. That expedition had discovered the Strait of Magellan, traversed the Indian and Pacific oceans, put to rest the hypothesis of the *Sinus Magnus*, and circumnavigated the earth for the first time. As a result, the earth became the scene of world history, and its Fourth Part (America) was distinguished from the Asiatic fourth peninsula. These discoveries took place within a European perspective interpreting itself for the first time as the center of human history and thus elevating its particular horizon into the supposedly universal one of *occidental culture*.[61]

For the modern *ego* the inhabitants of the discovered lands never appeared as Other, but as the possessions of the Same to be conquered, colonized, modernized, civilized, as if they were the modern ego's *material*. Thus the Europeans (and the English in particular) portrayed themselves as "the missionaries of civilization to all the world,"[62] especially to the "barbarian peoples."[63]

Europe constituted other cultures, worlds, and persons as objects, as what was thrown (*arrojado/jacere*) before (*ob/ante*) their eyes. Europe claimed falsely that the covered one (*el cubierto*) had been dis-covered (*des-cubierto*). *Ego cogito cogitatum*, but this *cogitatum* was Europeanized and immediately covered over (*en-cubierto*) with respect to its otherness. The Other was thus constituted as part of the Same.[64] The modern *ego* was born in its self-constitution over against regions it dominated. Fernandez de Oviedo exemplifies this subjection of the "Other" to "the Same":

> The people of these Indies, although rational [*sic*] and of the same branch of the holy ark of Noah, are made irrational [*sic*] and bestial by their idolatries, sacrifices, and infernal ceremonies.[65]

The Other is Oviedo's beast, Hegel's future, O'Gorman's possibility, and Albert Caturelli's *material in the rough*. The Other is a rustic mass dis-covered in order to be civilized by the European being (*ser*) of occidental culture. But this Other is in fact covered over (*en-cubierta*) in its alterity.

CHAPTER
3

From the Conquest to the
Colonization of the Life-World

> Their ultimate reason for destroying such an infi-
> nite number of different souls has been only to obtain
> gold, to stuff their coffers with wealth in a short
> period of time, and to attain a high status out of pro-
> portion to their persons. All this results from their
> insatiable greed and ambition. And so I must impor-
> tune Your Majesty not to allow these tyrants to real-
> ize what they have invented, pursued, and inflicted
> and what they call conquest.
>
> —Bartolomé de las Casas, *Brevissima relación*
> *de la Destrucción de la India*, Introduction

The third figure, *conquest*, involves neither an aesthetic nor a quasi-scientific relationship between person and nature as in the *discovery* of new worlds. Rather, this new practical, political, and military figure concerns person-to-person relationships. Instead of recognizing or inspecting new territories, drawing maps, or charting climates, topographies, flora and fauna, one dominates Indian persons and nations. Conquest (*conquista*) existed as a juridical-military term in Spain since the beginning of the reconquest in 718, according to the thirteenth-century *Partidas*. In 1479 the Catholic kings used the term by announcing that "we are sending certain of our troops for the *conquest* of the Grand Canary Island, against the Canarian infidels, the enemies of our holy Catholic faith."[1]

TOWARD A PHENOMENOLOGY OF THE "I CONQUER"

After the geographical recognition of a territory, one proceeded to control the bodies of the inhabitants, since they needed to be *pacified*, as it was customary to say in that epoch. In the Spanish world and later in the European world in general, it fell to the warrior to establish domination over others. The conquistador was the first modern, active, practical human being to impose his violent individuality on the Other. Vasco Núñez de Balboa was the first conquistador-colonizer in *tierra firma* (present-day Panama) and was subsequently assassinated in 1519[2] by Pedrarias, a Castillian noble of the second degree. But Hernán Cortés was the first who could really claim the name and who epitomized modern *subjectivity*. No conquest had taken place in the Caribbean, from Santo Domingo to Cuba, since no urban culture existed in those regions, but only scattered indigenous tribes and ethnic groups. The slaughter and seizure of small villages could not compare with subjugation of the Mexican empire.

Hernán Cortés, a poor Estremenian noble[3] born in Medellín in 1485 (the same year as Luther[4]), left home at fourteen to study letters in Salamanca. Later, Cortés, "tired of studying and lacking in money,"[5] decided not to leave for Naples but instead departed for the Indies. He arrived in 1504, one year after Bartolomé de las Casas and the same year in which the first African slaves were delivered on Hispanola. He spent five or six years in Santo Domingo as a plantation owner (*encomendero*), exploiting Indians on his farms.[6] Accompanying Diego Velázquez on the conquest of Cuba, Cortés "with the aid of his Indian servants seized a great amount of gold and became rich in a short time."[7]

After several more adventures, Cortés was finally appointed

captain in charge of the *conquest* of Yucatán, which had been discovered in 1517. From the coast, two previous expeditions had observed "buildings of stone invisible from the islands and people magnificently dressed."[8] Prior to this, the Spaniards had only observed nude Caribbean Indians lacking any weaving technology and more or less nomadic village cultures of food gatherers and fishermen dispersed from Terranova to Patagonia. Because of the Spaniards' focus on exploring the Pacific, it took them twenty-five years to notice the Mayan and Aztec cultures.

The Same violently reduces the Other to itself through the violent process of conquest. The Other, in his or her distinction,[9] is denied as Other and is obliged, subsumed, alienated, and incorporated into the dominating totality like a thing or an instrument. This oppressed Other ends up either being interned (*encomendado*)[10] on a plantation or hired as salaried labor on estates (*haciendas*) or, if an African slave, regimented into factories turning out sugar or other tropical products. Likewise, the conquistador constitutes and extends his own subjectivity through his praxis. Cortés "was mayor that year [1518] and felt happy and proud since he knew how to treat each person according to his own inclination."[11] Once Velázquez appointed him general captain of the conquest in recently discovered territories, Cortés immediatedly invested all his accumulated riches in the undertaking. Regarding Cortés's subjectivity, Torquemada comments:

> He began *to live as if he were* a captain; he arranged his house with a major-domo, valet, chief waiter, and other officials—all people of honor.[12]

The poor Estremenian noble has become *general captain*, and he knows it. His modern *ego* begins to constitute itself. He readies 11 ships, 508 soldiers, 16 horses, and 10 pieces of artillery for the enterprise of conquest. He envisions himself as Christendom's new Constantine:

> During this journey, Cortés carried a banner of black taffeta with a colored cross, and blue and white flames scattered throughout. He inscribed on the border of the banner: *We follow the cross and in this sign we shall conquer.*[13]

Cortés was astute at firing up his troops. In the elegant speeches he delivered before, during, and after battles, he spoke sincerely. Thus he created a profound *consensus* among his soldiers, who "with the fervor of his words were all the more incited and desirous of winning victory," comments Torquemada.[14] Departing Cuba February 18, 1519, he sailed the Yucatán coast and reached the eastern coasts of the Aztec empire (San Juan de Ulúa). There, according to Torquemada, he received reports about the Aztecs and their emperor Moctezuma. Moctezuma's spies had already informed him of the first two Spanish exploratory expeditions:

> All of us who were there saw gods arriving on the coast in great houses of water (which they call ships). . . . Motecuhzuma *remained alone, pensive, and quite suspicious of this great novelty in his kingdom. . . . and he called to mind his prophet's predictions.* . . . He began to believe that it was Quetzalcohuatl whom they once adored as a god . . . and who long ago had left for the far east.[15]

Moctezuma's ambassador, speaking to Cortés before he disembarked, expresses just this belief:

> They responded that they were Mexicans, who came from Mexico to seek the Lord and King Quetzalcohuatl who they knew was there.[16]

Cortés becomes aware for the first time that these people considered him a god and he begins to ponder his options.

> What are they trying to say when they say that he is their King and God, and that they wish to see him? *Hernán Cortés heard this, and with all his people he thought carefully about the situation.*[17]

The emissaries greeted Cortés as God and lord and "then prostrated themselves on the ground and kissed it":

> Our God and our Lord, you are welcome since for a long time we your servants and vassals have awaited you.[18]

Immediately "they put on his head a gold piece shaped in the manner of an armet and embedded with valuable stones." The first day the envoys were well treated. But on the second day, the Spaniards decided "to scare those messengers . . . by discharging their artillery and challenging them to fight." The legates, who did not hold the office of warriors in their highly institutionalized empire, remained terrified and refused to fight. They were tagged as *effeminate* and violently dispatched with the orders:

> That they go to Mexico to make it known that the Spaniards were coming to conquer (*conquistar*) the Mexicans, and at their hands all would die.[19]

Thus the two *worlds* met. The one, modern, composed of *free* subjects in a commonly decided accord; the other, the greatest empire of the new world, completely limited by its traditions, divinatory laws, rites, ceremonies, and its gods. The Mexicans repeatedly wondered:

> Who are these people, where do they come from, and why must they conquer us—we who hold power and inspire fear in all these kingdoms? . . . Motecuhzuma listened carefully to what these ambassadors said, the color of his face turned pale, and he manifested great sadness and dismay.[20]

The struggle was never equal:

> Cortés overlooked nothing when it came to how it might be possible to augment his own status. He ordered his armies to form in battle array, to fire their harquebuses, and to engage in cavalry skirmishes . . . but the thunder of the artillery was most impressive, since it was utterly new to these people.[21]

Such pyrotechnic theatricalization aroused awe among the religious-symbol-oriented Indians and disturbed them:

> Although warriors, they were not prepared to defend against invasions and maritime wars since they never anticipated that strange peoples would cross the sea, which they did not believe was navigable.[22]

Thus the Aztecs established *for the first time* a relationship with their Other, the outsider, the absolute stranger, coming forth like the sun from the infinite ocean of the East. The Aztec new age would commence with this relationship with an absolute stranger who was coming to conquer, subjugate, and kill. In this violent relationship the conqueror was pitted against the conquered, advanced military technology against an underdeveloped one. At this beginning of modernity, the European ego experienced a quasi-divine superiority over the primitive, rustic, inferior Other. The modern ego, covetous of wealth, power, and glory, reacted predictably when the emperor's ambassadors presented magnificent gifts of gold, precious stones, and other riches:

> Those who saw the presents were astonished to see such great wealth, and they wished to be presented to someone greater than this person or someone like him. Gold tends to enliven the heart and animate the soul.[23]

Upon reaching the first great city, Cempoalla:

> They entered and saw so many vibrant, happy people, whose houses were made of either adobe or lime and stone. The streets were filled with people who had come out to see them. They felt justified in calling this land New Spain. . . . The city was named Cempoalla, the greatest town.[24]

Cortés behaved like the Christians in the reconquest and the Catholic kings in the victory of Granada. He formed pacts with some, divided others, and slowly went about routing the enemy. In violent battles a mere handful of Cortés's soldiers demonstrated the techniques of warfare acquired through more than seven centuries of struggle against the Muslims in Iberia. They deployed firearms, powder cannons, bestial dogs trained to kill, and horses seemingly inspired by demons. They utilized duplicities, hypocrisies, lies, and political Machiavellianism with such efficacy that they disconcerted the Mexicans. The Mexicans, themselves experts in the domination of hundreds of villages, appeared ingenuous before modern humanity:

> The news that such strange people had arrived spread throughout the land . . . not because the Mexicans feared the loss of their lands but because they understood *that the world was ended.*[25]

Truly, a world was ending.[26] For that reason, it is totally euphemistic and vacuous to speak of the "meeting of two worlds," since the essential structure of one of them was destroyed.

Even though no one was permitted to look into Moctezuma's face, the emperor realized that he could not escape receiving Cortés at the great city's entrance. How imposing must the city have appeared with its tens of thousands of inhabitants and its army of one hundred fifty thousand to the three hundred Castillian soldiers! Bernal Díaz de Castillo writes:

> What men have there ever been with such daring? . . . The great Montezuma descended from his platform. . . . Cortés was told that the great Montezuma was coming . . . so he approached Montezuma, and they did each other homage.[27]

One can only imagine Moctezuma's feelings when he stood face to face with the conquistador who had freely and personally decided to confront the emperor who was considered a quasi god by his empire. Moctezuma, in contrast, was absolutely determined by the auguries, sorceries, astrological definitions, myths, theories, and other sources that revealed the designs of the gods. The free, violent, warlike, politically adept, juvenile[28] modern ego faced an imperial functionary, tragically bound by communal structures like a chained Prometheus.[29] Everyone else stared at the earth[30] in front of the emperor. The "I-conqueror" was the first ever with the freedom to look him in the face.

This "venturous and daring entrance into the great city of Tenustitlan, Mexico," took place on November 8, 1519,[31] but Cortés would return August 13, 1521, to seize and destroy it.[32] Then Cortés ordered Emperor Cuahutemoc, Moctezuma's humbled and conquered successor, to approach him:

> Cortés ordered the construction of the best stage possible to be covered with mats, blankets, and other seats. . . . Then they carried Guatemuz *before Cortés*, and, when Guatemuz did him homage, Cortés embraced him with joy.[33] When this meeting finished, Cortés declared himself *lord of Mexico and all its kingdoms and provinces.*[34]

Cortés lords it over an ancient lord, and at this point only Emperor Charles V exceeds him in power. The "I-conquistador" forms the protohistory of Cartesian *ego cogito* and constitutes its own subjectivity as will-to-power. With similar arrogance, the Spanish king will assert in law 1, of title 1, of book 1 of the *Recopilación de las Leyes de los Reynos de las Indias*:

> God our Lord because of his infinite mercy and goodness has served himself in giving us without merit such a great share in the *lordship of this world*.[35]

The king of Spain proceeded to sign "I, the King," with large, impressive letters in the *Reales Cédulas*. I personally have run across that signature several times in the Archive of the Indies at Seville. This ego's *lordship* (*señorio*) over the world was based in God.[36] Although the conquistador participated in the king's lordship, he surpassed even the king, because he had to opportunity to face another lord and lord it over him. The conquistador exerted his power by denying the Other his dignity, by reducing the Indian to the Same, and by compelling the Indian to become his docile, oppressed instrument. The conquest practically affirms the conquering ego and negates the Other as Other.

This conquest was extremely violent. From among Cortés's first allies in Zempoala no one survived, since a plague annihilated that heavily populated, vibrant, and happy city. This was its repayment for having allied itself with Cortés against Moctezuma. The conquistadores further leveled the village of Cholula. But nothing compares with Pedro Alvarado's treacherous massacre of the Aztec warrior-nobles. After Cortés departed from Mexico to battle Pánfilo Narvaéz, Alvarado invited the warriors to lay down their arms and partake of a feast in the great patio near the temples.

> The Spaniards took up positions at the exits and entrances . . . so that none of the Aztecs could leave. The Spaniards then entered the sacred patio and commenced murdering people. They marched forward carrying wooden and metal shields and swords. They surrounded those dancing and pushed them toward the kettledrums. They hacked into the drum player, cutting off both his arms. They then decapitated him, and his head fell to the ground at a distance. Swiftly the Spaniards thrust their lances among the people and hacked them with their swords. In some cases they attacked from behind, carving out entrails, which spread all over the earth. They tore off heads and sliced them open, leaving bodies lifeless. They wounded those partying in

the thighs, the calves, and the full abdomen. Entrails covered
the earth. Some Aztecs ran, but in vain, since their own intestines
wrapped their feet like a net and tripped them up. These victims could find no way to escape since the Spaniards slaughtered them at entrances and exists. Some victims attempted to
scale the walls, but they could not save themselves.[37]

Similar acts of cruelty still smolder in the memories of indigenous
people, who do not share the Spanish interpretation of the conquest.

THE "COLONIZATION" OF THE LIFE-WORLD

Colonization (*Kolonisierung*)[38] of the life-world, the fourth figure,
is not a metaphor, but carries strong, historical, real significance. A
Roman *colonia* (near the *column* of the law) was a land or culture
dominated by the empire and so forced to speak Latin, at least among
its elites, and to pay tribute. Latin America was the *first colony* of
modern Europe since Europe constituted it as its first periphery
before Africa and Asia.[39] The colonization of the indigenous person's daily life and later that of the African slave illustrated how the
European process of modernization or civilization really subsumed
(or alienated)[40] the Other under the Same. This Other, however, no
longer served as an object to be brutalized by the warlike praxis of
a Cortés or a Pizarro. Rather, the Spanish subjugated the Other
through an erotic, pedagogical, cultural, political, and economic
praxis.[41] The conqueror domesticated, structurized, and colonized
the manner in which those conquered lived and reproduced their
lives. Later Latin America reflects this colonization of its life world
through its mestizo race, its syncretistic, hybrid culture, its colonial
government, and its mercantile and later industrial capitalist economy. This economy, dependent and peripheral from its inception
and from the origin of modernity, gives a glimpse of modernity's
"other face" (*te-ixtli*).

Before Cortés arrived in Mexico, "toward the end of March
1519," some Mayan chiefs in Tabasco (Yucatán) offered him luxu-
rious gifts.[42] They also handed over "twenty women, among them
a very excellent woman, who was called doña Marina,"[43] la Malinche. This woman symbolizes the American Indian woman, who,
educated and fluent in Mayan and Aztec, would eventually mother

"a son from her master and lord Cortés."[44] A similar event took place later in Tlaxcala:

> These same old chiefs came back with five beautiful Indian virgins and five servants, all of whom were daughters of the chiefs. Even though they were Indians[!], they were beautiful and well dressed. . . . Directing himself to Cortés, the leader said: "This is my daughter, a virgin; take her for yourself." He gave her hand to him, and the other nine were given to the captains.[45]

The modern ego of the conquistador reveals itself as also a *phallic ego*.[46] No amount of idyllic fantasizing about erotic relationships between the conqueror and the conquered can ever justify injustices such as occurred in Tlaxcala. Such erotic violence simply illustrates the colonization of the indigenous life-world (*Lebenswelt*):

> The force and violence deployed in Mexico were unheard of in other nations and kingdoms. Indian women were compelled to act against their own will, married women against their husbands' will, young girls, ten and fifteen years-old, against the will of their parents. The greater and ordinary mayors or magistrates (*corregidores*) ordered them to leave their homes and husbands or to abandon parents who received no compensation for the loss of their daughters' services. These young women were conscripted to labor as far as eight leagues away in the houses, ranches, or workshops of plantation owners who often maintained them in concubinage.[47]

While the conquistador murders the male Indian and subdues him in servitude, he sleeps with the female, sometimes in the presence of her husband. The sixteenth-century practice of secret concubinage with Indian women was illicit, but permitted, never legal, but necessary for many Spaniards, who officially married Spanish women. In satisfying a frequently sadistic voluptuousness, Spaniards vented their purely masculine libido through the erotic subjugation of the Other as Indian woman.[48] As a result they colonized Indian sexuality and undermined Hispanic erotics since the double moral standard of machismo maintained the sexual domination of the Indian woman in tandem with merely apparent respect for the European wife. Two children were born from these unions: the mestizo bastard from the conquistador and Indian woman, and the legitimate *criollo*, or white person born in the colonial world.

Carlos Fuentes's narratives preeminently depict the contradiction experienced by the mestizo offspring of these erotics:

> Marina cries: Oh, leave now, my son, leave, leave, leave from in between my legs . . . leave, son of a violated mother. . . . My adored son . . . son of two bloods at enmity with each other. . . . You will have to struggle against all, and your struggle will be sad, because you will be fighting against part of your own blood. . . . However, you are my only heritage, the heritage of Malintzin, the goddess; of Marina, the whore; of Malinche, the mother; . . . of Mainxochitl, the goddess of dawn; . . . of Tonantzin, Guadalupe, mother.[49]

The colonization of the Indian woman's body is a thread in the same cultural fabric sustained by the exploitation of Indian male's body for the sake of a new economy. In this epoch of originary accumulation, mercantile capitalism will immolate and transform Indian corporeality into gold and silver. What Marx calls the *living labor* of the Indian is objectivated in the dead value of these precious metals:

> The year of the surprise of Innsbruck (1552) witnessed the opening of Spain's cautious floodgates in response to Charles V's tragic situation. . . . The Fuggers in Amsterdam received an official transfer of silver in 1553. . . . From the great monetary center of the Low Countries, particularly Amsterdam, American metal passed to Germany, north Europe, and Britain. One will never know fully the role which this redistribution of moneys played in a European expansion that Europe could not have produced by itself.[50]

But the gold and silver of nascent capitalism in Europe spelled death and desolation for America. July 1, 1550, Domingo de Santo Tomás writes from Chuquisaca (present-day Bolivia):

> Four years[51] before depleting the land, a mouth of hell was discovered into which a great quantity of people descended each year. These victims, sacrificed by Spanish greed to its god, work in the silver mine called Potosí.[52]

The mine's mouth represents metaphorically the mouth of Moloch requiring human sacrifice—a sacrifice not to the bloody Aztec god Huitzilopochtli but to to the invisible god Capital, the new deity of occidental, Christian civilization. The sacrificial capitalist economy commenced its five-hundred-year history by worshiping money as its fetish and by celebrating its earthly (unheavenly) religion during the week, instead of on the Sabbath, as Marx indicated in *The Jewish Question*. In order that the totality of this nascent economic system might secure free or cheap labor, it subsumed the subjective corporeality of the Indian and the African slave.

In this brief space, one can only suggest the agony of the long history of cultural, economic, and political colonization of Latin America. The colonizing ego, subjugating the Other, the woman and the conquered male, in an *alienating erotics* and in a mercantile *capitalist economics*, follows the route of the conquering ego toward the modern *ego cogito*. Modernization initiates an ambiguous course by touting a rationality opposed to *primitive*, mythic explanations, even as it concocts a myth to conceal its own sacrificial violence against the Other.[53] This process culminates in Descartes's 1636 presentation of the *ego cogito* as the absolute origin of a solipsistic discourse.

The Spiritual Conquest: Toward the Encounter between Two Worlds?

> The friars assumed responsibility for the destruc-
> tion of idolatry. They boasted that they were con-
> quistadores of the spiritual domain. And when the
> Indians observed the daring and determination with
> which the friars burned down their principal tem-
> ples and shattered their idols ... they knew that the
> friars must have had some reason for doing this.[1]

I now turn to two new figures: the *spiritual conquest* and the *encounter* of two worlds. By such terms, I refer to the power the Europeans exercised over the imagery (Sartre's *imaginaire*) of the conquered natives. Contradictions abounded, however, since the Spaniards preached love for religion (Christianity) in the midst of an irrational and violent conquest.

It is also difficult to understand how the Spanish could have cru-elly imposed cultural re-education and at the same time focused that re-education on a crucified, innocent victim, the memory that lay at the foundation of Christianity.[2] Further, while the conquest depicted itself as upholding the universal rights of modernity against barbarism, the indigenous peoples suffered the denial of their rights, civilization, culture, and gods. In brief, the Indians were victimized in the name of an innocent victim and for the sake of universal rights. Modernity elaborated a myth of its own goodness, rationalized its violence as civilizing, and finally declared itself innocent of the assassination of the Other.[3]

THE SPIRITUAL CONQUEST

One year after 1492, Fernando of Aragon requested of Pope Alexander VI to grant a bull conceding him dominion over the discovered islands. Conquistador praxis required divine legitimation. Cortés, too, like Descartes, needed God to escape the enclosure of his *ego*. When Cortés considered the numerical advantages the millions of indigenous Mesoamericans possessed against his handful of soldiers, he decided not to elict his army's valor and tenacity by an appeal to banal wealth or honor. Instead, he endeavored to give their sacrifices an ultimate significance, as is evidenced in his exhortation on the verge of the conquest of Mexico:

> We understand the task upon which we embark, and *through the mediation of our Lord Jesus Christ* we have to prepare ourselves fittingly for the battles to come and we will triumph in them. For should we be defeated (*which I hope God will not permit*), we will never escape, given our small numbers. Since we no longer have ships to flee to Cuba, *the only recourse left* to our fighting, strong hearts, is *to turn to God*. Beyond this, he [Cortés] drew several comparisons with the heroic deeds of the Romans.[4]

God provided the foundation (*Grund*) for their enterprise, just as Hegel later affirmed that "religion is the *fundament* of the state." God is thus used to legitimize actions that modernity would consider merely secular. After the Spanish had discovered the geographical space and conquered bodies geopolitically, as Foucault would say, they needed to control native imagery by replacing it with a new religious worldview. Thus the Spaniard could completely incoporate the Indian into the new system coming to birth:

mercantile-capitalist modernity. But the Indian remains modernity's exploited, dominated, covered-over "other face."

Before battling the Indians, the conquistadores read them the *requirement* (*requerimiento*), which promised to exempt the Indians from the pains of defeat if they would merely convert to the Christian-European religion:

> I *require* that you understand carefully this proclamation, take it utterly seriously, and deliberate about it for an appropriate amount of time. I require you to recognize the church as queen and superior of the world, to acknowledge the pope in the church's name, and to obey his majesty, the pope's vicar, who is superior, lord, and king of these lands. . . . If you refuse or try to protract this process by malicious delay, I certify that with the aid of God I will wage mighty war upon you in every place and in every way. . . . I will seize your women and sons and sell them into slavery. I will rob you of all your goods and do to you every evil and injury in my power.[5]

Of course, the Indian would have been unable to grasp this proposal, since it had been read in Spanish. The *earthly* defeat of the Aztec armies of Moctezuma or the Incans of Atahualpa would have signified that their gods had been conquered *in heaven*, as Mircea Eliade has pointed out. According to their mythic mindset, they were compelled to incorporate the conquering gods within their imagery. The Spanish conqueror, however, never entertained the idea of appropriating anything from the world of the conquered. As a unique exception, the Franciscans edited and presented more than two hundred works of indigenous *sacramental authors* in popular theaters—that is, in the atria of immense colonial churches. Generally, the Spanish regarded the entire indigenous imagery world as demonic and worthy of destruction. They interpreted the Other's world as negative, pagan, satanic, and intrinsically perverse. Since the Spanish considered indigenous religion demonic and theirs divine, they pursued a policy of tabula rasa, the complete elimination of indigenous beliefs, as a first step in replacing those beliefs with their own:

> Idolatry remained . . . as long as the temples of idols still stood. The ministers of demons had to flee there to exercise their offices. . . . So the Spaniards concentrated . . . on tearing down

and burning temples. . . . They began this practice in 1525 in Texcoco, the location of the most beautiful and towering temples. . . . Later they demolished the temples in Mexico, Tlaxcala, and Guexozingo.[6]

José de Acosta insisted that the Spaniards be cognizant of ancient indigenous beliefs to avoid being deceived:

> It is not only useful but totally necessary for Christians and masters of the law of Christ to know the errors and superstitions of the ancients in case the Indians employ them furtively.[7]

Similarly, the great founder of modern anthropology, Friar Bernardino de Sahagún, who recorded for forty-two years the ancient Aztec traditions in Texcoco, Tlatelolco, and in Mexico City, wrote in the prologue of *Historia general de las cosas de Nueva España*:

> In order to recommend medicines for the sick, a doctor must first know the humor or cause of the sickness . . . : in this case one must be familiar with these worthless and idolatrous sins, rites, and superstitions. . . . Those who excuse idolatry as a mere trifle, child's play, or something insignificant, ignore the very roots of this activity. Confessors neither ask about it, nor think that there is such a thing, nor know the language to ask proper questions, nor would they understand those who admit sins of idolatry.[8]

The twelve first Franciscan missionaries to Mexico in 1524 formally initiated the *spiritual conquest* in its strong sense. This conquest lasted approximately until the first provincial council in Lima in 1551 or Philip II's great meeting in 1568.[9] During this brief space of thirty or forty years, missionaries preached the Christian doctrine in urban regions throughout the continent. They touched more than fifty percent of the entire population, from the north in the Aztec empire in Mexico to the south in the Inca empire in Chile.

Since all Europe accepted as unreflectively valid the doctrine eventually recorded in the Catechism of Trent, the Franciscans were unable to present it with any veneer of rationality to those other cultures. Fernando Mires's recollection of the intercultural debate at Atahualpa, related by the Inca Garcilaso de la Vega, reveals that proper evangelization would have taken more time than the missionaries wanted to spend. After Father Valverde explained the *essence of Christianity*—much better expressed by Feuerbach—his Incan counterpart responded:

> You listed five preeminent men whom I ought to know. The first is God, three and one, which are four,[10] whom you call the creator of the universe. Is he perhaps our Pachacámac and Viracocha? The second claims to be the father of all men, on whom they all piled their sins. The third you call Jesus Christ, the only one not to cast sins on that first man, but he was killed. The fourth you call pope. The fifth, Carlos, according to you, is the most powerful monarch of the universe and supreme over all. However, you affirm this without taking account of other monarchs. But if this Carlos is prince and lord of all the world, why does he need the pope to grant him concessions and donations to make war on us and usurp our kingdoms? And if he needs the pope, then is not the pope the greater lord and most powerful prince of all the world, instead of Carlos? Also you say that I am obliged to pay tribute to Carlos and not to others, but since you give no reason for this tribute, I feel no obligation to pay it. If it is right to give tribute and service at all, it ought to be given to God, the man who was Father of all, then to Jesus Christ who never piled on his sins, and finally to the pope. . . . But if I ought not give tribute to this man, even less ought I to give it to Carlos, who was never lord of these regions and whom I have never seen.[11]

Such argumentative acumen threw the conquistadores and Father Valverde into confusion. They simply reverted to modern irrationality instead of presenting better reasons:

> The Spaniards, unable to endure this *prolixity of argumentation*[!], jumped from their seats and attacked the Indians and grabbed hold of their gold and silver jewels and precious stones.[12]

The feebly based spiritual conquest could only *replace* the ancient indigenous vision of the world without accommodating it. Hence, it differed from the first three centuries of Mediterranean Christianity which transformed Greco-Roman imagery *from within* by reconstructing it. As the mature fruit of such accommodation,

Christianity diversified in its Armenian, Byzantine, Coptic, Russian, and Latin versions.

At best, the Spaniards considered the Indians coarse, childlike, immature (*unmündig*), needy of patient evangelization. José de Acosta asserted that they were barbarians who "reject right reason and the common mode of humanity[13] and thus act out of barbarian crudeness and savagery."[14] He contrasted these Indians with the Chinese, Japanese, and East Indians, who, although barbarians, nevertheless deserved to be treated "analogously to the manner in which the apostles preached to the Greeks and Romans."[15] For this European life-world (*Lebenswelt*) taking itself as the parameter and criterion of rationality and humanity, the Aztecs and Incas appeared as an inferior grade of barbarians, "because they do not yet use Scriptures or know the philosophers."[16] The indigenous peoples outside American or Andean urban cultures constituted a third class of barbarians to be defined in this way:

> The third-class savages resemble wild animals. . . . There are infinite numbers of these in the New World. . . . For all those who are scarcely human or only half-human, it is fitting to teach them to be human and to instruct them as children. . . . One must also contain them by force . . . and even force them against their will (Luke 14:23) so that they might enter the kingdom of heaven.[17]

For this reason, the spiritual conquest was obliged *to teach them* Christian doctrine and to inculcate in them every day the principal prayers, commandments, and precepts until they knew them by rote. This spiritual conquest also imposed a different time cycle (liturgical cycle) and alternative notions of space (sacred spaces). The whole indigenous sense of ritualized existence underwent change.[18] The present-day, ecclesial-Vatican triumphalism which *celebrates* these events, ought to return to painful history and comprehend the ambiguity of this spiritual conquest. This conquest appears more as a coercive or hopeless religious domination, subjecting the oppressed to the religion of the oppressor, than as an adult's free conversion to a religious belief system he or she has come to recognize as superior.

ENCOUNTER OF TWO WORLDS?

The sixth figure consists in the euphemism of the encounter (*encuentro*) of two worlds,[19] of two cultures—an interpretation favored today by dominant Latin American *criollo* and mestizo classes. This figure elaborates a myth: the new world as a single culture harmoniously blending the European and the indigenous. The contemporary advocates of this figure are the white or *criollo* (or white souled) children of Cortés by a Spanish wife or the Malinche's children (the mestizos), both of whom control the reigning, hegemonic culture.

To speak of a *meeting* is to employ a euphemism, a Great Word as Rorty would put it, and to conceal the genocidal shock that devastated indigenous culture. The new syncretistic, hybrid, predominately mestizo culture was born neither from a freely entered alliance nor from steady cultural synthesis, but from the originary trauma of being dominated. If one wishes to affirm authentically this new Latin American culture, conceived in such ambiguous origins, it is imperative never to forget the innocent victims, the Indian women, the overworked men, and the crushed autochthonous culture. The idea of *meeting* covers over reality by occluding how the European ego subjugated the world of the Other.

A meeting between two cultures, an *argumentation community* in which all are respected as equal participants, was impossible. Rather the Spanish asymmetrically *excluded* the world of the Other from all rationality and all possible religious validity. Further, they justified this exclusion through theological reasoning only disguised as argumentation and based on the recognized or unconscious supposition that Christendom was superior to indigenous religion.

No meeting could have been realized because the Spanish totally disdained indigenous rites, gods, myths, and beliefs, and sought to erase them through the method of tabula rasa. Nevertheless, in the clarity/obscurity of everday practices a syncretistic religion formed, which not even the purest Inquisition could have snuffed out. Popular creativity shaped this mixed religion contrary to all the intentions of European missionaries.

I cannot condone dominant elites in Latin America or Spain who continue speaking of the meeting of two worlds.

The great Colombian writer Germán Arciniegas, whom I met in
Paris in 1964 during a Latin American week, also examines the ideology of a meeting in his *Con América nace la nueva historia:*

> America is the only continent whose precise date of origin is
> known and whose formation occurred through universal par-
> ticipation. Millions of *immigrant Europeans* created it when
> they came to build homes and take advantage of unheard of
> opportunities. They joined creative forces with Indians dream-
> ing of a republic and with Africans fleeing to find emancipation
> unknown in their homelands and among their own blood, which
> had enslaved them.[20]

First of all, since Arciniegas takes 1492 to be the beginning of
Latin America, he attributes no historical significance to the indigenous peoples with their splendid cultures. Secondly, Latin Americans are the sons of immigrants[21]—that is, *criollos* first and afterward
mestizos. Third, these immigrants are said to join with *emancipated*
Indians, as if the Indians had been dominated *before* the conquest
but suffered nothing *in* the conquest except what was necessary for
emancipation or modernization. Arciniegas construes the Indians
as republican participants in the the Enlightenment (*Aufklärung*).
Fourth, like Vieira,[22] a Portuguese theologian in Brazil, Arciniegas
believes that Africans freed themselves *by becoming slaves* (!) since
in Africa "their own blood had enslaved them" and they found freedom only when unshackled in Latin America.'Such revisionist history amounts to another Hegelian[23] rereading of Africa's history—but
now by a Latin American. For Arciniegas, there was no meeting, but
only the self-realization of the Europeans in American lands. In this
obviously *criollo*, Eurocentric interpretation, like O'Gorman's, the
indigenous peoples either disappeared or were transformed.

Miguel León Portilla, an organizer of the fifth centenary celebrations, suggested that these celebrations concentrate on the topic
of the meeting of two cultures. The 1988 debate in Mexico regarding the significance of 1492,[24] however, revealed much confusion
regarding the meaning of *meeting*. The different interpretations of
1492 reflect more or less explicitly held *ideological positions* of
authors or their institutions. Spain, for instance, has manifested a
preference to understand 1492 in terms of the meeting of cultures.

When Felipe González became prime minister of Spain's social democracy in 1982, his inaugural address promised a special celebration of the *discovery* in ten years. Spain, eager at that point to enter the European Common Market, claimed 1492 as one of its glories, on which it prided itself as no other European nation could. Spain now emphasizes this *glory* more than it did before, since it is promoting its own politics of integration with Europe.

Europe understands the last five hundred years in its own terms since its 1492 celebrations manifest little intent to comprehend or help Latin America, and since it fixed 1992 as the year for its progress in economic and political unity. Five centuries ago, Europe broke through the Islamic wall which had hemmed it in for eight centuries, and 1992 recalls a new cycle in world history initiated by Portugal and Spain. Since Spain could not celebrate the conquest, it focused positively on the ideology of meeting in order to buttress its politics of integration with Europe and its supposed openness to Latin America.

In 1984, I entered this debate denying the validity of the concept of *meeting* in a seminar organized in Mexico, "The Idea of the Discovery."[25] I prefer to understand 1492 as a covering over (*encubrimiento*), and I have stressed the need for Indian compensation (*desagravio*).

If the *meeting (encuentro)* of two worlds were to signify the new hybrid, syncretistic culture that the mestizo race is articulating, its content would be acceptable. Popular culture in its own creative consciousness would then be producing this meeting, and not the brutal event of conquest.

PART TWO

Transition:
The Copernican Revolution of
the Hermeneutic Key

At this second, intermediate stage, I will examine the *maximum of critical consciousness*, which Europeans were able to attain regarding their own actions (chapter 5). Then I will focus on the other completely distinct, indigenous perspective, which inverts the usual European understanding of 1492 (chapter 6).

CHAPTER
5

Critique of the Myth of Modernity

This war and conquest are just first of all because these barbaric, uneducated, and inhuman [Indians] are by nature servants. Naturally, they refuse the governance which more prudent, powerful, and perfect human beings offer and which would result in their great benefit (*magnas commoditates*). By natural right and for the good of all (*utriusque bene*), the material ought to obey the form, the body the soul, the appetite the reason, the brutes the human being, the woman her husband,[1] the imperfect the perfect, and the worse the better.

—Ginés de Sepúlveda, *De la justa causa de la guerra contra los indios*[2]

This claim that the conquest is "for the good of all" and of "great benefit" for the dominated, vanquished one, perfectly expressed the myth of modernity.[3] One defines one's own culture as superior and more developed and the other as inferior, crude, barbaric, and culpably *immature*.[4] While one culture may be superior to another in many aspects, the critical observer realizes that the criteria of this superiority are always qualitative and so uncertain in their application.[5] Even the violence inflicted on the Other is said to serve the emancipation, utility, and well-being of the barbarian who is civilized, developed, or modernized. Thus after the innocent Other's victimization, the myth of modernity declares the Other the culpable cause of that victimization and absolves the modern subject of any guilt for the victimizing act.

Finally, the suffering of the conquered and colonized people appears as a necessary sacrifice and the inevitable price of modernization. This logic has been applied from the conquest of America until the Gulf War, and its victims are as diverse as indigenous Americans and Iraqi citizens. Its features become evident at the birth of modernity, in the Valladolid dispute (1550), the most famous, consequential, and influential of the last five hundred years.

Historically, three theoretical-argumentative positions take up the questions of the inclusion of the Other in civilization's *communication community* and the sixteenth century's justification of the conquest: (1) modernization as *emancipation* (Ginés de Sepúlveda); (2) modernization as *utopia* (Gerónimo de Mendieta); and (3) a European critique of the *myth* of modernity (Bartolomé de las Casas).

MODERNITY AS EMANCIPATION

Ginés de Sepúlveda, the modern Spanish humanist, presents argumentation that is shockingly blunt, unabashedly cynical, and typically modern. He begins by denying that the Aztec or Incan urban centers, whose architecture dazzled the conquistadores, prove that the Indians are civilized:

> Many are deceived, but not I, since I regard these very institutions as proof of these Indians' rudeness, barbarity (*ruditatem barbariem*),[6] and innate servitude. Natural necessity

induces human beings to build houses, rationalize some behaviors, and engage in some species of commerce. That the Indians do these things proves that they are not bears or monkeys, and are not totally devoid of reason.[7]

He proceeds candidly to reveal the ideal of modernity in the light of which he judges the indigenous world:

> On the other hand, in their republic *no individual is entitled to own* a house or a field or to bequeath it *as a testament* to descendents. Everything belongs to their lords, whom they improperly name kings and whose judgment they follow more than their own. They submit completely to their kings' capricious will without being coerced and forfeit *their own liberty* voluntarily and spontaneously.[8] This abasement signals the servile, abject spirit of these barbarians. . . . The barbarous, uneducated, and inhuman character and customs (*ingenio ac moribus*) of these half-men (*homunculos*) preexisted *the arrival of the Spaniards*.[9]

For Sepúlveda, the root of indigenous barbarity lies in its nonindividual mode of relating to persons and things. The Indians know nothing of private possession (*ut nihil cuiquam suum sit*), personal inheritance contracts, and, above all, modernity's supreme characteristic: subjective liberty (*suae libertati*), autonomously resistant to the arbitrariness of rulers.[10]

Conquest emancipates by enabling the barbarian to depart from (Kant's *Ausgang*) *immaturity*, as the text opening chapter 5 suggests. Sepúlveda proffers a second justification for conquest:

> The second cause is to ban these barbarians' abominable lewdnesses (*nefandae libines*) and to save from serious injury the many innocent mortals they immolate every year.[11]

Inadvertently Sepúlveda passes from the concept of modernity to its myth.[12] Conceptually modern rationality affords an emancipative potential to civilizations with less developed instruments, technologies, practical politico-economic structures, and capacities for subjective expression. But, at the same time, this concept hides the domination or violence that modernity exercises over other cultures. Modernity justifies the Other's suffering because it saves many innocent victims from the barbarity of these cultures. Sepúlveda articulates with definitive and classical clarity the myth of modernity, whose argumentative stages (premises, conclusions, corollaries) follow:

(1) Europe is more developed;[13] its civilization is superior to others (major premise of all *Eurocentrism*).

(2) A culture's abandonment of its barbarity and underdevelopment through a civilizing process implies, as a conclusion, progress, development, well-being, and *emancipation* for that culture.[14] According to the *fallacy of development* [developmentalism], the more developed culture has already trod this path of modernization.

(3) As a first corollary, one defends Europe's domination over other cultures as a *necessary*, pedagogic violence (just war), which produces civilization and modernization.[15] In addition, one justifies the anguish of the other culture as the necessary price of its civilization and expiation for its culpable immaturity.[16]

(4) As a second corollary, the conquistador appears to be not only *innocent*, but meritorious for inflicting this necessary, pedagogic violence.[17]

(5) As a third corollary, the conquered victims are culpable for their own violent conquest and for their own victimization. They should have abandoned their barbarity voluntarily instead of obliging the victimizing conquistadores to use force against them. Hence, so-called underdeveloped peoples double their culpability when they irrationally rebel against the emancipatory conquest their culpability deserved in the first place.

While modernity's emancipatory concept is visible in stages 1 and 2, its myth is exposed in the Eurocentrism of 1, in the developmental fallacy of 2, and in stages 3 to 6. The *full* realization of modernity's *concept* demands that one surpass modernity in a project of *transmodernity*[18] which upholds negated alterity, the dignity and identity of the other cultures, and the covered-over (*en-cubierto*) Other. At the same time, one can negate the *myth* of modernity by modifying or denying the Eurocentrism of the major premise.[19] The myth propagates a *sacrificial paradigm* which calls for the sacrifice of the victim of violence for human progress—a key tenet for Kant and Hegel, but not for Marx.[20]

The myth of modernity perpetrates a gigantic *inversion*: the innocent victim becomes culpable and the culpable victimizer becomes innocent. Paradoxically, modern humanist Ginés de Sepúlveda and all subsequent modernity lapse into irrationalism by advocating not argumentation but violence as the means of including the Other in the communicative community. Sepúlveda appeals to the New Testament text in which the lord whose many banquet invitees fail to appear finally obliges or compels (*compelle*) the poor to enter. Saint Augustine adds a special interpretive twist, which Sepúlveda recalls:

> St. Augustine . . . adds: Christ illustrated this point suffi-
> ciently in the parable of the banquet. Those invited did not
> come and the father said to his servant: "Leave with haste
> and scour the plazas and city streets to find the poor and
> *introduce* them into the feast." . . . But since there was still
> space, the lord commanded the servant: "Go along the roads
> and through the fields and *oblige (compelle)* people to enter
> and fill my house." The lord thus revises his first order, *intro-
> duce them*, to the second, *oblige them*, for the later arrivals.
> This alteration signifies thus the two periods of the church.
> [Up to here Saint Augustine speaks, but Gines adds]— . . . I
> maintain that we are not only permitted to invite these bar-
> barians, violators of nature, blasphemers, and idolators [in
> brief, culpable ones]. But we may also *compel* them, so that
> under the bondage of Christian rule they might hear the apos-
> tles who announce the gospel to them.[21]

By *compel* Sepúlveda intended even the use of war to pacify indigenous peoples. Only afterward did he think it appropriate to "initiate them into Christianity and to imbue them with it, since one transmits that religion better by examples and persuasion than by force."[22] Hence, Sepúlveda recommends violence to insert the indigenous people within the communication community, but, once inside, they deserve to be addressed with rational argumentation. Thus, the Valladolid dispute deals with *how one enters* the communication community described by K.-O. Apel.

MODERNIZATION AS UTOPIA

Gerónimo de Mendieta authored this second major position on modernity, which manifests the influence of other early Franciscan missionaries in Mexico,[23] among whom were "spirituals," "Joachinists,"[24] and "millenarists." According to the author of the *Historia Eclesiástica Indiana*, the devil had immersed the Aztecs in paganism, idolatry, and enslavement just as he had done to the Hebrews in Egypt. Hernán Cortés, preceded by Christopher Columbus, was the Moses[25] liberating them from servitude in accord with modernity's emancipatory tendencies. Unlike Bartolomé de las Casas, the Franciscans favored waging war against the indigenous peoples if they opposed evangelization. Although they concurred with Ginés de Sepúlveda's defense of the conquest on the basis of Luke 14:15–24,[26] they disagreed on what was to be done afterward. While Ginés supported the Hapsburg monarchy, Mendieta strongly criticized Philip II for the *Babylonian captivity* he imposed upon the Amerindians.

Mendieta held that since the gospel had been preached to all peoples, the end of the world had been inaugurated, though one quite different from the Indian end of the world. Furthermore, although sinful Europe had betrayed Jesus Christ, the simple, poor Indians behaved as if untouched by original sin.[27] Mendieta envisioned them as reenacting the ideal church of the earliest era,[28] prior to Constantine and corresponding to Francis of Assisi's dream.

During the Mexican church's golden age from 1524 to 1564, it conserved those Aztec traditions that the Franciscans and Pedro de Gante deemed not to be in conflict with Christianity. The Franciscans conserved autochthonous languages, clothing, customs, and political structures. They undertook a modernizing project from the outside, from what was still intact after the conquest, in order to build a Christian community immune to Spanish influence. This essentially utopian project, similar to the Jesuit reductions, eventually spread throughout the continent, extending from San Francisco, Los Angeles, and San Antonio (in the California territory) to Bolivia and Paraguay of the Moxos and Chiquitanos.

Taking their cue from the alterity of the Indian, the Franciscan missionaries introduced the Christian religion, European forms of government, European technology, including iron plows and other instruments, the textile industry, horses and other domestic animals, alphabetical writing, and advanced architectural devices such as the semicircular arch. This *Indian monarchy*, as Torquemada designated it, placed the Indians under the emperor's political sway while granting them cultural independence under the Franciscans' paternal guidance.

However, the European colonizers were not at all satisfied with these paternalistic utopias set up by the Franciscans and later by the Jesuits in Paraguay on a larger and more developed scale. Gerónimo de Mendieta documents how the entire project failed when Spanish colonizers seized these indigenous communities after 1564.[29] During the reign of Philip II, these colonizers instated the "kingdom of silver" and the "Babylonian captivity." The modernizing utopias, which in part respected indigenous cultural exteriority, yielded to the *repartimiento*, a parceling out of Indians for governmental or private agricultural or mining enterprises. The *repartimiento's* economic exploitation of indigenous people reimposed what Mendieta had earlier dubbed the slavery of Egypt and restored the reign of mammon, or capital, according to Marx's interpretation.

THE CRITICISM OF THE MYTH OF MODERNITY

Bartolomé de las Casas surpassed modernity's own sense of criticism as represented by Sepúlveda, Mendieta, Francisco Vitoria, the great professor of Salamanca,[30] and later Kant. Las Casas exposed the falsity of inculpating the subjects for a supposed immaturity (*Unmündigkeit*) in order to legitimize modern aggression. He appropriated modernity's emancipatory meaning without partaking of its irrational myth, which attributed culpability to the Other. He denied the validity of any argument sanctioning violence in order to *compel* the Other to join the community of communication. Given the undisputed belief that within the communicative community only argumentation was appropriate, las Casas's concern focused on how the Other should *enter* the community and begin to *participate* in it. In this debate regarding the a priori conditions of participating in a rational community of communication, Sepúlveda endorsed an irrational first moment—war—to inaugurate argumentation. Las Casas insisted instead on rationality from the start of the dialogue with the Other.

For las Casas, the emancipation of indigenous peoples from past domination and their imputed bestiality or barbarity warranted neither violence nor Spanish colonization, which was totally out of proportion to all that preceded it. In contrast with the new servitude, the ancient order among the indigenous peoples[31] seemed like a lost paradise of freedom and dignity. He wrote in the prologue to the *Apologética Historia Sumaria*:

> Ultimately we have written to make better known all these nations . . . whom some have defamed . . . by reporting that they were not rational enough to govern themselves in a humane and orderly fashion. . . . I have compiled the data in this book to demonstrate the contrary truth.[32]

An opposite purpose motivated the great Franciscan anthropologist Bernardino de Sahagún to gather the most complete collection of Aztec beliefs and culture in his *Historia General de las cosas de Nueva España*:

> It is necessary to know how these people formerly practiced idolatry in order to preach against it or even to recognize it. Because of our ignorance, they now practice idolatry in front of us without our understanding it.[33]

For las Casas, it was possible to appropriate modernity without its myth as long as the Indians were not destroyed in their alterity. Rather than setting modernity against premodernity or antimodernity, the Spanish could have modernized by starting from alterity instead of from *the Same* of the system. Such a project would have constructed a system from the transsystemic moment of creative alterity. In *De Unico Modo*, las Casas expressed his critical method—a rationalism of liberation:

> Divine providence established once and for all a single, same method for teaching the true religion: the persuasion of the

understanding through reasoning, inviting, and gently moving the will.[34]

Las Casas answered thirty-five objections to this point in three hundred pages in only one chapter. To convince the gentiles about the true religion, one needed only to resort to rational argumentation and the testimony of a good life to avoid falling into a *performative contradiction.* This mode of conveying the true religion "ought to be common throughout the world and not distorted by sects, errors, or customs."[35] Las Casas formulated an absolutely universal principle based upon the autonomy of reason:

> The rational creature possesses a natural aptitude to be moved . . . to listen voluntarily, to obey voluntarily, and to adhere voluntarily. . . . Hence one should be permitted to consult one's own motives, free will, and natural dispositions and capacities as one listens to everything proposed.[36]

After thorough discussion, he proposed a second question for chapter 6:

> Some . . . believe it convenient and feasible to subject infidels to the dominion of Christians, whether they want it or not. After establishing their dominion, Christians are supposed to then preach the faith in an ordered manner. Thus, preachers would not oblige infidels to believe, but convince them by reason.[37]

Las Casas was preoccupied with the *rational* conditions not for arguing but for coming to participate in a community of argumentation in the first place. He added:

> But since no infidel and certainly no infidel king would prefer to submit himself voluntarily to Christians . . . undoubtedly it would be necessary to undertake war.[38]

Las Casas confronts the myth of modernity and future modernizations at their outset. Modernity as myth always authorizes its violence as civilizing whether it propagates Christianity in the sixteenth century or democracy and the free market in the twentieth. But this violence has its price:

> Evils accompany war: the clamor of arms, sudden, impetuous, and furious attacks and invasions; ferocity and grave

perturbations; scandals, deaths, and carnage; havoc, rape, and dispossession, the loss of parents or children; captivities and the dethronement of kings and natural lords; the devastation and desolation of cities, innumerable villages, and other sites. These evils leave kingdoms and regions mourning copiously, shedding tears, and gloomily lamenting their calamity.[39]

Las Casas refuses to impute to the indigenous people the *culpable* immaturity that Kant later ascribes to the unenlightened:

This war would only be just . . . if the people against whom it is waged deserved war because of some injury they inflicted on those waging it. But these infidels living in their country distant from Christian domains . . . have done nothing to Christians *for which they deserve to be attacked.* Thus, this war is unjust.[40]

Las Casas demolishes the nucleus of modernity's myth[41] and places the blame where it belongs, on those pretending to be innocent: the civilizing European heroes, especially their leaders:

The texts cited prove that those who give the orders are principally responsible for the grave and bloody crimes perpetrated upon the infidels. These who give orders sin more seriously than the rest.[42]

Las Casas attained the maximal critical consciousness by siding with the oppressed Other and by examining critically the premises of modern civilizing violence. In his view, a more developed Christian Europe would have displayed its pretended superiority over Others differently. It would have taken account of the Other's culture, respected the Other's alterity, and engaged the Other's free, creative collaboration. Las Casas's critical reason was buried beneath the avalanche of Philip II's strategic rationality and cynical realism. Subsequent modernity, enlightened (*aufgeklärt*) and critical within Europe's confines, availed itself of irrational violence when it came to what was outside Europe . . . even until now, at the end of the twentieth century.

CHAPTER
6

Amerindia in a Non-Eurocentric Vision of World History

He had already made the necessary *fundament-of-
        the-word*[1]
to-open-itself-in-flower.[2]
He had already made the unique love of the wisdom
        contained in his being-from-heaven[3]
to-open-itself-in-flower.
In virtue of his knowing that he-opens-himself in-flower,
he produced a song that would-open-in-flower,
a sacred song[4] in solitude.
Before the earth existed,
in the middle of the ancient night,
when nothing was known,
he produced a *sacred song* that would-open-in-flower
for himself in solitude.

     —Ayvu Rapyta of the Guaranís

It is now time to change skins and to see through new eyes. It is now time to put off the skin and the eyes of the *I conquer* which culminates in the *ego cogito* or the will-to-power. One's new hands are not those that clutch iron arms, and one's new eyes are not those looking out from the caravels of the *European intruders*,[5] who cry Land! with Columbus. The new skin is the soft, bronzed skin of Caribbeans, of the Andean people, of the Amazonians. The new eyes are those of the Indians who, with their bare feet planted on soft, warm, island sands, saw[6] in wonderment new gods floating on the sea as they approached. This new skin suffered punishment on the plantations and land distributions, rotted with strangers' plagues, and hung in shreds at the column where slaves were scourged. These slaves, once peaceful peasants in the African savannah, were sold like animals in Cartagena of the Indies, Bahia, Havana, or New England. The new eyes are those of the Other, of the other *ego*, of the *ego* whose history requires reconstruction as modernity's other face. This history begins in the Pacific Ocean.[7]

It is time to change skins like a serpent, not the perverse treacherous serpent tempting Adam in Mesopotamia, but the *plumed serpent*, the divine duality (Quetzalcóatl),[8] who changes skins in order to grow. It is time to put on methodically the skin of the Indian, the African slave, the humiliated mestizo, the impoverished peasant, the exploited worker, and the marginalized person packed among the wretched millions inhabiting contemporary Latin American cities. It is time to take on the eyes of the oppressed, those from below (*los de abajo*), as Azuela's well-known novel expresses it. It is time to turn from the *ego cogito* to the *cogitatum*, who also thought—even if Husserl or Descartes ignored him or her. Before being a *cogitatum*, this Other was a dis-tinct (*dis-tinta*) subjectivity, and not merely different in the postmodern sense.

FROM THE WEST TO EAST: AMERINDIA IN WORLD HISTORY

A historically and archeologically acceptable reconstruction is needed to correct the Eurocentric deviation that excludes Latin America from world history.[9] Such a reconstructed and full account of the histories of the civilizations that produced occidental Europe will unmask Hegel's vision of history not merely as a Eurocentric ideological invention but also as an inversion of the facts.

Indigenous American ethnic groups did not first appear in world history merely to provide a context for the discovery of America, contrary to the usual college and university history program that first mentions Indians in 1492. Such programs note that—in addition to islands, palm trees, and exotic animals—Indians, too, lurked on the beaches Columbus discovered. In order, however, to locate the Indians' real place in history, it is essential to return to the neolithic revolution, which witnessed the birth of agriculture and cities. This revolution, contrary to Hegel's proposal, began primarily in the West, first in *Mesopotamia* and later in *Egypt*, and then surged forward toward the East, usually with few contacts between civilizations. This revolution spread eastward to the Indus valley, to China's Yellow River valley, to the Pacific Ocean region, and finally into Mesoamerica, home of the Mayan and Aztec civilizations, and the southern Andes, where the Incas resided.[10]

In certain propitious places and moments, at least six[11] great urban civilizations arose and intersected at two contact zones (I and II in Figure 1). Although this presentation of world history might appear naive and familiar, it includes from its origin Latin America, Bantu Africa, and Asia. These other cultures do not serve merely as the ancient age anteceding European culture, but stand as pillars of world history in their own right, according to Alfred Weber's terminology. Moreover, the Mesoamerican and southern

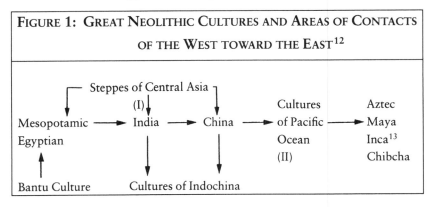

FIGURE 1: GREAT NEOLITHIC CULTURES AND AREAS OF CONTACTS
OF THE WEST TOWARD THE EAST[12]

Steppes of Central Asia

(I)

Mesopotamic → India → China → Cultures of Pacific Ocean (II) → Aztec → Maya

Egyptian   Inca[13]   Chibcha

Bantu Culture   Cultures of Indochina

Andes region experienced their own enlightenment (*Aufklärung*), which ought to fall under Jaspers's notion of axis time.

In the Mesopotamian region (Sumeria, Acadia, Babylonia), a high neolithic culture had developed irrigation and established the great cities of Ur, Eridu, Erech, and Larsa by the fourth millennium before the common era.[14] "Around 4000 B.C.E., the vast semiarid land bordering the eastern Mediterranean, reaching toward India, and centered in Mesopotamia, experienced the growth of several communities."[15] The Tel-el'Obeid culture extended over "all ancient western Asia, from the Mediterranean to the plateaus of Iran"[16] and formed the broth out of which Sumeria was born. King Mesilim of Kisch left traces of his glorious campaigns, motivated by struggles between Lagasch and Umma. Centuries afterward, King Eannatum solidified his power in 2700 B.C.E. and set in motion a succession of kingdoms and small empires. The Ziggurat of Ur, the most splendid temple of Sumeria, built in honor of Nannar, the moon, consisted of a garden shaped like a scaled pyramid and reminiscent of the immense way of the dead of Teotihuacan, Mexico. Although Enlil was adored in Nippur and An in Uruk, the mythic mountain of the Ziggurat formed the center of the universe, the meeting place of heaven, earth, and Hades (*Dur-An-Ki*).[17] This mythological-ritual vision and its symbolic discourse systematized into meaningful narratives reflected a highly critical rationality and enlightenment (*Aufklärung*). Likewise, according to Claude Lévi-Strauss, the structured myths of the Bororos and other Indian peoples of tropical Brazil represented a system of enormous, *rationally* codified complexity. Even though these mythologies fell short of those of Mesopotamia, Mexico, or Peru, they depended on "codes of second order, with the first order codes pertaining to language."[18]

Thus, a *rational* world of myth flourished in the great urban civilizations reaching from Mesopotamia to the southern Andes. Cortés confronted a rational consciousness at this same neolithic cultural level.

Centuries later, the famous Codex of Hammurabi (1728–1686 B.C.E.) laid down rationally universal ethical principles:

I have governed them in peace. I have defended them with
wisdom in such a way that the strong do not oppress the
weak and that they do justice to the orphan and widow.[19]

Egypt's[20] primordial myths sprang from the Bantu cultures,
which inhabited the deserts flanking the Nile.[21] Near the end of the
fourth millenium B.C.E. (around 3000 B.C.E.), the Bantu, African
negro "kingdom of the South" conquered the servant of Horus of
the North.[22] The first Tinita dynasty, which was named for the city
of This or Tinis near Abydos, initiated Egypt's national history on
a highly ethical footing, as is evident in the *Book of the Dead*:

I have given bread to the hungry, water to the thirsty, clothing
to the naked, a ship to shipwrecked, and offerings and liba-
tions to the gods. . . . Divine spirits, free me, protect me, and
do not accuse me before the great divinity Osiris![23]

For the Tinitas, the body and soul did not separate from each
other in death, but rather the *flesh* died and rose.[24] Such a belief
indicated that the flesh possessed absolute dignity and that to give
bread, water, or clothing constituted absolute *concrete* ethical
principles.[25] The principles did not mention housing for the home-
less since in Egypt's hot climate it was more important to have a
ship, which served as means for housing, the provision of food,
and transportation.

From the Indus valley (today Pakistan) to the Punjab, cultures
such as the Mohenjo-Daro and Harappa, with their murals dating
to 2500 B.C.E., prospered. The neighboring cities of Amri,
Chanhu-Daro, Jhangar, Jhukar, and Nal had divided themselves
into quarters and built streets eight meters wide. Although scholars have discredited the Indo-European/Aryan invasion of this
region, the whole area relied upon Sanskrit as its commercial and
sacred language. Also, in this period of the *Rig-Veda*, castes
supervened upon primitive modes of interrelationship.[26] Also, in
this axis time, Buddha criticized caste religion and embarked
upon the narrow path of contemplative life in community.

In China's Yellow River valley,[27] from the capital city of
Anyang, the Shang dynasty conquered the Yangtze, the Shansi,

and Shensi and ruled from 1523 to 1027 B.C.E. Confucius brought this culture to a high point by his wisdom, which Lao-Tse summarized in his *Tao Te Ching:*

> Calm signifies rest, and, when the principle of rest prevails, one fulfills duties. Rest means being at one with the self and at peace with oneself. The one at rest overlooks pains and fears, and enjoys a long life.[28]

The morality of the Tao order, the totality, governs for centuries. In addition to these achievements, the Chinese, as experienced navigators, traveled to eastern Africa and apparently as far as the western coasts of America. Does the ancient Catigara on Martellus's 1487 map correspond to the pre-Incan city of Chan on Peru's coast?[29] Is not this city, of which Arab and Chinese mariners had spoken in conversations with the Portuguese, evidence of a Chinese presence? At any rate, neolithic history progressed eastward to the coasts of the Pacific and was ready for its next major step.

THE PACIFIC OCEAN AND THE "CEMANAHUAC," "ABIA," "YALA," "TAHUANTISUYO"[30]

This new vision of world history, of the consistent progress of humanity, refuses to consider Africa and Asia as immature moments. It includes the Amerindian peoples who are now on the verge of migrating from the eastern Pacific region. These peoples from the extreme east of the Orient were Asians by race, language, and culture. It is crucial to follow their eastward movement to appreciate Amerindia's own authentic being in spite of efforts to deny it by everyday consciousness, college and university history programs, and Edmundo O'Gorman's anthropology. It took a similar effort by Amerigo Vespucci to recognize that America was a new world after Columbus had died affirming that he had reached Asia. Having acknowledged this eastward itinerary, one will never be able to claim again that only with America's *discovery* did its Indian peoples first claim their place in world history. Indeed, this ideological framework of discovery covered over Amerindia conceptually just as the genocidic invasion did so militarily.

The pillar cultures (Mesopotamia, Egypt, the Indus valley, the Yellow River, Mesoamerica, and the Inca zone) interlinked in different *contact areas*, such as the eastern Mediterranean[31] or, more importantly for the Eurasian continent, central Asia, numbered (I) in Figure 2.[32] This area began in the east with Mongolia, famous for the Gobi Desert and the domestication of horses in the fifth millenium B.C.E.,[33] and crossed eastern Turkestan or China (Sinkiang, from Dzungaria to the valley of Turfan, the Tarim) and western or Russian Turkestan (the Turan). It finally ran southward near Iran and then headed westward through the steppes north of the Black Sea until it reached Europe. This immense region of caravan routes, the Road of Silk, played a central role in Euroasian history until the sixteenth century. From this area, successive waves of invasions swelled forward: first the horsemen with arms of iron such as the Hittites or Hyksos, then the Archaeans, Dorians, and Ionians, and finally the Persians and the Germans. When the Turks, present in 760 B.C.E. in Turfan, dominated this region in the fifteenth century C.E., the Europeans sought contact with the Indian Ocean via the Atlantic, since the Muslim *fence* blocked any land access.

The Pacific Ocean, designated by Martellus's map as the mythic *Sinus Magnus* and numbered (II) in Figure 1, provided another *contact area* as important for the Spanish as for the Aztecs and Incas of the southern sea. Although for the Greeks this great sea marked the *horizon* of neolithic explorations, it functioned as the *center* of America's protohistory. In an interglacial epoch 50,000 years B.C.E., according to the latest estimates, numerous Asian migrations crossed the Bering Strait, traversed the Anadir valley, and forged the Yukon River. Thus they discovered[34] these lands and commenced America's protohistory (and not its prehistory[35]). Fleeing Asia under demographic pressures from the Gobi and Siberia, these migrants included representatives of the Australoid, Tasmanian, Melanesian, Protoindonesian, Mongoloid, and even Malayan-Polynesian races. The latest arrivals, the Eskimos, straddled both continents. The Amerindian, thus, is an Asian who originally settled the western coasts of the Pacific.

In addition, 1700 years B.C.E., proto-Polynesians from Burma, Java, other Indonesian islands, and southern China, launched forth on the great ocean and passed through Melanesia (New Guinea) and on to Samoa, whose fossil remains date to 800 B.C.E.. Some headed northeast (Micronesia) and others toward Hawaii, arriving in 124 C.E., others due east (Isles Marquises), and others southeast (Society Islands and Tuamotu, Tahiti, Pitcairn). Two invasions, the latter involving the Akiris, reached Easter Island, one hundred kilometers from Chile. During July and August, the Humboldt current in the South Pacific conveyed large balsa boats with as many as 150 persons from Tahiti to Easter Island or to the coasts of Chile or Peru in a matter of weeks. The equatorial current could also propel explorers from the Christmas Islands toward what would later be the Mayan and Aztec regions. In the North, one could hug the continental coasts, as did the Chinese, bridge the gap between northern Asia and Alaska, and descend along the California coast.

The ocean engendered a single cultural world. For example, the word *toki* means ax, an instrument for warfare or labor, on the islands of Tonga, Samoa, Tahiti, New Zealand, Mangareva, Hawaii, Easter Island, and among the Araucanians of Chile.[36] Likewise, the verbs *tokin* and *thokin* signify to mandate, to govern, to judge in all these locations. "According to our data and categories, we can deduce that the isoglossal semantic chain of *toki* extends from the eastern limit of Melanesia, across the Pacific islands, all the way to American territory where it shaped various cultures' vocables. During this entire trajectory, the meanings of this vocable have undergone indentical semantical transformation."[37] Similarly, Polynesian and Quechua, an Incan language, illustrate the following parallels: carry (*auki, awki*), medium (*waka, huaca*), eat (*kamu, kamuy*), old (*auki, awki*), warrior (*inga, inga*), strong (*puhara, pucara*).[38]

At other levels within what Schmidt and Graebner call the *circle of culture*, the similarities between Polynesian and Amerindians become even more astonishing.

Friederici has shown the identity of the *taclla*, the Peruvian agricultural shovel, even in its secondary details, with the Maori

taclla of Zealand. In southern Chile one drinks *kava*, the Polynesian national drink, called by the same name and likewise fer-
mented by chewing plant roots. Sticking out the tongue as a
sacred gesture bears similar religious meaning throughout the
Pacific area as far as India, whether one considers Easter Island's
cyclopean statues or Aztec sculptures. For instance,
Huitzilopochtli of the fifth age of the world, that of the rock of the
sun, sticks out his tongue, as can be seen in the expositions at
Mexico's Museum of Anthropology.

One could draw other comparisons, such as the identity or
similarity in blow-pipes, propellents, wooden clubs (*macanas*),
ring fingers (*anulares*), arches, slings, ropes, fishhooks, bridges of
liana vines, oars, rafts, double canoes, prow decorations, types of
dwellings, mortar, seats or pillows of wood, hammocks, mosquito
nets, hair brushes, fiber coats for protection against rain, textile
procedures, nasal ornaments, wooden drums, drum rhythms,
musical bows, flautas of bread, games of the most diverse type,
alcoholic drinks, terraced cultivations, types of irrigation, fishing
with poisons, religious offerings of shells, dances with masks,
mutilations, the meaning of instruments in ritual functions, and
liturgical music and lyrics.

Thus, the Pacific formed the *cultural center of the Amerindian
protohistory* and extended its influence throughout urban *nuclear
America* in Mexico, Guatemala, or Peru. In its protohistory,
Amerindia derived in part from the generative nucleus of the
Asian cultures of the Pacific. It would be a grave mistake to claim
that Amerindian cultures originated from Polynesia, since Mexican agricultural fossils dating to the eighth millenium B.C.E. have
been found in Texcoco Lake. I only suggest that the Pacific provided a context for cultural interchange after the origins of American humanity left Asia by crossing the Bering Strait. Opposite
Asia, sprawled an immense continental mass on which its diverse
inhabitants bestowed different names: the Cemanáhuac of the
Aztecs, the Abia Yala of the Cunas of Panama, the Tahuantisuyo
of the Incas. These are diverse autochthonous names for a continent already humanized in its totality when Columbus arrived.

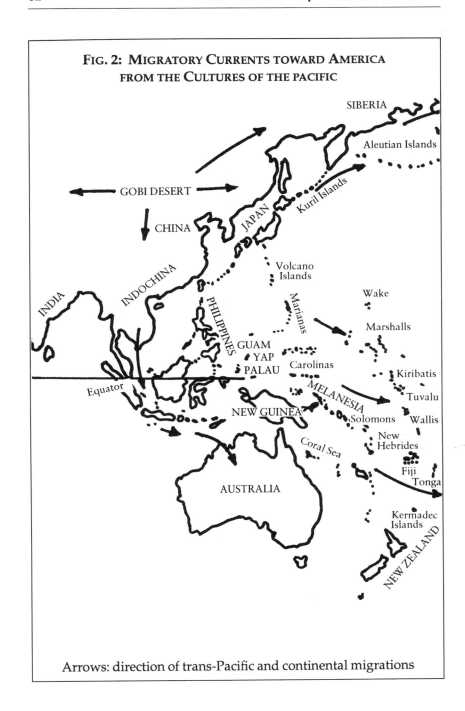

FIG. 2: MIGRATORY CURRENTS TOWARD AMERICA
FROM THE CULTURES OF THE PACIFIC

Arrows: direction of trans-Pacific and continental migrations

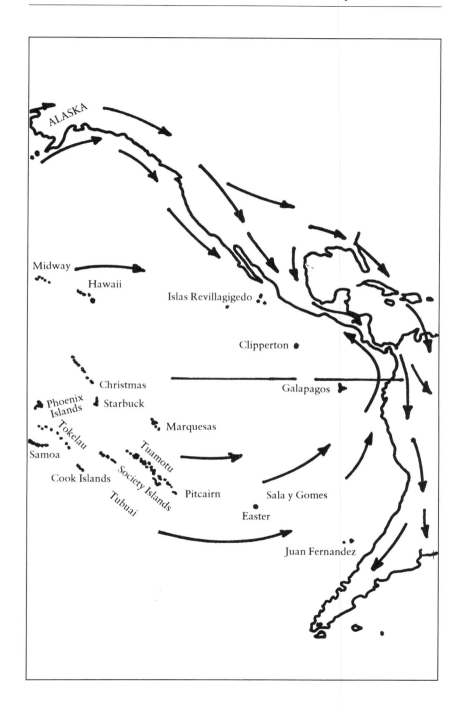

THE TEKOHA[39] OR WORLD OF THE AUTOCHTHONOUS AMERICAN PEOPLE

Beginning from the Pacific basin, the Amerindian peoples descended from Alaska for over fifty thousand years and scattered throughout the valleys near the Great Lakes or along the Mississippi, in the Missouri valley and on to Florida and the Antilles Islands or even to the Orinoco, the Amazon, and the Rio de la Plata—in brief, from Chicago to Buenos Aires. They populated the mountainous regions from the Rockies to the Sierra Madres of Mexico, which funneled migrants into enormous demographic concentrations. They moved on to the Andes as far as Tierra del Fuego. Originally Asiatic in race, language, and religion, they shaped new cultures during their long migratory passages and in the semiautonomous centers they established often without frequent exterior contacts.

All these cultures, from the simple fishers and food-gatherers of the extreme South (like the Alacaluf or Yahgan) to the Eskimos of the extreme North, recognized a heavenly mythic great divinity. They usually considered this divinity dual-natured as the great mother-father, or twin brothers or sisters, or as a combination of abstract principles. Although I lack the space to describe fully the Amerindian world, this amazing mythic similarity pervading the continent[40] helps to highlight Amerindia's place in history as the result of very early Asian migrations.

In my interpretation, these American peoples forming the continent's protohistory attained three levels of cultural development. At the *first level*, I would situate clans and tribes of fishers, hunters, and nomadic food-gatherers of the South[41] and the North.[42] At the *second level*, I would include agricultural villages, composed of clans, tribes, and (preurban) tribal confederations. This second level appeared in the Cordilleras to the south and southeast of the Incan empire extending as far as the Amazons. This level would also encompass such groups as the Tupi-Guaraní, the Arawaks, the Caribs, and the indigenous cultures of the plains, southeast, and southwest of the present-day United States. Nuclear or urban America, including the Inca empire and Mesoamerica with its Aztecs, Mayans, and Chibchas comprised the *third level*. This multilayered cultural world had *discovered* rivers, mountains, valleys, and plains, endowed them with names, and incorporated them within varied life-worlds. Amerindia was no *empty*, uncivilized, or barbaric world, but rather a *plenum* of humanization, history, and meaning.

The Tupi-Guaraní, who inhabited the Amazon forests in the Paraguay region, exemplify the second-level culture. Their external cultural manifestations might have seemed totally devoid of any development,[43] and José de Acosta might have classified them as barbarians in his third, most primitive sense.[44] They are, though, the Other, covered over (*encubierto*) by the discovery (*des-cubrimiento*), the diachronic and metaphoric 1492, which has steadily been sinking its roots throughout the continent since the fifteenth century. But modernity is not that distant from the existential Heideggerian world of the Guaraní, as Ayvu Rapyta expresses it in his *great song*.[45]

> The true Father Ñamandú, the first,
> with his knowing that opens-itself-as-a-flower,[46]
> engendered flames and tenuous fog
> from part of his own heavenly being,[47]
> from the wisdom in his heavenly being.
> Incorporated and raised up as human,
> he knew the *fundamental word* of the future
> from the wisdom in his heavenly being,
> and with his knowing that opens-itself-as-a-flower, . . .
> and he made that word part of his own heavenly being. . . .
> This is what Ñamandú, the true Father, the first, did.[48]

Guaraní existence revolved around a profoundly rational, mystical cult dedicated to the word: the word as divinity, the word as "the person's (*ayvu o ñe'e*) initial nucleus, the divine portion in which one participated."[49] The *word-soul*, forming a person's essence, was discovered in sleep,[50] and then interpreted and expressed in the community's celebration of the *ritual song*. Upon receiving a name, each Guaraní commenced a biography that unfolded that word "which keeps-standing[51] the flowing of speech."[52] The eternal word of Father Ñamandú founded and *made stand* each human existence when it *opened-in-flower* at birth, and this word guided each Guaraní's mode of being, or *teko*:[53]

> Oh, our First Father!
> From the beginning you knew the rules of our *mode
>   of being* (*teko*).
> From the beginning you knew the *fundamental word*,
> before the opening and appearance of the *earthly
>   dwelling* (*tekkoha*).[54]

The earthly dwelling referred to the place the Guaraní cleared[55] in the woods to construct their village, to plant crops, and to live humanly. In this dwelling, each Guaraní's word would unravel as a destiny bestowed by the fundamental word mysteriously hidden from its origin in the first father, the creator, who opens himself in flower.

This word, embedded in a system of total reciprocity, was always communitarian and economic:

> Beyond the ceremony, the Guaraní feast also functions as the concrete metaphor for a reciprocally lived economy. . . . Principles of egalitarian distribution direct the interchange of goods for consumption or use in such a way that the giver is obliged to receive and the receiver to give. In this social, dialogic exchange of goods, the prestige of the giver and joy of the receiver circulate among all participants. Hence, the Guaraní imitate the first fathers and mothers, who hosted and were hosted from the very beginning.[56]

In the feast the Guaraní celebrated the word inspired in their dreams by improvising and singing great mythic narratives and by joining as a community in the ritual great dance for days. The feast also embodied economic reciprocity, since whoever shared in the banquet was obliged to prepare it and to invite others.[57]

Since these forest peoples quickly exhausted their lands' productivity, they wandered as nomads. As a result, their celebrations of the word envisioned a land-without-evil:

> The expression: *yvy marane'y*, translated by modern ethnologists as land-without-evil, signifies either "untouched soil on which nothing has been built" or *ka'a marane'y*, "a mountain where no one has removed tree trunks or tampered with anything."[58]

On this land-without-evil, the Guaraní would not have to expel enemies, kill dangerous animals, or work in order to eat. In this imagined land, governed by perfect reciprocity, they would only have to sing, dance, and bring forth the *fundamental word* eternally. "The word in the Guaraní's soul, *ayvy*, meant word-soul or soul-word. The Guaraní's life and death depended on the life of his or her word, and one could measure successes and crises by the forms that word took. A Guaraní's history was the history of the word imposed with one's name, and each Guaraní would listen to that word, say it, sing it, or pray it until in death it became the word that *was, ayvukue*."[59]

How could one ever express all this to the conquistador of the Rio de la Plata or to the generous, profound Jesuits who built the magnificent Paraguay reductions? Those *barbarian*, indigenous peoples . . . deeply worshiped the eternal, sacred, historical word among the tropical forests. To know their world, one would have had to know their tongue, their word, and to have lived it. To dialogue with them, one would have to inhabit their world, their *tekoha*, so beautiful, profound, rational, ecological, developed,[60] and human. To establish the conditions necessary for the kind of conversation Richard Rorty recommends, one would have to discover the world of the Other. The inescapable difficulties of such mutual comprehension in no way proves the total incommensurability of the worldviews. However, when the conditions for such conversation were not even in place, as occurred among the Eurocentric conquistadores, conversation became impossible, as did any argumentation in a *real communication community*. Modern humanist Ginés de Sepúlveda shared the conquistador framework, as do contemporary rationalists who anticipate an easy dialogue or as does Jürgen Habermas, who has yet to develop a theory of the conditions of the possibility of dialogue. From the moment of Europe's discovery of America, the Europeans disgracefully covered all this over. Under the mantle of forgetfulness and barbaric modernization, Europeans have continued realizing that mythic 1492 throughout the continent.

I could have provided hundreds of examples of either less developed peoples such as the northern or southern nomads or

more developed ones such as those of nuclear America. The case
of the Guaranís, however, *indicates* the question, which I will pursue by carefully considering as an example the Náhuatl culture of
nuclear America.

EXCURSUS ON EUROPE AS PERIPHERAL TO THE ISLAMIC WORLD

Until 1492, present-day western Europe was *peripheral* and *secondary* to Islam. Western Europe, hemmed in by the Turks at
Vienna on the east until 1681, had never been the center of history. From Vienna to Seville in the west, Latin-Germanic Europe
never exceeded a hundred million in population, and thus always
fell short of China's population. This isolated culture failed in the
Crusades to recover its presence in the Middle East, the neuralgic
pole of Eurasian commerce. In what is now Palestine, the homeland of the holy sepulcher, caravan commerce arriving in Antioch
from China, Turan, and Chinese Turkestan used to intersect with
seafaring traffic from the Red and Persian seas. Via these routes,
Italian cities like Genoa (the city of Columbus and origin of several clandestine Atlantic discoveries since 1474), Venice, Naples,
and Amalfi connected with tropical Asia and India. Thus, when
Europe lost control of the eastern Mediterranean, Islam confined
it all the more to an isolated, peripheral status.

Islam commenced in northern Africa with the Almoravides[61]
and flourishing cities in Morocco and the Magrib. It passed
through Tripoli, the starting point of caravans heading south
toward the Sahara and the kingdoms of the savannah, such as Mali
or Ghana. Islam then extended to present-day Libya and Egypt,
later seized by the Ottomans. It spread to the Baghdad caliphate, to
Iran, which the Saffarid empire conquered, and further to northern
India, where the Mogol kingdoms built capital cities at Anra and
later Delhi, and produced splendid art, such as the Taj Mahal. The
Muslim world finally expanded to Malacca and, due to Islamic
traders, reached its limits when Mindanao in the southern
Philippine Islands converted at the end of the fourteenth century.
Thus, the Giving-of-Islam, the house of faith, sprawled between
the Atlantic and the Pacific Oceans. To be sure, Turkish invaders,
themselves Muslims, had broken the dorsal spine of the Arab-

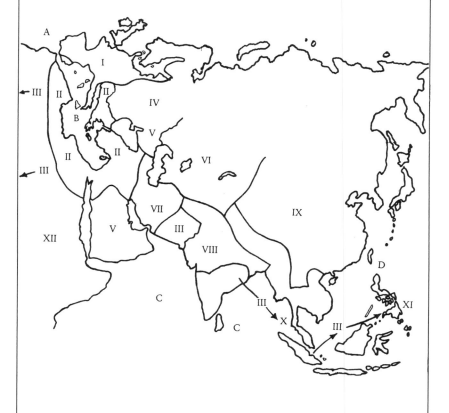

FIGURE 3

EUROPE PERIPHERAL TO THE ISLAMIC WORLD (1480–1500)

I	Peripheral Europe	IX	China
II	Ottoman Empire	X	Islamic traders
III	Other Islamic peoples	XI	Islamic Mindanao (Philippines)
IV	The Golden Horde (1480)	XII	Copts ("Prester John")
V	The Blue Horde (1480)	A	Atlantic Ocean
VI	Other Mogolian hordes	B	Mediterranean Sea
VII	The Saffarid Empire (1500)	C	Arabic Sea
VIII	The Mogol Empire (1600)	D	*Sinus Magnus* (Pacific Ocean)

Geographical source: Arnold Toynbee, *Historical Atlas*, from *A Study of History* (Oxford: Oxford University Press, 1962), vol. 11, pp. 132, 158, 164

Muslim commercial world. By occupying the Balkans, Greece, and Turkey, they had isolated the western parts of Islam from its east. Meanwhile, China had fallen into a profound economic crisis and the Mongols' golden horde dominated Russia (1240–1480). When the Turks took over Constantinople in 1453, Europe found itself surrounded and reduced to a minimal role.

Thus Hegel slips into myopic Eurocentrism when he speaks of Europe as the beginning, center, and end of world history.[62] Western Europe,[63] which never was the center of history, had to wait until 1492 to establish itself empirically as the center with other civilizations as its periphery. In my opinion, western Europe's bursting the bounds within which Islam had confined it, gave *birth* to *modernity*. In 1492 the European *ego* first transformed other subjects and peoples into its objects and instruments for its own Europeanizing, civilizing, and modernizing purposes.

Western Europe was the first to embark upon the conquest of the world. Russia under Ivan II, the Great, began an expansion through the northern taiga. Even though Ivan III founded the Kremlin in 1485, the Russians did not reach the Pacific Ocean until the early 1600s. In contrast, Europe broke the Muslim siege, which had been in effect since Mohammed's death in the seventh century A.D., and launched westward by the efforts of Spain and Portugal, which seized Ceuta in Africa in 1415.[64] Spain initiated modernity, even though western Europe later forgot and despised it, and even though Hegel ceased considering it part of Europe.

In the conquest of Mexico, the European ego first controlled, colonized, dominated, exploited, and humiliated an Other, another empire. It is important to view these events *from below*, from the viewpoint of the Other, from Indian perspective, from the horizon opened in this chapter that began with Asia and the Pacific. How did the Indian experience these Europeans, so marginal to Islam, as they pursued their triumphal course toward the center of world history?

From the Invasion to the Dis-Covery of the Other

In this third part, I will undertake a hermeneutic of 1492 from the Other's perspective. This date ceases being a historical moment and becomes a mythic, symbolic, metaphoric happening with rational significance.[1] The year 1492 becomes a text expressing Mayan and Aztec meanings awaiting interpretation. According to part 1, Western Europe *invented* the *discovery* in concurrence with Hegel's belief that civilization moved westward (Asia, Middle East, Europe, Atlantic, America) and as recognition and control of the continent between Europe and Asia. In contrast, for the civilizations that moved eastward (Middle East, Asia, Pacific Ocean toward America), 1492 took on metaphorical, mythic proportions. The year 1492 culminated in a parousia encounter with unknown gods (the first figure or *Gestalt*), who, when discovered to be human beings, came to appear as bestial *invaders* (second figure). At that point modernity's sacrificial myth of modernity supplanted the Aztec sacrificial myth, and the indigenous world experienced the *end of the world* (third figure). It is essential to interpret the significance of 1492 for indigenous peoples diachronically, since what began in the Carribean islands has not yet been completed among some Amazon tribes who *preexist the mythic 1492*. Although this other interpretation does not comprehend 1492 as a discovery of a new continent on the globe, it is extremely important for revealing the power of the myth of modernity for modernity's periphery. The proponents of Eurocentrism in Europe, the United States, Latin America, and other parts of the periphery, have yet to grasp this interpretation.

CHAPTER 7

From the Parousia of the Gods to the Invasion

> *In teteu inan in tetu ita, in Huehuetéutl* [Mother of
> the gods, Father of the gods, the ancient God],[1]
> lying[2] in the navel of the earth, enclosed[3] in
> turquoise. The God in the waters the color of the
> blue[4] bird, the God enclosed in the clouds,[5] the
> ancient God dwelling in the shadowy region of the
> dead,[6] the Lord of the fire and the year.
> —Song to Ometeótl, originary being
> of the Aztec *tlamatinime*[7]

To discuss the Aztecs' experience of 1492, it is essential to begin with their reflexive, abstract thought. This is especially true in view of the intercultural dialogue initiated in 1989 in Freiburg.[8]

THE TLAMATINI

Nomadic (of the first degree) or agricultural cultures (such as the Guaranís) had not sufficiently differentiated themselves to allow for the function of *philosopher*.[9] However, Garcilaso de la Vega in *Comentarios reales de los Incas* refers to such a role:

> Besides adoring the sun as a visible god through sacrifices or great festivals . . . the Incan kings and their *amautas* or *philosophers* [—comments Garcilaso de la Vega—] traced a path with their natural reason to the true, high God lord, creator of heaven and earth. . . . They called this God Pachacámac, a combination of *Pacha*, the universal world, and *Cámac*, present participle of the verb *cama*, meaning *to animate*, derived from the noun *cama*, meaning *soul*. By Pachacámac they designated the soul which animates the universal world as the human soul its body. . . . They held Pachacámac in greater veneration than the sun whose name they did not dare to utter. . . . For this reason, they neither constructed temples nor offered the sun sacrifices, but adored him in their heart and considered him an unknown God.[10]

The *amautas* performed special functions and considered Pachacámac (from the coast of Peru) or *Illa-Ticsi Huiracocha Pachayachic* (originary splendor, lord, master of the world) as the first principle of the universe. Among the Aztecs, the *tlamatini*[11] received a clearer social definition. Bernardino de Sahagún, in the tenth book of *Historia General de las cosas de Nueva España*, referred to the *tlamatini* after cataloging the offices of carpenter, stonecutter, mason, painter, singer.[12] Fernando de Alva Ixtlizóchitl mentions governors, judges, warriors, priests, and specifically delimited *wise ones*, designated by Sahagún as *philosophers* on the manuscript's margin:

> The philosophers, or wise ones, were responsible for depicting all that their sciences had achieved and for memorizing and teaching the songs conserved within their sciences and history.[13]

León Portilla presents some Náhuatl definitions of the *tlamatinime* who were educated in a scrupulously regimented academy called the *Calmécac*:[14]

> The *tlamatini* is a light and a thick firebrand that never smokes.[15] He is a pierced mirror, a mirror perforated on both sides.[16] His hue is black and red. . . . He is writing and wisdom. He is the way and true guide for others. . . . The truly wise person carefully maintains the tradition. He transmits wisdom and follows the truth.[17] Master of truth, he never ceases admonishing. He

makes wise the faces of others,[18] he makes them take on a face and develop it. . . . He holds up a mirror before others[19] . . . so that their own face appears. . . . He applies his light to the world.[20]. . . Thanks to him, the people humanize their desiring[21] and receive disciplined instruction.[22]

In addition, the Aztecs developed a negative description of the *false wise person*[23] and thus gave evidence of a conceptual thinking based on metaphors but exceeding mere mythic symbols.[24]

Young Aztecs left their families from ages six to nine in order to join the *Calmécac* community. In that absolutely regimented atmosphere,[25] they participated in dialogues and conversations with the wise ones (*Huehuetlatolli*).[26] They thus acquired a *wisdom already known* (*momachtique*) and the capacity to articulate an *adequate word* (*in qualli tlatolli*) with rhetorical discipline, as was learned in the Plato's academy or Aristotle's lyceum. The great work of the *Calmécac*, the *flower and song* (*in xochitl in cuícatl*), exhibited this discipline.[27] The *tlamatinime* inscribed this song in codices (*amates*), recited it with or without music, and danced to it. The divine communicated with *the earthly* (*tlaltípac*) in this song above all and also in dreams requiring interpretation.[28]

Among the fifteenth century Aztecs, the proto-philosophy of the *tlamatinime*, overlooked by the European and Latin American Enlightenment,[29] clashed head on with the sacrificial myth of Tlacaélel. That myth supported domination and militarism, and anticipated the myth of modernity, which would replace it. Because of the tension between these currents, Moctezuma, more a *tlamatini* than a military man, hesitated in his dealings with Cortés. The *tlamatinime* admired the European navigators and cartographers and, at the same time, experienced agitation over what they believed to be the parousia of the Gods. The vanquished Aztecs understood the conquest as a brutal invasion, colonization as the *sixth sun*, or the epoch of servitude, and the spiritual conquest as the death of their gods.

THE PAROUSIA OF THE GODS

Tlamatinime beliefs, such as that of the five suns, often coincided with popular convictions and those of the dominant political, warrior, and commercial classes.[30] However, the *tlamatinime* also developed highly conceptualized and abstract rationalizations, which underpinned their interpretation of the new arrivals from the East, where the sun (Huitzilopochtli) is born each day.

Beyond myths, Aztec reason affirmed that not one[31] but two (*Ome*) lay at the absolute and eternal origin of everything. From the start, the *divine duality* (*Ometeótl*), or simply the *duality* (*Oméyotl*), resided in the thirteenth[32] heaven, the *place of the duality* (*Omeyocan*). The *tlamatinime* would have disagreed with Hegel who posited first being and nothing which combined to form becoming and movement before any specific being (*Dasein*) came on the scene. In contrast, the *tlamatinime* conceived an origin already co-determined (*i-námic*[33] meant *one shares*) in the metaphoric manner[34] of *female-male*.[35] They fleshed out this origin's further determinations via a highly advanced process of conceptual abstraction:

> And also they said to him (1) *Moyucayatzin* (2) *ayac oquiyocux* (3) *ayac oquipic*, which means that no one created or formed it.[36]

Mendieta never grasped that these ontologically precise terms employed strict philosophical ratiocination far surpassing mere mythic reasoning. The first term (1) signified the *Lord who created himself*[37]; the second (2) indicated *no one made him*; and the third (3) *no one gave him his form*. The expressions of *flower and song* approximated an understanding of *Ometeótl* as *night-wind* (*Yohualli-Ehecátl*),[38] *he who is near and surrounds us* (*in Tloque in Nahuaque*),[39] *he who gives us life* (*Ipalnemohuani*). This less than complete explanation permits some comprehension of the text opening this chapter.

How did the *tlamatinime* explain the relation between the absolute ontological principle of divine duality and the phenomenal, temporal, terrestrial (*tlaltípac*) reality, in which we live as if *dreaming*? The divine duality unfolded itself through a *Diremption*[40] or *Explication* similar to the splitting of first principles characteristic of pseudo-Dionysius the Areopagite and Scotus Eriugena. "This god-goddess engendered four sons,"[41] each called *Tezcatlipoca*.[42]

These concrete, originary principles of the universe spread out in the direction of the four cardinal points as in Chinese ontology, Polynesian traditions, and the American cultures from the northern

Eskimos to the southern Incas or Araucanians. These principles included the East, red; the North, black, for the region of death; the West, white, for Quetzalcóatl; for fecundity, and life; the South, blue, for Huitzilopochtli of the Aztecs. Although these four Aztec principles resembled the pre-Socratic foursome of earth, air, water, and fire, each Aztec principle entailed more, since it dominated a world epoch. These previous four epochs had culminated in the present age of the fifth sun, the *Sun in movement,* Huitzilopochtli, the warrior god of the Aztecs:

> This sun, which follows four *movements,* this is our sun, in which we now *live.* . . . The fifth sun . . . is called the sun of *movement* because it moves upon its path.[43]

Movement (Y-olli) involved the *heart (Y-ollo-tl)* and *life (Yoliliztli).*[44] *All things live (Ipalnemohuani),* by Ometeótl via the sun, one of Tezcatlipoca's faces. Furthermore, humanity, the *macehuales,*[45] caught in the midst of the struggle among the four principles, could only survive by joining in solidarity with the reigning fifth sun. Nevertheless, these freely chosen efforts to secure oneself counted little in the Aztecs' tragic vision of existence, since everything was predetermined according to the *old rule of life (Huehuetlamanitiliztli).*

Love for Ometeótl regulated everything *on earth (tlaltípac):*

> Our lord, the lord surrounding us (*in Tloque in Nahuaque*), determines[46] what he desires, plans it, and diverts himself with it. What he desires now, he will desire in the future. He has placed us in the palm of his hand and moves us about at his fancy.[47]

Since humanity followed its necessary path[48] like the stars in heaven, the *tlamatinime* obsessively searched for the foundation[49] of reality where truth resided:

> By chance, are human beings the *truth?*[50] For all this, is our song not the *truth?*[51] Is what is standing (*está de pie*) by chance it?[52]

For the *tlamatinime, the only thing true on the earth (nelli in tlatícpac)* was the *flower and song* by which they communicated with the divinity in the community of the wise.[53] But one could achieve this founding of oneself in the divinity by other ways than the mystical-philosophical experience. For instance, the Aztecs devised a religious calendar to celebrate life's rhythms according to times of the day, festive days, thirteen day-long weeks, and even the lunar, solar,[54] and Venusian years.[55] The Aztecs assigned a protector divinity to each day, week, month, type of year, and their combinations. In order to calm the entire procession of hierarchized divinities passing through the heavenly circuit each day, the Indians offered worship of songs, rites, and sacrifices, and set up festive celebrations.[56] The Aztecs complemented their highly regulated lives by astrology[57] and by interpretations which endowed even anomalous experiences with significance.[58]

Whereas astrology supplied a divine rule a priori for every temporal (*in tlatícpac*) occurrence, by the hermeneutic of auguries the *tlamatinime* interpreted contingent, concrete, novel, empirical events a posteriori. That is, these auguries showed how the occurrence of past events had been necessary all along, how *they were unable to be any another way*, as Aristotle would say. Via such deterministic convictions, the tragic Aztec consciousness, shared by the people, the rulers, the warriors, and the *tlamatinime*, was assured of its fundamentation in Ometeótl's truth.

Against this background, Moctezuma comprehended the apparition of gods arriving on his coasts from the infinite *Teoatl* (Atlantic).

> Those who arrived in their ships came out of the sea (*teoatl*).
> . . . And when the Aztecs approached these men from Castilla[59]
> and faced them, the Aztecs ceremoniously kissed the land. . . .
> They believed that our lord Quetzalcóatl had returned.[60]

Moctezuma reasoned strategically to the conclusion that Cortés was Quetzalcóatl[61] when he received him in Mexico City. Although authors such as T. Todorov,[62] N. Wachtel,[63] M. León Portilla,[64] Octavio Paz,[65] J. Lafaye,[66] consider the emperor's attitudes to be wavering, contradictory, and scarcely comprehensible, they fail to explain sufficiently the rationality of his comportment. Moctezuma's comments are significant:

> Our lord, upon your arrival you seem fatigued and exhausted.
> You have come up to *your city*, to Mexico, to assume *your royal*

chair. Oh, for a brief time *your substitutes*, the lord kings Itzcaotzin, Motecuhzomatzin the elderly, Axayácac, Tízoc, and Ahuítztotl occupied *your throne*, but now they are gone. Oh, they exercised power over the city of Mexico and guarded the throne *on your behalf* for only a brief time. . . . No, I am neither dreaming nor awakening from a deep sleep. Now I am actually laying my eyes *on your face!* Five or ten days ago I felt anxiety and fixed my eyes on the region of the dead (*topa mictlan*) until you came among the clouds and mist. Our previous kings informed us who rule *your city* that you would return to take up again *your seat, your chair*. . . . Come, rest; take possession of *your royal houses*; relieve yourself.[67]

Moctezuma thus surrendered his throne to Cortés—exactly what Cortés desired. Well, not quite, since Cortés did not understand the offer and had no intention of occupying the throne. Faced with this novelty and subsequent ones, Moctezuma was repeatedly dismayed. Did Moctezuma behave *rationally*? Yes, *if one considers his world instead of projecting a Eurocentric perspective upon him.*

What possibilities[68] presented themselves to a man with his perspective, to an Aztec emperor, to a good warrior but a better *tlamatini*, to someone educated in the austere moral tradition of the wise *toltecas*? For an emperor as educated and refined as Moctezuma, the resources of his civilization afforded him three options:[69] (1) The recent arrivals were mere human beings—the least probable[70] from the Náhuatl hermeneutic perspective until later events confirming this hypothesis had occurred.[71] Moctezuma reasonably shelved this possibility *at first*, and he could have only known that this was actually an invasion if those later data had been available to him. (2) The only rational alternative was that they were gods. If so, which gods? Everything from the opinion of astrologers to that of the *tlamatinime* indicated that Cortés was Quetzalcóatl, possibly returning after having been expelled from Tula by the Toltecs and other peoples.[72] (3) In the third alternative, a variant of the second, this apparent Quetzalcóatl only masked the actual presence of the divine principle Ometeótl. This truly ominous event[73] would have spelled the end of the fifth sun.[74]

Faced with these possibilities, Moctezuma slowly decided as rationally as possible. He opted to offer the strangers homage by his gifts, and proposed that they reclaim what was theirs, even if that would cost him his throne. He knew full well that if he confronted these stangers disrespectfully, it would have implied his end.

> Preoccupied, Moctezuma caviled over these things; full of fear and terror, he fretted over what would happen to the city.[75]

By emancipating the empire's enemies in Zempoala or Tlaxcala, Cortés, whether divine or human, proved himself their valuable ally.[76] The warriors faithful to Huitzilopochtli, however, would have only commenced fighting on the side of their god if Cortés and his troops turned out to be merely human (possibility 1) or only if this seeming Quetzalcóatl had come to terminate the fifth sun (possibility 3). The people of Mexico-Tenochtitlan would lose nothing if Cortés were merely Quetzalcóatl reasserting control over his empire (possibility 2). Although different groups may have speculated about these possibilities, the ultimate decision rested with Moctezuma, and his options were limited.[77] If this was Quetzalcóatl (possibility 2), Moctezuma could only resign; in every other case, he could have cast his lot in with his warriors, but only after he had discredited the second possibility. So, motivated by clear stragetic rationality, Moctezuma, the great *tlamatini*, resolved to renounce his empire[78] and hand it over to Quetzalcóatl-Cortés: "Take possession of your royal house!"

Once again, he was surprised. When the Aztecs offered the new-comers food with blood, these strange gods disdained them. Their jubilance over gold seemed even stranger, especially since they irrationally melted down into ingots the precious metal that Aztec goldsmiths had so finely crafted, and which had earned Dürer's admiration in Holland. Instead of immolating their prisoners to their gods, they slaughtered them. The oddity that Cortés did not seize power over Mexico when offered it convinced Moctezuma that he was not prince Quetzalcóatl bent on recovering his temporal power (*in tlaltícpac*).[79] With the other possibilities still remaining, Moctezuma studied the situation carefully, since Cortés might have come at Ometeótl's behest to inflict the worst of all disasters, the destruction of the fifth sun. Therefore, Moctezuma at first endured humiliations in hopes of deferring the possibilities that the

Spaniards were only human beings who would place his life and his empire in jeopardy.

THE INVASION OF THE EMPIRE

Something occurred, though, which Moctezuma could not have anticipated and which required a posterior interpretation.[80] Because of this event, the situation appeared to be a case of the first possibility, a human invasion, even though the third possibility, that of the end of the world, remained in the background:

> Moctezuma was promptly advised that Pánfilo Narváez's armada from Cuba was approaching to make war on Cortés. The emperor, also cognizant that Cortés's reinforcement ships had arrived, summoned him, "Lord captain, your reinforcement vessels have arrived so that you might make battle preparations and depart as soon as possible."[81]

For the first time, Moctezuma became aware that numerous soldiers were available to reinforce Cortés and that all of them, including Cortés, were human.[82] If Moctezuma could persuade or compel these strangers to return from where they came, everything would have turned out well, with the empire, the traditions, the gods, and the fifth sun all intact. But two *new* events corroborated the invasion hypothesis and even implied a brand new fourth possibility: Cortés's defeat of Narváez and return to Mexico with reinforcements, and Pedro de Alvarado's massacre of the Aztec elites. These two events proved Moctezuma's error,[83] and tipped the balance in favor of the warriors inspired by Tlacaélel's sacrificial myth. These warriors had preferred to engage the Spaniards in war since they had believed that they were human from the start. Even though Moctezuma was finished, Cortés, ignorant of the Other, of Moctezuma and his highly developed *argumentative world*,[84] attempted to use him as before and squandered vital time.[85] Cortés gave the Aztecs time to ponder their discovery that he and his men were only human warriors, the front lines of an invasion of the *Cemanáhuac*, the world as the Aztecs knew it.

These events tested the *tlamatinime* vision of the world and disconfirmed and destroyed it. These occurrences discredited Moctezuma the *tlamatini* whose own physical death was only hours away, and they ushered in the parousia of the gods. Pánfilo Narváez and not Cortés proved as *no one before* had that an invasion was taking place, just as it fell to the lot of Amerigo Vespucci and not Columbus to discover America.

Tlacaélel, the Aztec Romulus and Remus,[86] was born in the year of the rabbit (1398), conquered the Tepanecas of Azcapotzalco and the Albalonga of Mexico-Tenochtitlan, in the year of Pedernal (1428), and so merited the title *the conqueror of the world* (*in cemanáhuac Tepehuan*).[87] He was responsible for reforming the empire, providing it with a cosmopolitan vision, and, unfortunately, interpreting it as requiring sacrifices from others for its flourishing.

> This office belongs to Huitzilopochtli, our god: to reunite and press into his service all nations with the strength of his breast and cunning of his mind.[88]

The Tezcatlipocas first revealed Ometeótl, the deity greater than the fifth sun or Quetzalcóatl, and the keystone in the Aztec sacrificial paradigm:

> And here is his sign, as it fell in the fire of the sun, in the divine firebox, there in Teotihuacan.[89]

According to the myth underlying this cryptic statement, the hummingbird god, Nanhuatzin, sacrificed his life by being immolated for all in the divine firebox. After a long night, he reappeared as the rising sun, Huitzilopochtli, a tribal god of the Aztecs. Through an imperialistic reformation that involved burning the sacred codices of all dominated peoples and rewriting their theogonies, Tlacaélel elevated this secondary warrior god to principal deity of Anahuac. The empire was founded to serve the existence and life of the sun. Since the sun's and all reality's movement, life, and heart related to blood (*chalchihuitl*), the Aztecs believed the life of the sun-Huitzilopochtli depended on human sacrifices. The Aztecs obtained their victims in the flower wars and their sacrifice justified the existence of the empire:

> There where the spears ring, where the shields clang, there are the white perfumed flowers, the flowers of the heart. The flowers

of the life-giver open their corollas, and the princes of the world
inhale the perfume of the life-giver: it is Tenochtitlan.[90]

By these myth-based human sacrifices performed in the greater
temple of Huitzilopochtli, Tlacaélel's empire collaborated in main-
taining the universe and prolonging the life of the fifth sun. Once
the empire recognized Cortés as only human, the warriors launched
a war against the intruders in order to prolong the fifth sun.

> The Spaniards departed at night on the feast of Techíhuitl. It
> was at that time that they died in the canal of the Toltecs. There
> we attacked them furiously.[91]

The Aztecs achieved little by expelling Cortés from the city on
the Spaniards' "sorrowful night."[92] Immediately after this, the plague
broke out, and the Aztecs interpreted it as ominous. In addition, the
invaders reorganized forces in Tlaxcala, and, like the Catholic kings
in Granada, Cortés set about debilitating Mexico. After a seige for
months, the Spaniards expelled the Aztecs from Tenochtitlan, cor-
nered them in Tlatelolco, and vanquished them:

> Broken spears clutter the roads; horses scatter. Houses stand
> with their roofs torn off and their walls reddened with blood.
> Brain matter spatters their walls, and worms swarm the streets
> and plazas. The waters are red, as if dyed, and taste of salt-
> peter.[93] The Mexicans, totally routed and needing water, flee to
> Tlatelolco like women, groaning and shedding copious tears.
> Where are we going? Oh, friends! Is it true?[94] They abandon
> Mexico City, as smoke ascends and the haze expands. . . . This
> is what the life-giver has done in Tlatelolco.[95]

The invasion was complete, and the warriors overpowered. Over
the years, this same tragedy befell the Mayas and the Incas of Atahualpa,
and despair spread from Tierra del Fuego to Alaska. The Spaniards
installed modernity by emancipating those oppressed by the Aztecs
and by denying their bloodthirsty gods any more victims. The sixth
sun had dawned. A new god, however, inaugurated a new sacrificial
myth. The myth of Tlacaélel yielded before the no less sacrificial myth
of the provident hand of God who harmoniously regulated Adam
Smith's market. To secure F. Hayek's myth of perfect competition, it
will be necessary to destroy the *monopoly* of workers' unions.

CHAPTER 8

From the Resistance to the End of the World and the Sixth Sun

And they said: Now we have come to *tlatzompan*, the end of the world, and these newcomers will remain. There is no hope for anything else since our ancestors predicted what has happened.
—Gerónimo de Mendieta,
Historia Eclesiástica Indiana[1]

The parousia of the gods (first figure) ended Moctezuma's empire, and the European invasion (second figure) extended its tentacles throughout the continent. The American *resistance* (third figure), more fierce and prolonged than many believe, would not triumph, in most cases because the indigenous people lacked interpretive flexibility and military technology. Even though the Amerindians faced the *end of the world* (fourth figure), they believed that a new cosmic era would take up the thread of eternal becoming. The *sixth sun* (fifth figure) was now commencing, and we in the periphery have lived the last five hundred years under its sway.

THE RESISTANCE

We cannot give an adequate account of this theme so important for the social block of the oppressed. A historian tells us:

> Traditional history presents the conquest as a prodigy achieved by a handful of valiant men who for the sake of God and Castille and with only their presence dominated thousands of primitive savages. A simple consultation of the chronicles discloses that a ferocious and systematic opposition began immediately after the surprise and confusion of the initial encounter. The battle ensued as soon as these gods whose arrival had been announced by the tradition turned out to be only earthly invaders. Indigenous men and women offered decisive, brave, and often suicidal resistance . . . to firearms, horses, and dogs trained to feed on Indians and tear them cruelly to pieces.[2] . . . Since so few of the resistance heroes have been remembered, we wish to revive the memory of all those who defended their land and liberty.[3]

Instead of following the resistance step by step,[4] I will indicate a few instances. In Santo Domingo on Hispanola, the site of the *celebration* of the discovery and evangelization of America in 1992, the following chiefs governed five small kingdoms: Guarionex, Guacanagarí (traitor to his own people and friend of Columbus), Caonabo, Behechio (brother of the brave and beautiful Queen Anacaona), and Catubanamá. When the Spaniards left by Columbus in Fort Navidad set about robbing, raping, and killing Indians, Caonabo initiated the hemisphere's first resistance by attacking the fort and punishing its denizens. In addition, the Spanish had forced Cibao, Caonabo's hometown, to pay a large tribute because of its wealth in gold. They also required the Indians to wear about their necks a copper coin recording the date they had paid the tax. Since the tribute was excessive and the sign of tribute-payment degrading,[5] Caonabo provoked a rebellion and prepared for war.

However, the Spaniards achieved by treachery what they could not win through arms by summoning Caonabo to receive a gift from Columbus and capturing him. He drowned en route to Spain when the ship carrying him sank. Although the other chiefs struggled for years in diverse forms, one by one they were defeated and their populations disappeared at a rapid rate. Only Guaracuya, called Enriquillo as a young student of the Franciscans, eluded the Spaniards until his death by waging guerrilla warfare in the mountains.

Concluding this sad history, the bishop of Santo Domingo in its first synod in 1610 felt no need to provide for the Indians *because not a single Indian remained.* Furthermore, the first rebellion of African slaves in the Americas occurred in Santo Domingo on the property of Diego Columbus, the admiral's son.

Great acts of heroism were displayed by chiefs Hatuey in Cuba,[6] Argüeibana and Mabodomoco in Puerto Rico,[7] Cemaco and Urraca in bloody battles at Veragua and the Darién,[8] and Nicaroguán in Nicaragua.[9] In Mexico,[10] Xicontencatl in Tlaxcala and Cacama in Texcoco withstood the Spanish as did the hundreds of thousands of soldiers who battled to the death in Náhuatl cities surrounding Mexico until young Cuahutemoc's execution. The Mexicans opposed the Spaniards often to the last man and woman,[11] and entire villages committed suicide rather than surrender.

The Mayas prolonged their subtle insurrection until the twentieth century.[12] Distinguished heroes include Tecum Umán, a sixteenth-century Quiché killed in Quetzaltenango by Alvarado, Jacinto Canek, an eighteenth-century Mayan, and Lempira in Honduras.[13] In Florida[14] the indigenous peoples were indomitable. In Venezuela[15] chiefs Guaicaipuro and Yaracuy refused to submit to the ferocious invasion launched by the Welzers, German traders. Tundama of Duitama and others combatted avaricious pearl hunters in northern Colombia[16] (Santa Marta and Cartagena) and the greedy Sebastian de Belalcázar in the south (from Pasto and Cali to Popayán). These Spaniards had pursued their devastating search for riches to the point of disintering Chibcha mummies to rob them.

In the Tahuantisuyo, the Incas confronted the most cynical European treacheries with a longer and more fierce opposition than the Aztecs offered.[17] Rumiñahui, the emperor's brother, defended Quito valiantly, only to die under torture. General Quizquiz repeatedly routed the Spaniards, and General Calichima's bravery resulted in his being burned alive. Manco Cápac led a new generation of Incans by beseiging Cuzco for eight months before taking refuge in Vilcabamba in the Andean cordillera. Fighting until the seventeenth century, these Incan refugees left the Machu Pichu as a testimony to their resolve. Túpac Amaru's rebellion in 1780,[18] the last before emancipation from Spain, proved that the Incan refusal to capitulate continued without interruption.

In Rio de la Plata,[19] only five hundred of Pedro de Mendoza's twenty-five hundred troops survived after the Querandís and Guaranís attacked them and burnt Buenos Aires in 1534. While the Guaranís also rebuffed the Spaniards in Paraguay, the Calchaquís obstructed their path in northern Argentina. Many nomad indigenous peoples in the Pampas skillfully deployed the horses abandoned by Mendoza against the Spaniards. The Mapuches (Araucanians) of Chile seized Patagonia and held it until Julio Roca embarked upon his 1870 *desert invasion* with the support of Remington rifles and the Morse wireless telegraph.

In Chile,[20] the Mapuches (Araucanians) triumphed as no other indigenous peoples due to their political organization and war pacts modeled on the Polynesian *toki*. Lautaro, son of Curiñancu, and Caupolicán, who defeated the conquistadores, excelled among the Mapuches, who impeded European and *criollo* occupation of southern Chile until the nineteenth century. The ravaged Tucapel fort marked the enduring southern boundary of the conquest.

While political-military control clearly had passed into the hands of the invaders in the great empires, the resistance persisted throughout the colonial epoch. In these empires, a new figure, the end of the world, succeeded the resistance, as the vanquished indigenous peoples recognized that one epoch had finished and another had begun.

The End of the World (the Tlatzompan, the Pachakuti)

The annihilation of the resistance compelled diverse peoples to interpret the new state of things with the resources of their world visions. The Aztecs, for instance, had anticipated their own tragic dénouement when the very arrival of the strangers under Cortés's authority evoked terror and weeping. Almost from the start, they interpreted these events as foreboding the end of the world and the fifth sun.

> They huddled together for meetings and discussions, and every
> person wept for the other. With heads drooping, they would
> burst into tears whenever they greeted each other.[21]

Moctezuma had pondered the third possibility of those listed in
chapter 7—namely, that Quetzalcóatl had returned to declare the
fifth sun's demise, but he sought to set it aside until the end. Instead,
he hoped that Quetzalcóatl, prince and wise man, had come again
to take over his throne. This option was preferable to failing at the
historical mission of the Aztecs over which Tlacaélel had obsessed—
the prolongation of the fifth sun by the sacrifice of blood (*chalchíhu-
atl*). Signs were to accompany the end of the fifth sun:

> Four movements precede the fifth sun. . . . As the old ones say,
> in it there will be movement of the earth and a hunger from
> which we will perish.[22]

One day the four movements (*nahui ollin*) and the epoch of the
fifth sun, the era of the Aztecs[23] and their god Huizilopochtl, would
come to an end. According to the Náhuatl cosmovision, everything
had been regulated from eternity, and there could be no unforeseen
or accidental changes. Besides, the passage to a new epoch was to
occur catastrophically through a radical hecatomb, which the Incas
called *pachakuti*[24] and which would instantaneously revolutionize
the universe. To postpone this tragedy:

> The sacrifice and the war of the flowers which provided victims
> to maintain the sun's life were their two central preoccupations
> and the axes of personal, social, military, and national life.[25]

For the Mayans and according to their account of the Katunes,
the Spaniards' arrival signified the end of an epoch of peace, pros-
perity, and song.

The Incas summed up the end of the world by *pachakuti*, a word
that spread doom as it circulated throughout the empire upon the
arrival of the invaders.

The Guaranís understood the end of the world in terms of the
end of the forest and of the elimination of any future time. This
absolute evil (*mba'e maquá*) similar to such great evils as the great
flood (*yporû*) had already begun insofar as modernizing forces were

destroying the forests and preventing the Guaranís from reproducing their lives in accord with their traditions:

> The worst of all the colonial evils would have been simply to deny the Guaranís their own land. Where would they have gone? The circle of devastation was closing in on the east and the west. Land which had not been traveled upon, exploited, violated, or built upon—the ideal of the *land without evil (yvy marane'y)*—no longer existed. The whites had converted forests and mountains into farm land and claimed it for their own. The earth had become evil; the *mba'e mequá* covered everything.[26]

The Guaraní fate was more ruinous than that of the Aztecs, Mayans, or Incas whose urban cultures had acquired high agricultural capacities with which to resist colonization.

THE INCONCLUSIVE DIALOGUE

Tragic resignation replaced defiant resistance. A narration claimed:

> The dogs consumed three *tlamatinime* of Tezcocano originally from Echécatl.[27] They had come to the Spaniards to hand themselves over. No one had obliged them. They had come carrying only their papers with paintings.[28] They were four, one fled; three were attacked in Coyoacán.[29]

Only today can we imagine the humiliation, the lack of respect, the tragedy these wise men experienced. They had intended to hand over the treasures of their culture and its traditional mystical world vision to illiterate, brutal, and uneducated invaders.[30] Christianity did not accommodate these indigenous cultures in the way that it transformed the Hellenist and Roman cultures into Byzantine, Coptic, Georgian, Armenian, Russian, or Latin-German forms of Christendom around the fourth century C.E. In contrast, the Amerindian cultures were torn up from their roots.

Therefore, the manuscript of the *Colloquios y Doctrina Cristiana*[31] possesses particular value since it gives an account of a historic dialogue. For the first and only time, the *tlamatinime*, those few remaining alive, were given the opportunity to enter into a somewhat respectful debate with educated Spaniards, the twelve recently arrived Franciscan missionaries. In this dialogue, the *reason of the*

Other faced the *discourse of modernity* as it was coming to birth. The argumentation lacked symmetry and fell short of Apel's ideal *argumentative community* since some participants were the conquered and others the conquerors. In addition, the arguing parties differed in their cognitive development in unexpected ways. While the *tlamatinime* had received a highly sophisticated education in the *Calmécac*, the friars, although very select and excellent religious, were not their equals. Although during the dialogue it might have seemed as if the Indians were mute and the Spaniards deaf, power rested with the Spaniards because of the conquest. Therefore, the Spaniards never attained the quality of argumentation on which Bartolomé de las Casas insisted in the *De Único Modo* and so they interrupted the argumentative dialogue and resorted to indoctrination. They treated the *tlamatinime* in the same way that catechists treated children when imparting doctrine to them in Seville, Toledo, or Santiago de Compostela.

The *tlamatinime*, on the other hand, produced a magnificent piece of rhetorical art *(flower and song)*, filled with beauty and logically structured into six parts.[32] They commenced with a greeting and introduction to the dialogue:

> Our much esteemed lords: What travail have you passed through to arrive here.[33] Here, before you, we ignorant people contemplate you.[34]

After the rhetoric, they then asked:

> What shall we say? What *should we direct to your ears?*[35] Are we anything by chance? We are only a vulgar people.

After briefly establishing the framework, they proceeded to the second part, an elaboration of the precariousness of dialogue, in response to the missionaries' initial proposal. That proposal had presented an unsophisticated catechism of beliefs which would have been acceptable only to someone who already believed in Christian doctrine, but it would have been incomprehensible to the Other. The real flesh and blood Other in this dialogue inhabited another culture, language, religion, and hermeneutical space. The *tlamatinime* continued:

> Through the interpreter[36] we will respond by returning the-nourishment-and-the-word[37] to the lord-of-the-intimate-which-

surrounds-us.[38] For his sake, we place ourselves in danger. . . . Perhaps our actions will result in our perdition or destruction, but where are we to go?[39] We are common mortals.[40] *Let us now then die, let us now perish* since *our gods have already died.*[41] But calm your heart-of-flesh, lords, for we will break with the customary for a moment and open for you a little bit the *secret,*[42] the ark of the lord, our God.

In the third part, they state the question to be discussed, the marrow of the dialogue:

> You have said that *we do not know* the lord-of-the-intimate-which-surrounds-us, the one from whom the-heavens-and-the-earth come.[43] You have said that our gods were not *true* gods.

The *tlamatinime,* as good rhetoricians, center the discussion on the essential question of the divine (the lord or our gods) as the truth of humanity and the whole Aztec world. In this question about what is actually the comparative history of religions, the wise Aztecs have more to say than their contemporaries might have thought. The Jewish *Yahweh* and the Roman *Father God* (Jupiter) were uranic gods of the type frequently worshiped by shepherds, nomads, or farmers,[44] and not all that different from Ometeótl, Pachacámac (as Garcilaso showed), and the Toltec, Aztec, or Incan diurnal gods (the sun, Huitzilopochtli or *Inti*).

The fourth part of their argument presents aspects significant for a consensual (not consensualist) theory of truth:[45]

> We respond that we are perturbed and hurt by what you say, because our progenitors never spoke this way.[46]

The *tlamatinime* then assert three defenses for their deities: from *authority,* from intramundane *meaning,* and from *antiquity.* They first cite authority:

> Our progenitors passed on the *norm of life*[47] they held as *true*[48] and the doctrine that we should worship and honor the gods.

These gods were part of a coherent meaning system:

> They taught . . . that these gods give us life and have gained us for themselves[49] . . . in the beginning.[50] These gods provide us with sustenance, drink and food including corn, beans, goose

feet (*bledos*), and *chia*, all of which conserve life. We pray to these gods for the water and rain needed for crops. These gods are happy . . . *where they exist*, in the place of *Tlalocan*, where there is neither hunger, nor sickness, nor poverty.

Finally they appeal to antiquity:

And in what form, when, where were these gods first invoked? . . . This occurred a very long time ago in Tula, Huapalcalco, Xuchatlapan, Tlamohuanchan, Yohuallichan, and Teotihuacan. These gods have established their dominion over the entire universe (*cemanauac*).

In the fifth stage, the *tlamantinime* conclude:

Are we now to destroy the ancient *norm of our life?*—the *norm of life* for the Chichimecas, the Toltecs, the Acolhuas, and the Tecpanecas? We *know* to whom we owe our birth and our lives.

After discussing their feelings about life, they assert: "We refuse to be tranquil or to believe as truth what you say, even if this offends you."

These wise men do not accept as true what the Spaniards proposed to them, since they find valid contrary reasons that support their own way of life. The sixth segment terminates this *flower-and-song*, this piece of rhetorical-argumentative art:

We lay out our reasons to you, lords, who govern and sustain the whole world (*cemanáhualt*). Since we have handed over all our power[51] to you, *if we abide here, we will remain only prisoners*. Our final response is do with us as you please.

Those prisoners who ended up their discourse in their fatherland today complete half a millennium in the hands of a modern humanity which dominates the world. Since they were never taken seriously in the only exchange they had, the dialogue has remained definitively interrupted.

THE SIXTH SUN, A GOD WHO IS BORN DRIPPING WITH BLOOD[52]

What could possibly remain after after the end of the world? The beginning of a new age, another sun or *katun*, as the Mayas called it—the sixth sun. In *El Libro de los libros de Chilam Balam* of the Mayas it is written:

> The eleventh *Ahuau Katun*, the first to be explained, is the initial *katun*. . . . In this katun the red-bearded strangers arrived, sons of the sun, the white colored ones. Ay! Let us mourn that they came from the East! . . . Ay! Let us mourn that they came, these great gatherers of rocks . . . who explode fire from their arms' extremities.[53]

The Mayas recognized the dawn of a new epoch:

> The eleventh *Ahau* begins this account because it was passing when the strangers arrived . . . those who brought the Christianity that ended the East's power, caused weeping to rise to heaven, and filled the corn bread of the *katun* with sorrow. Yaxal Chuen's throat was slit in his own epoch. . . . All those singing, men and women, old and young, were dispersed throughout the world.[54]

The Mayans grasp immediately the sense of the new *katun*:

> In this epoch these strangers will exact tribute. . . . In the *katun*, enormous labor will be forced upon us and the hangings will begin. . . . With the burden of battle, the tribute, and Christianity and its seven sacraments, which appear in conjunction with the tribute, the great travail of the peoples starts and misery is established upon the earth.[55]

The Mayans date this new *katun*:

> One thousand five hundred and thirty-nine years, 1539. To the east is the door of the house of Don Juan Montejo, who established Christianity in Yucalpeten, Yucatán.[56]

These strangers were not going to leave, and the Amerindians knew that they would have to live under them in the future *katun*.

Everywhere, in the Caribbean, in New Mexico to the north, and in Araucanian territory to the south, the invaders carried on the same way. They no sooner seized Tenochtitlan than, before doing anything else, they revealed the meaning of new sun:

> They requisition gold, asking the Indians if by chance they have a little gold, if they have hidden it in their shield or in their war insignias, or if they are keeping it somewhere.[57]

Filipe Guaman Poma de Ayala has described similar scenes among the Incas:

> All day long all they did was think of the gold, silver, and the
> riches of Peruvian Indians. Because of their greed, they seemed
> desperate, stupid, crazy, deprived of all judgment. Sometimes
> they could not even eat, so obsessed were they with gold and
> silver. When it seemed that there was no more gold or silver to
> be seized, they would celebrate.[58]

A new god ascended on the horizon of this new epoch. He began
his triumphal march in the heavens, not under the sacrificial sign
of Huitzilopochli, but under the auspices of modernity's sacrificial
myth. This new god was *capital* in its mercantilist phase, which pre-
vailed in Spain in the sixteenth and seventeenth centuries and later
in Holland. This new fetish metamorphosed, acquiring its industrial face in eighteenth-century England and its transnational embod-
iment in the twentieth-century United States, Germany, and Japan.

The Portuguese in Africa and Asia and the Spaniards in Latin
America craved gold and silver, the world-money by which they
grew richer throughout the entire world that had just been recognized as a planet. The Portuguese and Spanish had invented a world
market, E. Wallerstein's *world-system*, which spread its clutches
worldwide and consumed its new sacrificial victims in every corner
of the earth. A kind of mimetic desire[59] prompted each conquistador to hunt what every other conquistador hunted, even though such
greed resulted in civil wars, such as that between Pizarrists and the
Almagrists in Peru. During the period of capitalism's originary accumulation, this mimetic desire inspired these first modern individuals to horde without limits the universal medium of the new system,
money.[60] Money, the abstract equivalent of every value, whether in
Arabia, Bantu Africa, India, or China, flowed toward Europe, which
heaped up exchange value. Money facilitated the transference of
value and eventually the dominion of North over South and the center over the periphery. The new world order, born in 1492 as the
sixth sun, concealed from its own actors the sacrificial myth that
demanded no less blood than Huitzilopochtli:

> Capital is *dead* labor that, vampirelike, only lives by sucking
> living labor, and it lives the more, the more labor it sucks.[61] The
> discovery of gold and silver in America, the extirpation, enslave-
> ment, and entombment in mines of the aboriginal population,

the beginning of the conquest and looting of the East Indies, the turning of Africa into a warren for the commercial hunting of black skins, signalized the rosy dawn of the era [the "sixth sun"] of capitalist production.[62]

Using another metaphor, the author of *Capital* writes:

If money, according to Augier, "comes into the world with congenital blood on the cheek," capital comes dripping from head to foot, from every pore, with blood and dirt.[63]

In its rational nucleus, modernity entails the emancipation of humanity from cultural immaturity. As a world encompassing myth, however, modernity exploits and immolates men and women in the peripheral, colonial world as it first did with the Amerindians. Modernity hides this victimization, though, by claiming that it is the necessary price of modernization.[64] The act of liberation rationalizes modernity by transcending and deconstructing its irrational myth. As a practico-political program, liberation surpasses both capitalism and modernity in search of a new transmodernity characterized by ecological civilization, popular democracy, and economic justice.

Although Octavio Paz in his "Crítica de la Pirámide"[65] (critique of the pyramid) compared Aztec sacrifices with the contemporary Mexican system, he did not imagine that perhaps all of modernity demands a "Crítica de la Pirámide." The year 1492 ushered in a new era which has been immolating the colonized peoples of the periphery, or the so-called Third World, on a new god's altar:

In actual history, it is notorious that conquest, enslavement, robbery, murder, briefly violence, play the great part.[66]

The Multiple Visages of the One People and the Sixth Sun

The invasion and colonization excluded several visages (*rostros*), historical subjects, and oppressed peoples from the hegemonic community of communication. These make up the other face (*te-ixtli* in Náhuatl) of modernity as do the Others covered over (*encubierto*) by the discovery, the oppressed within peripheral nations (and so doubly dominated), and the innocent victims of sacrificial paradigms. This social block, as Gramsci dubbed it,[1] form a people, a historical subject, evident in such moments as the national emancipation movements in the early nineteenth century. In those movements, the *criollos* rebelled against the Spanish and Portuguese bureaucracies and commercial powers to win their own independence.

In this emancipation, all the dominated classes, the *social block of the oppressed*, took on the physiognomy of a historical subject and realized an authentic political revolution. Later, as the century progressed, the *criollos* transformed themselves from being dominated to dominating the neocolonial, peripheral order. Their class mediated the domination externally imposed by the centers of industrial capitalism, England and France in the nineteenth century and the United States beginning with the end of the second so-called world war.

In this epilogue I wish to indicate aspects not treated in the previous chapters and deserving future consideration. I wish to focus on the multiple visages which pertain to the single Latin American people and which modernity has overlooked.

The first protagonists of Latin American history subsequent to the cultural shock of 1492 were *the Indians*,[2] who still remained invisible to modernity. Although the invasion changed their lives by introducing iron instruments such as the ax, which transfigured agriculture and domestic labor, they have prolonged their resistance for five centuries. The Spaniards brutally and gratuitously exploited them on the *encomiendas* (estates), in the *repartimientos* (apportionments of Indians) for agriculture or mining, including the Andean *mita* (slave labor), and on the *haciendas*, where they received hunger wages. The Indians had to recompose entirely their existence to endure the inhuman oppression that was their lot as the first victims of modernity, the first modern holocaust, as Russell Thornton called it.

Although the European invaders numbered a hundred thousand at the end of the sixteenth century, one percent of the total population, they controlled strategic cities, roads, ports, and mountains. The daily life of the rest of the population, however, eluded the colonizers in spite of their ingressions[3] into the indigenous collective unconscious via the reductions and the doctrines of the missionaries. With their numbers reduced and their elites extirpated, the poor indigenous population survived, unable to revive its previous splendor. The colonial government systematically dominated this population while ceding them a traditional, communitarian proprietorship over some lands. Nineteenth-century liberalism, however, struck a second fatal blow against the Indians by enshrining an abstract, bourgeois, individualist, civic life, instituting private property in the countryside, and suppressing communal modes of living.

It was not surprising when the Indigenous Salvadoran Association (ANIS), in the First Spiritual and Cultural Meeting (*encuentro*), repudiated on February 11, 1988, the *"foreign invasion* of America." They called for "a stop to the genocide and ethnocide of subpeoples and subcultures, and totally rejected the celebration of the five-hundred-year-old *foreign invasion.*"[4]

Earlier, on March 6, 1985, the Indian Council of South America, in its Declaration of the International Commission CISA for the Human Rights of the Indian Peoples, wrote:

> We are certain that the genocide perpetrated on the Jews by the Nazis under Hitler will eventually appear as miniscule. We are certain that all political and ecclesiastical leaders of the Spanish Empire will be condemned to death on the gallows or to perpetual chains. We are certain that perpetual justice will be done.[5]

In an *indigenous consultation* in Mexico sponsored by CENAMI in October 1987 and focusing on *five hundred years of evangelization in Mexico*, the indigenous peoples concluded:

> We have been deceived into thinking that the discovery was good. The *day of the race (Día de la raza)*—[the denomination of the October 12 festivals]—we are now clear about its consequences. We need to distribute to local communities some literature[6] concerning what really happened so that we can all become more aware of why we are enslaved.[7] There is no need for festivities on October 12, since we are in mourning. Pope John Paul II has supposedly requested a novena to prepare for the celebration, but our response is that *he can listen to what we have to say. The pope's role is to serve the church, and we are the church.*[8] Today the conquest continues with all its terror and sorrow.[9] We do not want to celebrate a festival, since the missionaries did not come as brothers, as the gospels say, but as part of the Spanish conquest that enslaved us. We are sad.[10]

In 1992, five hundred years later, the Indians would still concur with Bartolomé de las Casas who wrote in the sixteenth century:

> In their treatment of the Indians, the Spaniards acted as if they were starved wolves, tigers, and cruel lions rushing upon defenseless animals. The Spaniards have done nothing these forty years

[today we ought to say, these five hundred years] except break them in pieces, kill them, cause them anxiety, afflict them, torment them, and destroy them. They have employed strange, new, and diverse cruelties neither seen, nor read about, nor heard of before.[11]

Some Peruvian Indians invited by some Spanish groups to Seville to reflect on 1492 protested near Columbus's tomb in the cathedral until the police were called in and imprisoned them. A little afterward, one commented to me, "We are used to this, but we did not expect to be treated this way, today, here!" Although there may not be many indigenous witnesses at the Seville international exposition, this imprisonment symbolizes how Spanish, Portuguese, Christian, modern Europeans perpetrated the first holocaust of the violent myth of modernity.

This example of modernity's cruelty, invisible to one concentrating only on its emancipative, rational, enlightened (*aufgeklärt*) nucleus, pales when one turns to the sufferings of the peaceful African peasants. Slave traders caged these peasants like beasts and transported them as cargo in boats across the Atlantic. In this cruelest of histories,[12] modernity subjected thirteen million Africans to the *treatment*[13] by immolating them as a second holocaust[14] for capital, the new god of the sixth sun. The first slaves arrived from Spain in Santo Domingo in 1504, but their service altered when the cycle of sugar replaced the cycle of gold in Hispañola in 1520. The Spaniards imported African slaves to labor on sugar, cocoa, and tobacco plantations, to live and die in sugar mills, and thus to provide capitalism with its originary value through their objectivated labor.

South of the Sahara, flourishing kingdoms[15] once produced gold and transported it across the desert by caravans that traded in the Islamic and Christian Mediterranean. With the discovery of the Americas and the unearthing of new and more productive gold and silver mines, these kingdoms faced a crisis. Complicit with the merchants of nascent European capitalism, these kingdoms collaborated in hunting (*caza*) free African peasants and selling them for arms and other products. In the famed *triangle of death*, ships left London, Lisbon, The Hague, or Amsterdam with European products, such as arms and iron tools, and exchanged these goods on the western coasts of Africa for slaves. They then bartered these slaves in Bahia, Hispanic Cartagena, Havana, Port-au-Prince, and in the ports of the colonies south of New England for gold, silver, and tropical products. The entrepreneurs eventually deposited all that value, or coagulated human blood in Marx's metaphor, in the banks of London and the pantries of the Low Countries. Thus modernity pursued its civilizing, modernizing, humanizing, Christianizing course.

In Cartagena—as in English, Portuguese, or French colonies—slave traders stripped Africans naked, herded men and women together, and displayed them in the market place. Purchasers punched their bodies to assess their constitution, fingered their masculine or feminine sexual organs to determine their health, and examined their teeth. These buyers, having calculated their size, age, and strength, paid with gold coins the value of their persons for life. Then they were branded by fire. No other people in human history and in such numbers were ever so reified as merchandise; no other race was treated this way. Another glory of modernity!

The slaves, however, resisted continually, and many finally attained liberty. The thousands of Afro-Brazilians populating the *quilombos* (liberated territories) and defying colonial armies and the many Jamaican slaves who took refuge along the Pacific coasts of Central America provide evidence of the resistance. The enslaving-colonial order, nevertheless, met every intention of flight or emancipation with systematic brutality. The French—revolutionaries only in their own nation in 1789—promulgated *Le Code Noir ou Recueil des Reglaments rendus jusqu'à présent*,[16] which protracted for decades the suffering of Afro-Caribbeans in Haiti, Guadalupe, and Martinique. In this prototypical document, mercantilist capitalism, sprung from the modern bourgeois revolution, upheld its *rights*. Modernity has shown its double face even to this day by upholding liberty (the essential liberty of the person in Hobbes or Locke) *within* Western nations, while at the same time encouraging enslavement *outside them*. European Common Market politics, closed in upon itself, expresses this double face in new guise. Modernity's other face shows up on the map tinted with negritude in the southern United States, the Caribbean, the Atlantic coast of Central

America, the north and east of Colombia, the Pacific coast as far south as Ecuador, the three Guyanas, and Brazil, home of sixty million Afro-Brazilians.

Transplanted Africans, who are accustomed in the Caribbean area to keep the *umbilical cord* of a newly born child in a little box or bury it in the earth,[17] created a new, syncretistic culture. The world music of rhythm, from the blues to jazz to rock, expresses Afro-American culture. In Latin America, African-Latin American religious expressions from Haitian voodoo to Brazilian *candomble* and *macumba* reflect the transplantation of slaves.

The third visage of those from below is that of the sons of Malinche, the mestizos,[18] as Carlos Fuentes calls them, the sons and daughters of Indian women (the mother) and Spaniards (the dominating male). Latin America must live out its subsequent cultural history and politics with the ambiguity of this new denizen who is neither Indian nor European. In *El laberinto de la soledad*, which speaks of the loneliness of the mestizo, Octavio Paz in the 1950s vents his own uncertainty:

> The Hispanist thesis that we have descended from Cortés and not the Malinche belongs to the patrimony of several extravagant people who are not pure white themselves. On the other hand, *criollos* and maniac mestizos spread about equally untrustworthy indigenist propaganda to which the Indians themselves have never paid much attention. Mestizos[19] prefer to be neither Indian nor Spaniard, nor to descend from either group. They do not affirm themselves as mestizos but as abstractions, as if they were only human beings. They begin in themselves and wish to be children of no one. . . . Our popular cry[20] betrays us and reveals the wound that we alternately show or hide without indicating why we separate from or negate our mother or when that rupture occurred.[21]

In contrast to Africans, Asians, American indigenous peoples, and even white North Americans, all of whose culture, race, and identity are evident, most Latin Americans are, as Paz indicates, neither Amerindian nor European. There are more than two hundred million people of this mixed-race heritage who have developed this continent and marked it with their history. These mestizo sons and daughters celebrate their five hundreth birthday in a way that neither

Indians, nor Europeans, nor Africans, nor Asians can. The Indians, who call them *ladinos* in some places, hate them because they are given priority as *lord*, even though they are not white. The Europeans and their *criollo* sons and daughers despise them likewise for not being white. In the midst of such contradictions, the mestizo, nevertheless, represents what is unique, positively or negatively, to Latin American culture. The mestizo is responsible for building Latin America, Luso-Hispanic America, Hispano America, Ibero-America as a cultural block beyond mere geography (South America, Central America, North America, and the Caribbean).

Mestizos live in their own flesh the contradictory tension of modernity as both emancipation and sacrificial myth. Following in the footsteps of their father Cortés, they have pursued the project of modernity through the eighteenth-century Bourbon colonial Enlightenment, the nineteenth century's positivist liberalism,[22] and through the developmentalism of modernized dependence after the populist and socialist crises of the twentieth century. But they will always fail unless they recover the heritage of their mother, the Malinche. Mestizos must affirm their double origin, as the peripheral, colonized, victimized other face of modernity and as the modern ego which lords it (*enseñorea*) over the land invaded by Cortés. As the majoritarian race, mestizos make up that part of the social block of the oppressed who are entrusted with *the realization* of Latin America. However, the mestizo culture cannot claim to exhaust in itself all Latin American culture.[23] Nevertheless, the project of liberation needs to be mindful of the cultural-historical figure of the mestizo, the third visage and other face of modernity. While not suffering to the extent of the Indian or African slave, the mestizo cannot escape the structural oppression resulting from cultural, political, and economic dependence at national and international levels.

The *Nican Mopohua*,[24] although originally Náhuatl according to the Indian Antonio Valeriano, mediates between the indigenous and mestizo/*criollo* cultures. It announces the beginning of the sixth sun, even as it tries to offer hope for the poor and the oppressed.[25] In this text, the Guadalupe-Tonantzin says to Juan Diego:

> To you, to all of You together who dwell in this land . . . I have come here to hear your laments and to remedy all your miseries, pains, and sufferings.

The Virgin, the Tonantzin (our little mother) of the oppressed Aztecs, directs herself to Juan Diego, the Indian par excellence, and not to the Spaniards who *have recently come here*. Juan Diego, calling himself a *"string, a step ladder without boards, excrement, a loose leaf,"*[26] becomes the subject and protagonist of this apparition:

> The Virgin is an Indian. In addition, she appears to the Indian Juan Diego on a hill that before had been a sanctuary dedicated to Tonantzin. . . . The conquest coincides with the apogee of the worship of the masculine deities: Quetzalcóatl . . . and Huitzilopochtli. . . . The defeat of these gods . . . produced among the faithful a longing to return to ancient feminine deities. . . . This Catholic virgin is also Aztec mother, and so the indigenous pilgrims call her Guadalupe-Tonantzin. Her principal task does not involve guarding the earth's fertility, but serving as the refuge of the forsaken.[27]

Quickly after this, thanks to Miguel Sánchez's *Imagen de la Virgen María Madre de Dios de Guadalupe milagrosamente aparecidea en México* (Mexico: 1648), the mestizos and *criollos* appropriate this indigenous image to affirm their identity against the Spaniards and the Europeans. She symbolizes the unity of the Latin American people, a social block of the oppressed, a unity at once dispersed and contradictory:

> Across the bridge extending between Tepeyac[28] and St. John's Apocalypse,[29] the eighteenth-century[30] preachers and nineteenth-century revolutionaries present themselves.[31] . . . Miguel Sánchez does not hesitate to assert that the image of Guadalupe is originary to this country and that she is the preeminent *criollo* woman. . . . Sánchez was . . . certainly a fully self-conscious *criollo*[32] patriot.[33]

Although the symbol of María Guadalupe united diverse classes, social groups, and ethnic groups at a critical juncture in the constitution of the nation state, the mestizos and *criollos* have appropriated it. Nevertheless, she has functioned as the mother of a free nation filled with contradictions, threatening its future development.

One can speak of the native elites as a fourth, dominated visage. These *criollos*, white sons and daughters born to Spaniards or

Portuguese in the new world, suffered under the Hapsburgs and later the Bourbons or under the Portuguese kings in Brazil. By the end of the eighteenth century, as they became accutely aware that their own historical project was being frustrated, they took charge of the *emancipative project*. José de San Martín in El Plata, Simón Bolívar, a wild (*montuano*) conservative in Venezuela and Nueva Granada, and the priest Miguel Hidalgo in New Spain were all *criollos*. *Criollos* in the new world had known and lived its rivers, mountains, and woods as their own since their birth. But they knew them differently than indigenous peoples, who held them as ancestral gods; than African slaves, who recognized them as strange, possessed by slaveholders, and far distant from their native Africa; and than depreciated mestizos. *Criollo* consciousness was happy, basically undivided, even though partially dominated by peninsulars, royalists, *gapuchines*, and Hispano-Lusitanos. This hegemonic class at the start of the nineteenth century galvanized into a historical people in arms a contradictory social block of oppressed peoples including Indians, African slaves, *zambos* (sons of Indians and Africans), mulattos (sons of whites and Africans), and mestizos (sons of whites and Indians).

The Latin American people undertook the adventure of emancipation against France,[34] Spain,[35] or Portugal,[36] and in Jamaica, Curaçao, and other Latin American colonies, they stood up to England and Holland. To a great extent, Latin Americans experienced their historical unity via the negation of their colonial past and in common cause against a common enemy. This nineteenth-century emancipative process, hegemonized by the *criollos* in Luso-Hispanic America, rapidly fell apart, however. The *criollos* simply were not adept at taking up, subsuming, or affirming the historical projects of indigenous peoples, emancipated African slaves, mestizos, and other groups in the oppressed social block. Therefore, Simón Bolívar's dream of an easy unification under the hegemony of the white race was only a fantasy:

> Of the fifteen or twenty million inhabitants who find themselves spread out on this great continent of indigenous, African, Spanish, and mixed-race nations, the white race is the smallest

minority. But this race possesses the intellectual qualities that
makes its influence seem equal to the other races in the eyes of
those unacquainted with this race's moral and physical qualities. The composition of these qualities produces an opinion
most favorable to union and harmony among all inhabitants,
in spite of the numerical disproportion between the races.[37]

In spite of Bolívar's conviction that the whites could reconcile
these diverse races and cultures, the *criollos* ended up monopoliz-
ing the power in the new national states after the independence
movements. A new oppressed social block replaced the former, as
the *criollos* took up the roles of dominators, conservatives, federal-
ists, liberals, or unitarians. As a result, everyone, with the greater
or lesser participation by mestizos, indigenous peoples, and mulattos, formed classes and groups dependent not upon Spain or Portugal, but upon England, France, and finally the United States.[38]
While awareness of dependence could have sparked an *assumptive*[39]
project, such a project would have fallen short of a project of liberation encompassing indigenous peoples, Afro-Latin Americans, peasants, workers, and marginal peoples—in brief, modernity's *other
face*. The projects of national emancipation, heirs of the emancipation movements led by *criollos* in the nineteenth century, have produced the modern nation-state. But the purposes of indigenous and
Afro-Latin American groups still await integration into a future
Latin American project of liberation.

After the emancipation consummated between 1821 and 1822
from Mexico to Brazil, new visages took the stage as the ancient
poor people of the colonial era reappeared as if with new clothing.
The fifth visage, the peasants,[40] were simple indigenous people who
had departed from their communities, or they were empoverished
mestizos, *zambos*, or mulattos who had dedicated themselves to the
land. These small proprietors often owned more or less unproductive land plots or shared *ejidos* [government plots of land] without
real competitive possibilities. Propertyless, poorly paid laborers from
the countryside also belonged among the "laborers directly engaged
with the land." In the earlier twentieth century, more than 70 percent of the Latin American population dwelt in the countryside and
suffered exploitation at the hands of large landlords of the *criollo*

oligarchy. In Mexico, the peasants rose up in revolt between 1910 and 1917, and even when their leaders Francisco Villa and Emiliano Zapata were assassinated, the *cristeros* revived the revolution. To this day peasants in other regions lack land as can be seen in the thirty million *northeasterners* in Brazil, who occupy land illegally and destroy the tropical Amazon forest in order to eat.[41] Finally, the modernizing advance of the unplannable free market supposedly governed by Adam Smith's mythic, provident hand of God, prevents isolated peasants from reproducing their life in the countryside and impels them toward the cities. Here the destiny of the sixth sun—capital—enables them to be transformed into other visages of the other face of modernity.

Workers make up the sixth visage.[42] The industrial revolution took place primarily in England in the mid-eighteenth century after Spain and Portugal had inaugurated mercantile capitalism at the end of the fifteenth century. The industrial revolution, however, reached Latin America only at the end of the nineteenth century[43] and unfolded there as an originally dependent industrial revolution.[44] Therefore, the national bourgeoisie of Latin American countries, who construct unitarian projects for conservative or liberal constituencies or populist ones that are not really popular, find themselves enmeshed in a *weak* capitalist system. Within the international capitalist system, they end up structurally transferring value to the central capital and its metropolitan centers, to England first, to the United States since 1945, and last to the giants of transnational capitalism such as Japan, Germany, and the European Common Market. According to the clear and yet insufficiently elaborated position of Mauro Marini, weak capital superexploits (*sobre-explota*) its laborers.[45] That is, weak capital increases excessively labor hours and augments absolute surplus value by heightening the intensity and rhythm of labor (a derived type of relative surplus value) and by disproportionately diminishing absolute and relative salaries (the minimal salary is $45 monthly in Haiti, $60 in Brazil, and somewhat more than $100 in Mexico).[46] All this occurs because peripheral capital must compensate for the value it transfers to central capital.[47]

The entire discussion about modernity and postmodernity, whether in Habermas, Lyotard, Vattimo, or Rorty, omits any reference

to this entire problematic and displays a lack of world consciousness typical of Eurocentric and North American philosophies. World
capital exploits most of all these millions of Latin American, Asian,
or African laborers. Hegel foresaw these miserable masses in his
Philosophy of Right when he predicted that bourgeois society would
resolve its contradictions by seeking solutions beyond its borders:

> The amplification of that articulation is reached by means of
> colonization, to which, spontaneously or systematically, the
> developed bourgeois society is pushed.[48]

Marx amplifies Hegel by this further reflection:

> Accumulation of capital is, therefore, increase of the prole-
> tariat.[49] The law [of the accumulation of capital] establishes
> accumulation of misery (*Akkumulation von Elend*) corre-
> sponding with accumulation of capital. Accumulation of wealth
> of one pole is, therefore, at the same time accumulation of mis-
> ery, agony of toil, slavery, ignorance, brutality, ethical degra-
> dation, at the opposite pole—that is, on the side of the class
> that produces its own product as capital.[50]

Obviously in 1992 the mythology of a free market of perfect
competition holds Marx in disrepute.[51] Marx's stock is particularly
low since he explains how the misery of the people (indigenous peoples, Africans, mestizos, peasants, laborers) of peripheral nations is
proportional to the wealth of the rich within both peripheral and
central capital. The myth of modernity ignores all this.

One ought not forget the seventh visage of the other face of modernity, the marginal ones.[52] Due to weak, peripheral capital's transference of value, it not only superexploits salaried labor but also
fails to employ an enormous relative and absolute overpopulation,[53]
a *reserve labor army*. These structural weaknesses in Latin American countries produce an urban marginality growing by the millions
in large cities such as São Paulo, Mexico City, Buenos Aires, Santiago, Lima, Bogotá, Rio, or Guadalajara, as well as in cities like New
Delhi, Cairo, or Nairobi.

This contemporary phenomenon of marginality, a modern but
more serious version of the *lumpen*, reveals disfigured visages, the
unjust outcome of what Habermas and others have called late

capitalism (*Spätkapitalismus*). Even careful historians and philosophers neglect the systematic linkages between postindustrial, service-oriented, financier, and transnational late capitalism and peripheral capitalism. Industrialized peripheral capitalism subsumes living labor by offering minimum subsistence salaries to competing marginalized ones who must sell themselves at subhuman prices, like the illegal *braceros* in the United States. The quality of these marginal lives with respect to food, clothing, habitat, culture, and sense of personal dignity falls well below that of the festive and populated city of Zempoala, which Cortés entered in 1519. Five hundred years finds millions of marginal persons in Mexico City yearning to have the food, the clothing, and dignity characterizing those who inhabited Mexico-Tenochtitlan. I am here recommending neither a return to the past nor a folkloric or preindustrial project such as Gandhi's. I simply desire to show modernity's other face, the structural product of its myth, and to recognize that myth for the sacrificial, violent, and irrational myth it is.

During the long history from 1492 to 1992, the era of the sixth sun, the Latin American people, the social block of the oppressed, have struggled to create their own culture.[54] Any attempt at modernization which ignores this history is doomed to fail, since it will be overlooking its own other face.[55] Furthermore, people seeking to modernize will encounter difficulties in that sector which modernity has always exploited and oppressed, and which has paid with its life for the accumulation of originary capital and central capitalism's development. In the name of modernity's rational and emancipatory nucleus, which can free one from an immaturity that is not culpable, I wish to deny modernity's Eurocentric, developmentalist, sacrificial myth.

Therefore, any merely assumptive liberating project will favor the *criollos*, behave conservatively on behalf of large landholders, and uphold a liberalism that denies the indigenous, Afro-Latin American, and colonial past. Authentically liberating projects must strive to lead modernity beyond itself to transmodernity. Such projects require an amplified rationality which makes room for the reason of the Other within a community of communication among equal participants, as envisaged by Bartolomé de las Casas in the 1550 Valladolid debate.

Within such projects, all ought to be welcomed in their alterity, in that otherness which needs to be painstakingly guaranteed at every level, whether in Habermas's *ideal speech situation* or Apel's *community of ideal or transcendental communication.*

This book serves only as a historico-philosophical introduction to an intercultural dialogue that will encompass diverse political, economic, theological, and epistemological standpoints. Such a dialogue endeavors to construct not an abstract universality, but an analogic and concrete world in which all cultures, philosophies, and theologies will make their contribution toward a future, pluralist humanity.

Modernity began in 1492 with Europe thinking itself the center of the world and Latin America, Africa, and Asia as the periphery. The year 1492 carries a different, non-European significance in the peripheral world.

In analyzing these topics, I have sketched the historical conditions for a theory of dialogue. Such a theory should not (1) fall into the facile optimism of rationalist, abstract universalism that would conflate universality with Eurocentrism and modernizing developmentalism, as the Frankfurt School is inclined to do; nor should it (2) lapse into the irrationality, incommunicability, or incommensurability of discourses that are typical of many postmoderns. The philosophy of liberation affirms that rationality can establish a dialogue with the reason of the Other, as an alterative reason. Today, such rationality must deny the irrational sacrificial myth of modernity as well as affirm (subsume in a liberating project)[56] the emancipative tendencies of the Enlightenment and modernity within a new transmodernity.

APPENDIX
1

DIVERSE MEANINGS OF THE TERMS
Europe, The Occident, Modernity, Late Capitalism

(1) Barbarian *Europe* versus Greece, Hellenicity. Asia is a province of Anatolia, present-day Turkey, and nothing more. According to this oldest and first meaning, Europe signifies the uncivilized, barbarous, nonpolitical, and nonhuman.

(2) The *Occident*, the Latin Roman Empire including Africa as its southern provinces, versus the Orient, the Hellenist sector of the Roman Empire. Asia belongs to the oriental empire, including Ptolemaic Egypt, which is distinct from Africa. There is no relevant concept of Europe.

(3) Constantinople in the seventh century distinguishes the Christian Roman Empire from the Islamic Arab world. Both worlds study classical Greek, and the Arabs in Baghdad and Cordova immerse themselves in Aristotle more than the Christians. There is no concept of Europe. Constantinople is neither Occidental nor European in opposition to Asia and Africa.

(4) *Latin Europe* versus the Arab World. The Arabs consider Aristotle their philosopher more than the Christians do, but Christian Latins such as Abelard, Albert, and Thomas begin to take interest. Aristotle is considered neither Occidental nor European. Slowly Europe begins to distinguish itself from Africa, now Muslim and

black, and Asia, now Muslim. Constantinople and Greek Orthodoxy constitute the Orient.

(5) During the Italian Renaissance after the fall of Constantinople in 1453, the Latin Occident and Greek Orient united against Turks, Arabs, and Muslims, distinguished the Turks from Hellenism, and forgot their Arab-Hellenistic linkages. The equation is born: the *Occident* = Hellenistic + Roman + Christian. According to Toscanelli's letter of 1474, the Occident thinks of confronting the Orient across the Atlantic.

(6) After 1492, *Europe* consolidates definitively in the sixteenth century and distinguishes itself from America, Africa, and Asia. The Islamic world from Vienna to Granada had hemmed in Latin-Germanic Europe until now. But now, for the first time, with the discovery of the fourth part of the world, America, Europe declares itself as the center. The other three parts, America, Africa, and Asia—commence their history as the periphery. The Orient consists of the continent between Asia Minor, the sea of the Arabs (Indian Ocean), and the sea of the South (the Pacific).

(7) In the eighteenth century, the notion of the Occident (somewhat in confusion since number 2) combines with Hellenicity (which in number 1 had been the anti-Europe) and Europe-as-center, with its peripheral colonies. Hegel expresses most articulately this philosophico-theological ideology, and for the first time the concept of *Occidental Europe* appears.

(8) Occidental culture (or civilization) comes to include North America, which shares Europe's colonialist, racist, and nationalist tendencies, whether instantiated in Nazism or the CIA. The North American ideological notion of the occidental hemisphere nevertheless excludes the South—namely, Africa and Latin America—which geographically pertain to that hemisphere. Although the United States restricts its interest to the northern occidental hemisphere, *occidental culture* could encompass Latin America or at least its elites, whether *criollo* or mestizo, as Edmundo O'Gorman thinks.

(9) Even though the Occident arrogates to itself the tag *Christian*, as the *occidental and Christian culture or civilization*, *Christianity* has nothing occidental about it. Like Islam and Judaism, Christianity was born in the Semitic world, and geographically and culturally

deserves to be called oriental and Asian, especially given its oriental status in the Roman Empire. Christianity's origins are more oriental than Hellenism, which at first was not European at all. The syncretistic, ideological, and contradictory expression *occidental and Christian culture or civilization* is both anti-Semitic—excluding Jews as did Hitler and the integrisms of the center and the periphery— and also antisocialist, since Lenin's revolution and socialism succeeded only in the Orient. Orient-Occident form the ideological poles of the cold war at the end of the second so-called world war, which was only an intercapitalist war of the center.

(10) The concept of modernity rises to prominence at the end of the fifteenth century or the beginning of the sixteenth in works such as *Mundus Novus*. However, the terms *new* and *modern* only suit the culture of Europe (meaning number 6) and the Occident (number 7) after the eighteenth century. This Europe-as-center quickly excludes Spain and Portugal, which constitute southern Europe, never mentioned by Hegel.

(11) The eighteenth century provides the scenario for the concept of the industrial, capitalist, cultural system. Max Weber understands modernity through the bureaucratization and secularization proper to capitalism. A new equation emerges: modernity = European (meaning number 6) + occidental (meaning number 7) + capitalist (meaning number 11).

(12) *Spät-kapitalismus* (in Habermas's sense) functions as an advanced stage of capitalism and of modernity in the midst of the twentieth century.

Many people employ these twelve possible meanings unreflectively, without attending to their contamination by Eurocentrism and the developmentalist fallacy.

TABLE 1						
THESE TWELVE MEANINGS AND THEIR HISORICAL DERIVATION						
IN ANTIQUITY	7TH CENT.	12TH CENT.	15TH CENT.	16TH CENT.	18TH-19TH CENT.	20TH CENT.
1, 2	3	4	5	6, 10	7, 8, 9	9,12

APPENDIX
2

Two Paradigms of Modernity

Semantically the word *modernity* carries two ambiguous significations.

(1) For its first and positive conceptual content, modernity signifies rational emancipation. The emancipation involves leaving behind[1] immaturity under the force of reason as a critical process that opens up new possiblities for human development.

(2) But, at the same time, in its secondary and negative *mythic*[2] content, modernity justifies an irrational praxis of violence. The myth follows these steps: (a) Modern civilization understands itself as most developed and superior, since it lacks awareness of its own ideological Eurocentrism. (b) This superiority obliges it to develop the most primitive, uneducated, barbarous extremes. (c) This developmental process ought to follow Europe's, since development is unilineal according to the uncritically accepted developmental fallacy. (d) Since the barbarian opposes this civilizing process, modern praxis ought to exercise violence (a just colonial war) as a last resort in order to destroy any obstacles to modernization. (e) This domination produces

its diverse victims and justifies its actions as a sacrifice, an inevitable and quasi-ritual act. Civilizing heroes transform their victims into holocausts of a salvific sacrifice, whether these victims are colonized peoples, African slaves, women, or the ecologically devastated earth. (f) For modernity, the barbarian is at *fault*[3] for opposing the civilizing process,[4] and modernity, ostensibly innocent, seems to be emancipating the fault of its own victims. (g) Finally, modernity, thinking itself as the civilizing power, regards the sufferings and sacrifices of backward and immature[5] peoples, enslaveable races, and the weaker sex as the inevitable costs of modernization.

(3) To overcome modernity, one must deny its myth. I seek to overcome modernity not through a postmodern attack on reason based on the irrational incommensurability of language-games. Rather, I propose a transmodern opposition to modernity's irrational violence based on the *reason of the Other*. I hope to go beyond modernity by discovering as innocent the so often denied and victimized other face of modernity. This innocent victim of modernity's ritual sacrifice convicts modernity of sacrificial violence and proves that its essential, constitutive features are those of the conquistador. To deny modernity's innocence and to affirm the alterity of the Other, the inculpable victim, reveals the other face hidden and yet essential to modernity. This Other encompasses the peripheral colonial world, the sacrificed Indian, the enslaved black, the oppressed woman, the subjugated child, and the alienated popular culture—all victims of modernity's irrational action in contradiction to its own rational ideal.

(4) By denying the *civilizing myth and the innocence* of its concomitant violence, one recognizes the injustice of Europe's sacrificial praxis within and outside itself. At the same time, one overcomes the limitations of *emancipative reason* via a *liberating reason*, purified from the Eurocentrism and developmentalist fallacy ingredient in hegemonic processes of modernization. The discovery of the ethical dignity of the Other purifies Enlightenment rationality beyond any Eurocentric or developmentalist communicative reason and certainly beyond purely strategic, instrumental rationality. Liberating reason declares the victims innocent beginning from the affirmation of their alterity as an identity in

the exteriority even though modernity has denied them as its own contradiction.

Thus I hope to transcend modern reason not by negating reason as such, but by negating violent, Eurocentric, developmentalist, hegemonic reason. The worldwide liberation project of trans-modernity differs from a universal, univocal project that seeks to impose violently upon the Other the following: European rationality, unilateral machismo, and white racism, and which conflates occidental culture with the human in general. In transmodernity, the alterity, coessential to modernity, now receives recognition as an equal. Modernity will come into its fullness not by passing from its potency to its act, but by surpassing itself through a corealization with its once negated alterity and through a process of mutual, creative fecundation. The transmodern project achieves with modernity what it could not achieve by itself—a corealization of solidarity, which is analectic, analogic, syncretic, hybrid, and mestizo, and which bonds center to periphery, woman to man, race to race, ethnic group to ethnic group, class to class, humanity to earth, and occidental to Third World cultures. This bonding occurs not via negation, but via a subsumption from the viewpoint of alterity[6] and in accord with Marx's reversal of Hegelian *Aufhebung* through the concept of subsumption.

This subsumption intends neither a premodern project, nor a folkloric affirmation of the past, nor the antimodern project of conservatives, rightists, Nazis, fascists, or populists. Nor does it envision a postmodern project negating modernity and all rationality only to topple into nihilist irrationalism. This transmodern project really subsumes modernity's rational emancipative character and its negated alterity even as it rejects modernity's mythic character and its irrational exculpation of self and inculpation of its victims. Modernity began in certain medieval European cities under the impetus of the Renaissance proponents of the *Quatrocento*. But modernity could only take off when sufficient historical conditions were in place: 1492, its empirical spreading over the world, its organization of colonies, and its usufruct over the pragmatic, economic lives of its victims. Modernity came to birth in 1492—that is our thesis. Its real surpassing, as subsumption and not merely Hegelian *Aufhebung*, transcending its Eurocentrism on behalf of its negated alterity. This new project of transmodernity implies political, economic, ecological, erotic, pedagogic, and religious liberation.

I propose two contradictory paradigms: mere Eurocentric modernity and modernity subsumed in a world horizon. While the first paradigm functions ambiguously as emancipative and mythically violent, the second, transmodern paradigm embraces both modernity and its alterity. According to Tzevan Todorov's *Nosotros y los otros*,[7] *nosotros* refers to Europeans, and *los otros* refers to the peoples of the periphery. Modernity defined itself as emancipative with respect to its *we* without averting to its mythic-sacrificial behavior toward its *Others*. Montaigne aptly captured the paradox:

> We can call them barbarians with respect to our rules of reason, but not with respect to us, who exceed the entire species in barbarity.[8]

Two Paradigms of Modernity

(Schematic simplification of the moments determinative for both paradigms)

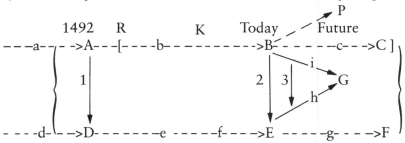

Read diachronically from A toward G and from a to i

I) Most relevant determinations:

A: Europe at the moment of discovery (1492).
B: The European modern present.
C: Project of realization (Habermasian) of modernity.
P: Project of postmodern nihilism.
D: The invasion of the continent (of Africa and Asia later).

F :   Project within the dependent new world order.
G: World project of liberation (transmodernity).
R :   Renaissance and Reformation.
K :   The *Aufklärung* (industrial capitalism).

II) Relations with a certain direction or arrows:

a :   European, medieval (or premodern) history.
b :   Modern European history.
c :   Praxis of the realization of C.
d :   Amerindian history (also that of Africa and Asia).
e :   Mercantilist colonial and dependent history.
f :   History from the peripheral world to industrial capitalism.
g :   Praxis of the realization of F (developmentalism).
h :   Praxis of the liberation or of the realization of G.
i :   Praxis of solidarity of the center with the periphery.
1, 2, 3 : Historical types of domination (of A over→D, etc.).

III) The two paradigms of modernity:

[]   Eurocentric paradigm of modernity [R→K→B→C].
()   World paradigm of modernity/alterity (toward
           transmodernity): (A/D→B/E→G).

APPENDIX
3

FROM THE DISCOVERY OF THE ATLANTIC UNTIL 1502

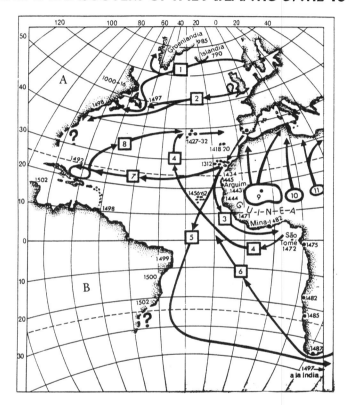

1: Route of the Vikings. 2: English voyages of Juan Casoto. 3: The route to Guinea. 4: *Volta de Mina* or the return route from Guinea. 5: Route to India, depending on circumstances; established beginning about 1500. 6: Return route from India (beginning from Ecuador and coinciding with the *Volta de Mina*). 7 and 8: Departure and return of Columbus's first trip 1492 (including American coastal areas known in 1502, the discovery dates of points on the African and new world coasts, and the two first permanent African trading posts [*feitorias*] of the Portuguese). 9, 10, and 11: Principal kingdoms Islamicized in sub-Saharan Africa, from which caravan routes headed northward.

[Source: Guillermo Céspedes del Castillo, *América Hispánica (1492–1898)* in *Historia de España*, by Manuel Tuñon de Lara (Madrid: Labor, 1983), vol. 6, p. 46.]

APPENDIX
4

MAP OF THE FOURTH ASIATIC PENINSULA OF HENRY MARTELLUS (FLORENCE, 1489)

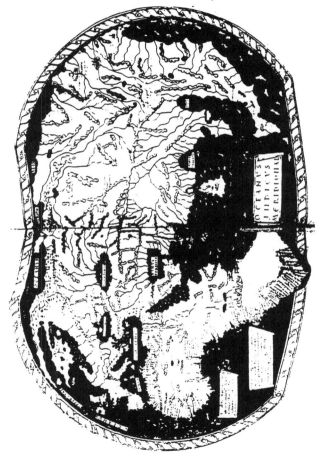

[Source: Gustavo Vargas Martínez, *América en un mapa de 1489,* unpublished (Bogotá: 1991); Paul Gallez, *Cristóbal de Haro: banqueros y pimenteros en busca del estrecho magallánico* (Bahía Blanca: Instituto Patagónico, 1991) and from the same author, *La Cola del Dragón: América del Sur en los mapas antiguos, medievales y renacentistas* (Bahía Blanca: Instituto Patagónico, 1990).]

MAP OF THE FOURTH ASIATIC PENINSULA OF HENRY MARTELLUS (FLORENCE, 1489)

(with a clarification of explanations)

[Source: Gustavo Vargas Martínez, *América en un mapa de 1489*, unpublished (Bogotá: 1991).]

Notes

Preface

1. Richard Bernstein, *The New Constellation* (Cambridge: MIT Press, 1992).

2. Albrecht Wellmer, "The Dialectic of Modernity and Post-Modernity," *Praxis International* 4 (1985): 338.

3. Charles Taylor, *The Sources of the Self, The Making of the Modern Identity* (Cambridge: Harvard University Press, 1989).

4. Stephen Toulmin, *The Hidden Agenda of Modernity* (New York: Macmillan, 1990).

5. Jürgen Habermas, *Der philosophische Diskurs der Moderne* (Frankfurt: Suhrkamp, 1988).

6. This metaphysical-substantialist, diffusionist thesis of a "substance" invented in Europe and expanding throughout the world commits the reductionistic fallacy.

7. *Auf dem Boden* means "within one's regional horizon." I wish to show that Europe developed as the center of a world-system in modernity. It did not evolve internally into an independent entity unto itself, as Eurocentrists contend.

8. This *we* refers to Eurocentric Europeans.

9. Max Weber, "Vorbemerkung zu den Gesammelten Aufsatzen zur Religionssoziologie," in *Soziologie, weltgeschichtliche Analyzen, Politik* (Stuttgart: Kroner, 1956), p. 340. He continues: "Neither scientific,

artistic, governmental, nor economic evolution have led elsewhere to the modes of rationalization (*Rationalisierung*) proper to the Occident" (ibid., p. 351). Thus, Weber contrasts the Babylonians, who did not mathematize astronomy, with the Hellenes, without recognizing that the Hellenes learned from the Egyptians. He argues that science rose in the West in contrast to India and China, but he forgets the Islamic world from which the Latin Occident, in particular the Oxford Franciscans and the Paduan Marsilios, learned Aristotelianism and the experiential, empirical attitude. One could easily falsify Weber's Hellenic, Eurocentric arguments by taking 1492 as the ultimate example of the pretended superiority of the Occident over other cultures. I will take up this problematic extensively in the second chapter of the *Ethics of Liberation* that I am preparing.

10. André Gunder Frank, "The Shape of the World System in the Thirteenth Century," in *Studies in Comparative International Development* 22/4 (Winter 1987); "A Theoretical Introduction to 5000 Years of World System History," in *Review* (Binghamton) 13/2 (1990): 155–248; and A. G. Frank, B. K. Gills, eds., *The World System: From Five Hundred Years to Five Thousand* (London, New York: Routledge, 1992).

11. In disagreement with A. G. Frank, I would not use the term "world-system" for the anterior moments of the system. I prefer to speak of an *interregional* system.

12. Emmanuel Wallerstein, *The Modern World-System* (New York: Academic Press), vol. 1 (1974), vol. 3 (1989); *The Politics for the World Economy* (Cambridge: Cambridge University Press, 1984).

13. Wallerstein, *The Modern World-System*, vol. 2, chaps. 4–5.

14. Ibid., vol. 3, chap. 3.

15. See my soon-to-be-published *The Underside of Modernity: Apel, Ricoeur, Taylor, Rorty and the Philosophy of Liberation*, translated by Eduardo Mendieta (New York: Humanities Press, 1995).

16. I have published several works on this theme: "Was America Discovered or Invaded?" in *Concilium* 200 (1988): 126–34; "The Expansion of Christendom, Its Crisis and the Present Moment," *Concilium* 144 (1981): 44–50; "Modern Christianity in the Face of the 'Other': From the 'Rude' Indian to the 'Noble Savage,'" *Concilium* 130 (1979): 49–59; "Las motivaciones reales de la conquista," *Concilium* 232 (1990):

403–15; "Del descubrimiento al desencubrimiento: Hacia un desagravio histórico," in *Concordia* (Frankfurt) 10 (1986): 109–16; "Otra visión del descubrimiento: El camino hacia un desagravio histórico," in *Nueva Epoca*, vol. 3, no. 9, Cuadernos Americanos (Mexico: UNAM, 1988), pp. 34–41; "1492: Diversas posiciones ideológicas" in *1492–1992: La interminable conquista: Emancipación e Identidad de América Latina* (Mexico: Joaquin Martiz, 1990), pp. 77–97.

17. An Argentinian Jew, from my homeland, provided some of the initial funds to defray the costs of Horkheimer's institute. The labor invested by the Argentinian cowboy and farmer in beef and wheat was transferred to Germany and helped originate this prestigious school. In the name of these poor half-Indians and cattlemen who invested their lives on Argentinian plantations, I write this book. In addition, a poor socialist carpenter, a Lutheran from Schweinfurt am Main, arrived in Buenos Aires in 1870 seeking work, security, and peace: he was named Joahnnes Kaspar Dussel. Argentina received him without obstacles and opened opportunities for him so that he could raise a family and die here: he was my great-grandfather. When strangers arrive in Germany these days, Germany repudiates them, expels them, and treats them like enemies! This country has forgotten the hospitality offered *to its poor* in the nineteenth century in other lands!

18. See the meaning of *compellere* in the Valladolid dispute 1550, chapter 5 here.

19. His departure point is "we liberal Americans," but not "we Aztecs faced with Cortés," or "we Latin Americans faced with North America in 1992." In such cases, *not even the conversation* would be possible.

20. Pedro de Alvarado will employ a similar sacrificial violence in the slaughter of May 23, 1520, in México-Tenochtitlán.

21. The Spanish Europeans saw riches where there were none, as if there were an infinite mirage of gold in this nascent world mercantilism.

22. The letter of Bishop Juan de Medina y Rincón, Michoacán, of October 13, 1583 (*Archivo General de Indias*, Seville, Mexico, p. 374).

23. I have delivered lectures on the meaning of 1492 in Seville and Pontevedra in Spain during October 1991; at Maryknoll College near New York City, in the seminar entitled the "Columbus Paradox"; at UCLA in Los Angeles; in the Cole Lectures at Vanderbilt University in

Tennessee; at the University of Feiburg, Switzerland; and at other universities in Germany, Austria, Mexico, Bolivia, and Colombia.

Part 1

1. Germán Marquinez Argote defended a thesis, the *Interpretación del "Cogito" cartesiano como modelo de hermenéutica lationamericana* (Bogotá: University of Saint Thomas Aquinas, 1980), in which he compared the "I conquer" with the "I think." He provides cogent texts showing the awareness Descartes had that his world had actually discovered a new world.

Chapter 1: Eurocentrism

1. The Spanish word *desarrollismo* is not directly translatable into German or English. Its root (*desarrollo*) does not permit the construction of a pejorative, as, for example, *scientificism* (*Szientifizismus*) or *scientificist* (*szientifizist*). One would need something like *developmentism* or *developmentalism* to signify the ontological position that Europe's development is assumed to be the model for every other culture. Thus, the developmentalist fallacy deploys neither sociological nor economic categories, but rather fundamental philosophical ones. For Hegel, too, there is a necessary movement of being as it pursues its inevitable development. Eurocentrism and the developmentalist fallacy are two aspects of the same world-view.

2. The fact of the exit (*Ausgang*), the exodus, is interesting as a process of emancipation.

3. Kant, *Was heisst Aufklärung?*, A, 481.

4. The end of every work: "The History of the World is the process of the *development* (*Entwicklung*) of the Spirit—it is a true *Theodicy*, the justification of God in History."

5. Hegel, *Die Vernunft in der Geschichte*, Second Draft (1830), C, c: in *Samtliche Werke*, ed. J. Hoffmeister and F. Meiner (Hamburg, 1955), p. 167; English version: *Lectures on the Philosophy of World History, Introduction: Reason in History*, trans. H. B. Nisbet (Cambridge, London, New York, Melbourne: Cambridge University Press, 1975), p. 138. See Martin Bernal, *Black Athena. The Afroasiatic Roots of Classical*

Civilization (New Brunswick: Rutgers University Press, 1987–1991), especially "Philosophy of Universal History of Hegel," vol. 2.

6. From Hegel the concept of development passed to Marx and from him into economy and sociology. I return to the philosophical content of this word which, as I say, is its oldest element. An *underdeveloped* country, ontologically, is nonmodern and pre-Enlightenment, according to Hegel.

7. Hegel, *Samtliche Werke*, Appendix 2; p. 243; English, p. 197. I will show that this development of history from the East is purely ideological; it is a constitutive moment of Eurocentrism. This view of history has been imposed in all the programs of history, high school to university, not only in Europe and the United States, but also in Latin America, Africa, and Asia. At times even socialist revolutions have disgracefully concurred in such Eurocentrism, perhaps because of Marx's own Eurocentrism, at least until 1868 [*El último Marx (1863–1882)* (Mexico: Siglo XXI, 1990), chap. 7]. In that year Marx opened up the problematic of peripheral Russia in response to Danielson and the Russian populists.

8. *Das Kind hat keine Vernünftigkeit, aber die reale Möglichkeit zu sein. . . . Der Mensch war stets eine Intelligenz . . . gleichsam in Zentrum von allem* (in Hegel, *Samtliche Werke*, Second Draft, C, b; p. 161; English, p. 133). *Die erste Gestalt des Geistes ist daher die orientalische. Dieser Welt liegt das unmittelbare Bewusstsein . . .* (Ibid., Appendix 2; p. 244; English, p. 198). The immediacy (*Unmittelbarkeit*) of the consciousness of the child as possibility means that the child cannot be the center, only the periphery.

9. Ibid., Appendix b; pp. 199–200; English, pp. 162–64.

10. Antonello Gerbi, in his work *La naturaleza de las Indias Nuevas* (Mexico: FCE, 1978), shows that the Europeans and Hegel himself thought that even the geology and the flora and fauna were more brutal, primitive, and savage among the Indians.

11. Hegel, *Samtliche Werke,* Appendix b, pp. 209–10; English, pp. 170–71.

12. In the next chapter, I will this show that this trinitarian division of the world, which Hegel and Columbus shared, is medieval and premodern.

13. Hegel, *Samtliche Werke*, Appendix c; p. 210; English, p. 171.

14. *Nachdem wir die Neue Welt und die Träume, die sich an sie*

knupfen können, gehen wir nun zur Alten Welt über. Sie ist wesentlich der Schauplatz dessen, was Gegenstand unserer Betrachtung ist, der Weltgeschichte (in Hegel, *Samtliche Werke*, Appendix c; p. 210; English, 171).

15. Ibid., p. 212; English, p. 173.

16. Ibid., p. 218; English, pp. 176–77.

17. Ibid., pp. 231–34; English, pp. 188–90.

18. One can see that Fukuyama extracts this expression from Hegel [Francis Fukuyama, *The End of History and the Last Man* (New York: Free Press, and Toronto: Maxwell Macmillan Canada, 1992)]. Fukuyama advances the thesis that the United States and the free capitalist market, after the collapse of the real socialism of the north since 1989, is the model to follow with no alternative. This model is the *end of history*. Similarly, Hegel believed that Europe was the center of history.

19. Hegel, *Samtliche Werke*, Appendix b; p. 235; English, pp. 190–91.

20. Ibid., Appendix c, p. 240; English, p. 195. With this, one sets aside the importance of the fifteenth to the eighteenth centuries, the epoch of mercantilism, which is the subject of this book.

21. Ibid.

22. Ibid.

23. Hegel, without realizing it, evokes the pathos that the *discovery* of the new world produced in Europe at the end of the fifteenth century. He projects upon the German past the concept *modern*—a concept current at the finding of the new world and originating with reference to Latin America. But Latin America has no place in his vision, although this is not so with the later Anglo-Saxon "America," which forms a second-level Occident for Hegel, and therefore does have its place in world history.

24. Hegel, *Vorlesungen über die Philosophie der Geschichte*, in *Werke* (Frankfurt: Suhrkamp, 1970), bk. 12, p. 413; English version: *The Philosophy of History*, rev. ed., trans. J. Sibree (New York: Colonial Press, 1900), p. 341.

25. Ibid., pp. 413–14; English, pp. 341–42.

26. Ibid., p. 414; English, p. 342.

27. See ibid., p. 417; English, p. 345. This is the "Joachinism" of Hegel.

28. Ibid., p. 417; English, p. 345.

29. Ibid., IV, 3, 3: p. 538; English, p. 455.

30. F. Nicolin-O. Pöggeler and F. Meiner, eds., *Enzyklopadie* (Hamburg: 1969), #346.

31. Ibid., #347.

32. Ibid., # 550, p. 430, Hegel writes: "Diese Befreiung des Geistes, in der er zu sich selbst zu kommen and seine Wahrheit zu verwirklichen geht, und das Geschaft derselben ist das höchste und absolute *Recht.* Das Selbstbewusstsein eines besondern Volks ist Träger der diesmaligen *Entwicklungsstufe* des allgemeinen Geistes in seinem Dasein and die objektive Wirklichkeit, in welche er seinen Willen legt. *Gegen diesen absoluten Willen ist der Wille der andern besondern Volksgeister rechtlos, jenes Volk ist das weltbeherrschende* [italics are Dussel's]. English version: *Hegel's Philosophy of Mind,* part 3 of *Encyclopedia of the Philosophical Sciences,* trans. William Wallace (Oxford: Clarendon, 1971), p. 281.

33. *Rechtsphilosophie,* #246 in *Enzyklopadie*; English translation: *Hegel's Philosophy of Right,* trans. T. M. Knox (Oxford: Clarendon Press, 1952), p. 151.

34. *Enzyklopadie* #248, English, pp. 151–52. Europe, then, *occupies* other territories. Hegel does not think that this signifies that it is necessary to capture these other peoples.

35. When Europe suffered from *overpopulation* or an excess of poor and wretched people, it sent them to the Third World. Today it does not permit them to enter Europe, and it closes its frontiers.

36. Júrgen Habermas, *Der philosophische Diskurs der Moderne* (Frankfurt: Suhrkamp, 1988), p. 27; English version: *The Philosophical Discourse of Modernity, Twelve Lectures,* trans. Frederick Lawrence (Cambridge: MIT Press, 1987), p. 17.

37. Ibid., p. 27; English, p. 29.

38. He speaks of discovery, but does not give it any importance (for example, in ibid., p. 13, German edition; p. 5 in English).

39. *Die Vernunft in der Geschichte,* in Hegel, *Samtliche Werke* Appendix a: Afrika, p. 213; English, pp. 173–74.

40. See Appendix 2 herein regarding these authors. See *Dialektik der Aufklärung* (Frankfurt: Fischer, 1971); Max Horkheimer and Theodor Adorno, *Dialectic of Enlightenment,* trans. John Cumming (New York:

Herder and Herder, 1972). The position of Jürgen Habermas is expressed in his "The Entwinement of Myth and Enlightenment: Max Horkheimer and Theodor Adorno," in *The Philosophical Discourse of Modernity*: German, pp. 130 ff. ; English, pp. 106 ff.

Chapter 2: From the Invention to the Discovery of the New World

1. Edmundo O'Gorman, *La invención de America* (Mexico: FCE, 1957, p. 12.

2. From the book cited in note 1. See the reaction of Wilcomb E. Washburn, "The Meaning of the *Discovery* in the Fifteenth and Sixteenth Centuries," in *The American Historical Review* 1 (1962): 1–21.

3. In Heidegger's meanings, as explained in *Sein und Zeit*.

4. In the meaning of the later Husserl.

5. In meanings number 4 and 5 of Appendix 1.

6. Africa was then the Muslim black world; Asia began with the Muslim Turkish world and extended to areas slightly known from such merchant expeditions as that of Marco Polo or from Franciscan missionaries such as Juan of Montecorvino (who traveled as far as Peking and died in 1328). [See Pierre Chaunu, *L'expansion européen (XIIIe, XIVe, XVe siècles)* (Paris: PUF, 1968)]. The Franciscans were in China until 1370, and they obtained much information that was eventually transmitted to Rome.

7. See the "Excursus on Europe as *Periphery* of the Muslim World," in chapter 6.

8. Columbus had been in the eastern Mediterranean, in the northeast of Europe, on the coasts of Guinea in Africa, on the Madeira Islands, always in the company of Genoan or Portuguese navigators. See Paolo Emilio Taviani, *Cristoforo Colombo, La génesi della grande scoperta* (Novara: Instituto Geográfico de Agostini, 1982); Kirkpatrick Sale, *The Conquest of Paradise* (New York: Plume, 1991); Daniel Boorstin, *The Discoverers* (New York: Vintage, 1985); Alvin Josephy, *America in 1492* (New York: Alfred Knopf, 1992); Samuel Elliot Morison, *Admiral of the Ocean Sea* (Boston: Little, Brown, 1972).

9. ". . . from one a very great river flowed out. It was about five fathoms deep and the water very sweet, in so much quantity" [*Diario del*

Primer y Tercer Viaje de Cristóbal Cólon, version of B. de las Casas (Madrid: Alianza, 1989), p. 182]. A little later he writes: "I say that, if it does not proceed from the Earthly Paradise, it comes and proceeds from an infinite expanse of land, next to the South Wind, concerning which now there has been little attention. Morover, I am quite sure in my heart that here, where I indicated [where the Orinoco begins], is the earthly Paradise, and I base myself on the reasons and authorities of the Scriptures" (ibid., 192).

10. As a mere anecdote, I recall now that family of my mother, Ambrosini Siffredi, my great-grandparents, were originally from this city, *geneises*, and they immigrated to Argentina at about the same time and for the same motives that moved my German great-grandfather: they were poor Europeans of the nineteenth century.

11. See *Die grossen Entdeckungen*, ed. E. Schmit (Munich: C. H. Beck, 1984), vol. 2, pp. 105–9.

12. ". . . This present year of 1492, after Our Highnesses have put an end to war with Moors, who were ruling in Europe, and after they have finished the war in the great city of Granada. There, in this year . . . and as a result of armed force, the royal flags of Our Highnesses fly from the towers of Alfambra" (*Diario del Primer y Tercer Viaje de Cristóbal Colón*, in the cited version, p. 41).

13. See his letter of 1474 in *Die grossen Entdeckungen*, vol. 2, pp. 9–13.

14. See Appendix 4.

15. Arrow 1 of the map in Appendix 3.

16. Arrow 7 of the map in Appendix 3.

17. Arrow 3 of the map in Appendix 3.

18. Arrow 5 of the map in the same appendix.

19. Martín Fernández de Navarrete, *Colección de los viajes y descubrimientos* (Madrid, 1825), vol. 2, p. xvii.

20. In his map Martellus (Appendix 4) designates one area *Tartaria per totum*. The *Kanes*, Mongol warrior/leaders, dominated Kiev and Moscow. The European Renaissance scholars believed that the domain of the Mongols extended to the extremes of Asia. Hence, Columbus searched for the kingdoms governed by the *Kanes*, in China.

21. According to Roman tradition, Prester John had asked to establish contacts with Rome. Martellus (Appendix 4) also inscribed in the region north of the *Sinus Magnus* the following: *Hic dominat Presbiter Johannes imperator totius Indiae.* Roman tradition also mentioned the Copts of Ethiopia who spread out from the east of Africa toward eastern Asia.

22. Columbus was well aware of the efforts and the pleasures the kings experienced in the taking of Granada. Boabdil still resided on the peninsula, and hundreds of thousands of Muslims, the Moors, refused to comply with their fate.

23. This is the meaning of the "expeditions of the *discoveries.*"

24. *Diario del Primer y Tercer Viaje de Cristóbal Colón*, in the version of B. de las Casas, ed. cit., p. 41.

25.Martellus in Appendix 4 identifies South America with China (Cataio, Quinsaii, Mangii). The *Sinus Magnus* replaces the Pacific Ocean, and the Orinoco and Amazon Rivers are thought to branch throughout the south of China.

26. Ibid., p. 57.

27. Ibid., p. 58, October 13, 1492.

28. I underline and refer to meanings 5 and 7 of Appendix 1. For O'Gorman the concept of occidental culture has not been clarified (see other examples of the use of these words in *La invención de América*, pp. 15, 98–99, etc.). O'Gorman comments: "The invention of America and subsequent historical developments present the effective possibility of the *universalization of the Western culture* as the only program [*sic*] for history. Only this program can include and bind all peoples, provided it is adopted for its own sake and not as the result of imperialist and exploitive imposition" (ibid., p. 98). Such Eurocentrism is typical among the elites of the periphery.

29. Ibid., p. 34.

30. In Columbus's time this peninsula (the "Golden Chersonesus," today Malacca) was thought to be small and located approximately where it is. This peninsula turned inland south of the coasts of China and opened on the *Sinus Magnus*. Columbus thought he had discovered it, but he lacked evidence. Gustavo Vargas Martínez, in *América en una mapa de*

1489, unpublished (Bogotá: 1991), equated the second Golden Chersonesus with both China and South America (as is suggested in Martellus's
map in Appendix 4).

31. In its world historical sense, this second voyage is distinct from
the first. This second one formally initiates the conquest—although I
will only use this figure in regard to the conquest of Mexico. Bartolomé
de las Casas reports Columbus's comments on the second voyage: "In a
few days seventeen great ships were prepared in lower Cadiz . . . and
they were well supplied and *fitted out with artillery and arms* [Dussel's
italics]. I am designating several chests for the gold and other riches
belonging to the Indians [of Asia!]. Fifteen hundred men arrived, all or
the majority under pay of your Highnesses" [*Historia de las Indias*, vol.
1, chap. 40 (Madrid, 1957), pp. 139–40]. No longer is Columbus
merely a Mediterranean merchant; now he is a warrior with arms, soldiers, and cannons. The kings *employ* these soldiers, *unemployed* since
the taking of Granada. The kings employ them to get rid of them by
sending them to the Indies. No sooner has the reconquest that began in
718 drawn to a close, than a new conquest is initiated.

32. The continental mass A of the map of Appendix 3. "Mangi"
appears on the map of Martellus (Appendix 4).

33. The region indicated in the map of Martellus (Appendix 4) as the
fourth peninsula (the continental mass B of Appendix 3).

34. The first is the Arabic peninsula; the second, the Indian; the third,
the Chersonesus (Malacca); and the fourth South America, as a continua-
tion of China on Martellus's map.

35. The passage toward India (Appendix 3) was supposed to lie
between mass A and B.

36. *Lettera Rarissima*, in Navarrete, *Colección*, vol. 1, pp. 303–4 (see
also in *Die grossen Entdeckungen*, vol. 2, pp. 181–83).

37. O'Gorman, *La invención de América*, pp. 64–65.

38. The Atlantic was designated the Western Ocean on the 1474
Behaim-Globus (see *Die grossen Entdeckungen*, vol. 2, p. 12) with the
Antilles at its center. Only when Balboa came across a new ocean on the
other side of the Isthmus of Panama in 1513 was the oceanic sea divided
into the "Sea of the South" (the future "Pacific" of Magellan) and the
"Sea of the North" (to the north of Panama, the Caribbean, the Atlantic).

These findings confirmed that America was the new world which Amerigo Vespucci had discovered somewhat earlier. The little *Sinus Magnus* turned out to be the enormous but unexplored Pacific Ocean.

39. Meaning 4 in Appendix 1.

40. Transition from meaning 4 to meaning 7: "Eurocentrism."

41. Imagine explaining to the common European that the Adamic myth had been created in Iraq, upon which the occidental and Christian civilization has dropped seven hundred thousand tons of bombs. It would seem cruel to have buried such a sacred place under bombs.

42. Just as Freud attempts to describe real sexuality, but objectively analyzes only macho sexuality, so O'Gorman sets out to depict American historicity but ends up presenting it in terms of the very Eurocentrism he criticized.

43. O'Gorman makes use of Aristotle's doctrine of potentiality and actuality. So does Alberto Caturelli in *América Bifronte*, the most hair-raising, reactionary interpretation, from the extreme Right, of America as nonbeing, as *in the rough*. Europe is being; America is matter or potency. Hegel, too, thought of America as pure potency and nonbeing.

44. That *form* is the occidental culture. The form is the actuality in good Aristotelian fashion.

45. O'Gorman, *La invención de América*, p. 93. O'Gorman's descriptions betray his Eurocentric ontology: "Europe, in whose image and likeness America was invented, has its principle of individualization in its own culture. But this particular culture does not suppose a mode of being exclusive and peculiar to Europe, since it assumes that it has universal significance" (ibid., p. 97). Regarding this tension in Europe between particularity and universality, O'Gorman observes: "in that [tension] the historical primacy of western culture is rooted [*sic*]. . . . Since this culture individualizes a determinate being, Europe is perpetually and internally threatened. It is threatened precisely by the very thing that particularizes it—namely, that its own universal significance overflows it" (ibid.). For O'Gorman Europe (in meaning 6 of Appendix 1), a particularity, bears in its womb a universality, occidental culture (meaning 8 of Appendix 1). Paradoxically, occidental culture seems to pass from particularity to universality without novelty or fecundation from some alterity. In reality, the European particularity with its pretension to universality imposes itself

violently upon other particularities such as Latin America, Africa, and Asia. Latin Americans, such as O'Gorman, can express such Eurocentric positions because dominant elites ever since Cortés, his *criollos*, and his mestizo descendents have introjected the dominator.

46. Passage from meaning 5 to meaning 6 in Appendix 1.

47. According to O'Gorman, Latin America as a European invention realizes its own authenticity by imitating European modernization and so passing from potency to act. O'Gorman obviously commits the developmentalist fallacy.

48. See among others Fernand Braudel, *The Mediterranean and the Mediterranean World in the Age of Philip II* (New York: Harper and Row, 1973), vol. 1–2; idem, *The Wheels of Commerce in Civilization and Capitalism, 15th–18th Century* (London: Collins, 1982), vol. 2; Emmanuel Wallerstein, *The Modern World-System. 1: Capitalist Agriculture and the Origins of the European World Economy in the Sixteenth Century* (New York: Academic Press, 1974).

49. The opening to the Atlantic results in an immense revolution. See Pierre Chaunu, *Séville et l'Atlantique (1504–1650)*, 11 vols. (Paris: 1957–1960).

50. See "Catigara" (today approximately in Peru) in Martellus's map (Appendix 4). Arnold Toynbee locates Catigara near Macao [*Historical Atlas and Gazette*, in *A Study of History* (London: Oxford University Press, 1959), p. 131]. China and South America are similar.

51. Letter of July 18, 1500 (Vespucci, *Cartas*, 98; O'Gorman, p. 122).

52. Following the trajectory of arrow 5 as far as the question mark in Appendix 3, but perfectly portrayed in 1489 by Martellus (Appendix 4).

53. See Pierre Caunu, *Conquête et exploitation des Nouveaux Mondes* (Paris: PUF, 1969), pp. 177 ff. The Portuguese mastered the Islamic or Arabic sea between 1500 and 1515. Amerigo Vespucci learned of this from Alvarez Cabral who returned from India in 1501 to the Cape Verde Islands.

54. See *Die grosse Entdeckungen*, vol. 2, pp. 174–81.

55. We have already indicated this mass in Martellus's map, Appendix 4.

56. Vespucci asserts that he arrived as far as 50 degrees southern latitude; that he discovered new stars; and that he had come across a continent

with so many strange animals that they would not have been "able to enter into Noah's Ark," etc. (*Die grossen Entdeckungen*, pp. 176–77).

57. "I have sailed around a fourth part of the world" (ibid., p. 176). O'Gorman denies that this statement refers to a "fourth continent" (*La invención de América*, p. 125), but, what other idea could the idea of a fourth part refer to except a new continent?

58. See chapter 6, Excursus.

59. O'Gorman, *La invención de América*, p. 62. For O'Gorman, there is nothing original about this event. However, he fails to notice that Vespucci's sense of the world is new since now the new and old world form part of a one world system. The old-world has disappeared, since there exists a new horizon embracing both old and new worlds. Modernity emerges in Vespucci's consciousness: old world and new world (new particularity) = a new planetary world, a new universality. Eurocentrism identifies the old world as the center of the new planetary world.

60. I am still discussing only the continental mass of South America. The mapmakers still confused North America with ancient China as if it were a part of Asia possibly united to this southern land mass (see *Die grossen Entdeckungen*, pp. 13–17). Until the beginning of the nineteenth century, Spain, Portugal, and Latin America spoke of the *Western Indies* but never America. The latter name was conferred by the rising northern European powers who had forgotten about Spain and Portugal since the end of the seventeenth century.

61. Ontological and theological/providentialist meaning of European civilization in Hegel.

62. Hegel, *Philosophie der Geschichte*, in *Werke* (Frankfurt: Suhrkamp, 1970), vol. 12, p. 538.

63. "Barbarischen Voelkern" (ibid.)

64. This was the incipient theme for the philosophy of liberation in 1969. All my works analyze this thesis, especially *Para una ética de la liberación latinoamericana* (Buenos Aires: Siglo XXI, 1973), vols. 1–2, and the three succeeding volumes, which I completed before my exile from Argentina in 1975. I relied on the later Heidegger in the late 1960s, then the Frankfurt School, especially Marcuse, and finally Emmanuel Levinas's ethics. On the basis of Levinas, I developed that five-volume ethics from the viewpoint of the Other (*Autrui*) as Indian, as dominated woman, and as the educationally alienated child. My ethics analyzes the violent nega-

tion of the Other who is American by the Same who is European. In 1982 Tzvetan Todorov produced *La conquête de l'Amérique. La question de l'autre* (Paris: Seuil) in which he developed masterfully the same thesis. *Desintegración de la Cristiandad colonial y Liberación* (Salamanca: Sígueme, 1978) commented on Las Casas's prophetic text that "God must pour down upon Spain fury and wrath" for injustices committed in the Indies. I concluded: "Bartolomé respects indigenous persons in their exteriority . . . which indicates his ability to overcome the system to open himself to the exteriority of the Other as Other" (p. 147). Todorov took up the theme again, repeating the same texts (without citing their source) and the same words (pp. 255 ff.). The book reiterates my theoretical position for more than twenty years. The question of the apparition and negation of the Other as a *covering over* (*encubrimiento*) has preoccupied me since 1990. But since this repeated idea has been published only in Spanish, it will not receive extensive publicity, and so will follow the destiny of many ideas originating in dominated and peripheral cultures.

65. *Historia General y Natural de las Indias*, bk. 3, chap. 60.

Chapter 3: From the Conquest to the Colonization of the Life World

1. Silvio Zavala, *La filosofía de la conquista* (Mexico: FCE, 1977), p. 24.

2. Carl Ortwin Sauer, *Descubrimiento y dominación española del Caribe* (Mexico: FCE, 1984), pp. 369 ff. ; Georg Friederich, *El caracter del descubrimiento y la conquista de América* (Mexico: FCE, 1987).

3. *Hidalgo* means *son of someone* or at least a person who has recently entered the ranks of the nobility. I will follow the account of Fray Juan de Torquemada, *Monarquía Indiana*, bk. 4, vol. 2 (Mexico: UNAM, 1975), which focuses "On the Conquest of Mexico": "In the year of the birth of our Lord Jesus Christ, 1519, when Pope Leo X governed the church in highest pontificate in Rome and, the very Catholic Emperor Lord Charles V, being monarch of the Christian princes . . . the most famous and no less venturesome captain Hernando Cortés landed on this land of Anahuac"(p. 7).

4. Ibid. Torquemada adds: "Luther was born in Islebio of Saxony. Fernando Cortés was born in Medellín in Spain. . . . This Christian captain was born so that he might bring an infinite multitude of peoples into the

Roman Catholic Church" (p. 7). Torquemada's anti-Lutheran crusade reveals better than Weber or Habermas modernity's two faces: Reformation Europe and the "other face," the periphery. My vision, like Torquemada's, is more universal, encompassing Europe and Latin America. Further, Torquemada's mention of the 1485 consecration of the Aztecs' *major temple* (ibid., Prologue, p. 8) suggests that God, having listened to the "affliction of these miserable [Aztec] people," called Cortés from his mother's womb "as a new Moses for Egypt" (ibid.). While I disagree with Torquemada and de Sepúlveda's interpretation that the conquistador was a liberator, I wish to highlight the awareness that now things move in *three* scenarios: the European center (Luther), the Hispanic world (Cortés), and the Aztec empire (Mexico).

5. Ibid., chap. 1, p. 13.

6. This word we could today translate as "business."

7. Torquemada, *Monarquía Indiana*, p. 16.

8. Ibid., cap. 3, p. 19. It is obvious what most enthused this Cuban expedition: "The people talked about nothing else those days; they seemed like King Midas who delighted solely in gold and silver to the extent that his interest could not be aroused by anything else" (p. 21).

9. In my *Philosophy of Liberation* (Maryknoll, N.Y.: Orbis, 1981) in the final "Index of Concepts," I distinguish between *difference* internal to the totality and *distinctness* pertaining to real alterity.

10. An aspect of the colonial Latin American economy also utilized to subjugate Muslims in Andalusia. Indians, "interned on plantations (*encomendado*)," served at the disposition of the conquistador, who also mandated them to search for gold in rivers or to toil in mines as in the *mita* (slave labor) of Peru. Thus modernity initiated new and diverse modes of domination in the world periphery.

11. Torquemada, *Monarquía Indiana*, chap. 4, p. 32.

12. Ibid., chap. 7, p. 37.

13. Ibid., p. 39. Cortés evidently seemed to fancy himself the new Constantine, founder of the *New Christendom of the Indies*, as Toribio de Mogrovejo, archbishop of Lima, would write years later, although in a critical vein.

14. Ibid., chap. 8, p. 41.

15. Ibid., chap. 13, pp. 58–59. In chapter 6 here, I will try to unfold Moctezuma's world in greater detail than Torquemada.

16. Ibid., chap. 14, p. 63.

17. Ibid.

18. Ibid.

19. Ibid., p. 64.

20. Ibid., chap. 13–14, pp. 66–67.

21. Ibid., chap. 16, p. 70.

22. Ibid.

23. Ibid., chap. 17, p. 73.

24. Ibid., chap. 19, p. 81. "Because of the place's grandeur and the beauty of its buildings, some called it Seville; others referred to it as the Villa of Vices due to its freshness and its abundance of fruits" (p. 82).

25. Ibid., chap. 22, p. 91. The text continues: "They said that the signs and prodigies witnessed . . . could only portend *the termination of the world*, and thus great was their sadness." For Hegel Europe was the origin and goal of history, while for the Indians Europe's modernizing presence spelled the termination of their world. The meaning of things is reversed when one views them from modernity's other face. (see chapter 8 of the present work).

26. See chapter 8.

27. Bernal Diáz del Castillo, *Verdadera Historia de los sucesos de la Conquista de la Nueva España*, chap. 88 (Madrid: Biblioteca de Autores Españoles, 1947), vol. 2, p. 83

28. This ego is both tempted but free, like Adam in Paul Ricoeur's analysis of the Adamic myth; see my *Para una ética de la liberación latinoamericana* (Buenos Aires: Siglo XXI, 1973), vol. 2; see also my *El humanismo semita* (Buenos Aires: EUDEBA, 1969).

29. See my *El humanismo helénico* (Buenos Aires: EUDEBA, 1975).

30. "When he returned with his lord, we all watched them [the Aztecs] *who had fixed their eyes on the earth and instead of looking at him looked idly at the wall*" (Díaz del Castillo, *Verdadera historia*). No one looked in the face of the emperor; the emperor looked at all but never saw himself looked at. Now, suddenly, all the conquistadores, not only

Cortés, but even the least important soldier, such as Bernal Díaz del Castillo himself, looked at him face to face, as if he were their equal. The emperor stood silent and terrified, not because they did not respect him but because they had violated the divine mandates; it was indeed the end of the world.

31. Ibid., p. 84.

32. Cortés marched with "two hundred thousand Indians from friendly, confederated cities, nine hundred Spanish infantrymen, eighty horses, seventeen pieces of lightweight artillery, thirteen brigantines, and six thousand canoes. Less than one hundred Spaniards died(!), a few horses, and not many Indian allies . . . but one hundred thousand Mexicans died(!) . . . without counting those who perished from hunger or plague" (Torquemada, *Monarquía Indiana*, cap. 1, p. 312). The proportion resembles that of the 1991 Gulf War; 120 U. S. marines in contrast to more than 100,000 Iraqi soldiers perished, without counting civilian deaths through fratricidal battles, hunger, and sicknesses. Five hundred years later, modern violence maintains its proportions.

33. Díaz del Castillo, *Verdadera historia*, chap. 156, p. 195.

34. Torquemada, *Monarquía Indiana*, chap. 102, p. 311.

35. See this citation and its commentary in *Filosofía ética latinoamericana* (Mexico: Edicol, 1977), vol. 3, p. 41.

36. Hegel wrote: "Religion is the fundament (*Grundlage*) of the state" as well as of the Christendom attacked by Kierkegaard and Marx for many of the same reasons.

37. *Informantes de Sahagún*, Códice Florentino, bk. 12, chap. 20 (version of Angel María Garibay). It would be interesting to compare this slaughter with the conquest of Massachusetts. Did (Catholic) Spain treat its conquered any differently than (Anglican) England? Neal Salisbury, *Manitou and Providence: Indians, Europeans, and the Making of New England, 1500–1643* (New York: Oxford University Press, 1982); Edward Johnson, "Wonder-Working Providence of Sion's Savior in New England," in Heimert-Delbanco, *The Puritans in America* (Cambridge: Harvard University Press, 1985); John Eliot, *John Eliot's Indian Dialogues: A Study in Cultural Interaction*, ed. Henry W. Browden and James Ronda (Westport, Conn.: 1980).

38. This would be the fourth figure (*Gestalt*) after invention, discovery, and conquest.

39. E. Wallerstein, *The Modern World-System* (New York: Academic Press, 1974), pp. 300 ff., advances the thesis: "The European world-economy: *Periphery* versus *Arena*." For Wallerstein, fifteenth–sixteenth century Russia, Poland, and Eastern Europe form Europe's periphery. The Portuguese colonies in Brazil, Africa, and Asia function as an external arena. Only Hispanic Latin America and North America lie in the external *periphery*: "The Americas formed the periphery of the European world economy in the sixteenth century, while Asia remained an *external arena*" (p. 336). The entire economy between 1546 and 1640 rested on massive exploitation of silver, the first world money, and in a lesser measure gold. Wallerstein writes, "We have defined a world-system as one in which there is extensive division of labor. . . . World economies then are divided into core states and *peripheral areas*" (p. 349). This is the absolute origin of the first world *system* in a strict sense, but the sense here differs from N. Luhmann's or J. Habermas's notion of system.

40. See my *Filosofía de la Liberación*, 2, 5: "Alienation."

41. Max Weber never imagined that in the archive of the Indies in Seville one can find 60,000 files (more than 60 million papers) on the Spanish bureaucracy in Latin America from the sixteenth to the nineteenth centuries. Spain represents the first modern, bureaucratized state. Díaz del Castillo reports that during the battle against Tlaxcala and with his supplies running low, Hernán Cortés "appointed a soldier by the name of Diego de Godoy to be *the court clerk of his majesty* [!] and ordered him to observe what was happening so he could report it if necessary. For they will not demand an account of the wounds and deaths as long as the war continues into the immediate future, but they will ask for it in peacetime" (Díaz del Castillo, *Verdadera historia,* chap. 64, p. 56). Cortés insists that his clerk keep such records to enable Cortés to defend himself against future possible accusations. In spite of his worry about such accusations, Cortés does not hesitate to hurl his troops into the fray with the cry "Santiago y a ellos (Saint James be with us and at them)." Cortés thus injects the apostle James, patron of reconquest, into the war against the Tlaxcaltecas, just as Muslims appealed to Mohammed in holy war against infidels. What would the poor apostle James have thought, as ethically rigorous and close to Jesus as he was, to see himself inserted into such military conflicts?

42. Ibid., chap. 36, p. 30.

43. Ibid.

44. Ibid., cap. 37, p. 32. I will say more about the son of Malinche later, since he is the Latin American properly speaking, the mestizo of a syncretist or hybrid culture.

45. Ibid., chap. 77, p. 68.

46. "La erótica latinoamericana," in *Filosofía ética latinoamericana* (Mexico: Edicol, 1977), vol. 3, p. 60: "The *phallic ego* establishes a world totality and defines the woman as a passive object, as non-I, nonphallus, or as the castrated one. The masculine Totality assigns her the lot of someone dominated and reduced to nonbeing."

47. Unedited from the letter of Juan Ramírez, bishop of Guatemala, March 10, 1603 [*Archivo General de Indias* (Seville: Audiencia de Guatemala), 156].

48. Michele de Cuneo received from Columbus a Carib virgin as a gift: "He went to the room of Briseida, who was nude according to her customs, and he derived great pleasure by amusing himself with her. The fierce little woman defended herself bitterly even with her fingernails. Our valiant Michele then grasped a cord and thrashed her so well and mightily that she cried out. . . . When he had mastered her, Michele smiled with satisfaction and said: 'I wonder what she is like when she starts making love'" [quote of Antonello Gerbi, *La naturaleza de las Indias Nuevas* ((Mexico: FCE, 1978), p. 49; I have translated from the Italian and omitted parts of the text]. Such acts display the cynical sadism inflicted upon undefended indigenous women.

49. "Todos los gatos son pardos," in *Los reinos originarios* (Barcelona: Barral, 1971), pp. 114–16.

50. Fernand Braudel, *El Mediterráneo y el mundo mediterráneo* (Mexico: FCE, 1953), vol. 1, pp. 406–8.

51. In 1545 the most bountiful silver mine of all modern times was discovered in Bolivia.

52. *Archivo General de Indias*, Audiencia de Charcas, p. 313.

53. See Appendix 2.

Chapter 4: The Spiritual Conquest

1. Gerónimo de Mendieta, *Historia Eclesiástica Indiana*, 3, chap. 21 (Mexico: Ed. S. Chavez Hayhde, 1945), vol. 2, pp. 72–73.

2. Christians in the Roman Empire were innocent victims for the sake of the crucified Christ even as Roman Empire that assassinated Christ judged them culpable. The Europeans now represented a modern, violent Christendom that preached the innocent Christ whom Christians were assassinating in the Indian.

3. See Appendix 2.

4. Bernal Díaz del Castillo, *Verdadera historia de los sucesos de la Nueva España*, (Madrid: Biblioteca de Autores Españoles, 1947) chap. 59, p. 51.

5. See my introduction to *Historia General de la Iglesia en América Latina* (Salamanca: Sígueme, 1983), vol. 1/1, p. 337.

6. Gerónimo de Mendieta, *Historia Eclesiástica Indiana*, 3, cap. 20; vol. 2, pp. 70–71.

7. José de Acosta, *Historia natural y moral de las Indias*, in *Obras* (Madrid, 1954), p. 139.

8. B. de Sagahún, *Historia General de las Cosas de Nueva España* (Mexico: Porrúa, 1956), vol. 1, p. 27.

9. In *The Millennial Kingdom of the Franciscans in the New World* (Los Angeles: University of California Press, 1956), John L. Phelan proposes another date: "The period 1524–1564 was the Golden Age of the Indian Church, just as the time between Moses and the destruction of Jerusalem by the Babylonians was the Golden Age of the Jewish monarchy" (p. 39). The year 1564 marked the arrival of new authorities who destroyed the Franciscans' missionary achievement, at least according to Gerónimo de Mendieta's millenarist and apocalyptic interpretation. For Mendieta, Philip II inaugurated a new Babylonian captivity, also known as the age of silver. Gustavo Gutiérrez explains the great meeting in *Dios o el oro de las Indias* (Salamanca: Sígueme, 1989), pp. 68 ff. The vice regents Velasco in Mexico and Toledo in Peru established the definitive colonial order and completed the spiritual conquest.

10. Within the Aymara and Quechua cultures, it is well known that each number (unity, dualism, trinity, quadrality, etc.) possessed profound theological meaning. Jorge Miranda-Luizaga, "Andine Zahlzeichen und Kosmologie. Ein Versuch zur Deutung des alt-andinen Schöpfungsmythus," 1991, p. 15 (unpublished and presented in a seminar in Aachen), soon to be published.

11. José de Acosta, *Comentarios Reales de los Incas*, in *Obras* (Madrid: BAE, 1960), vol. 3, p. 51 [Fernando Mires, *La colonización de las almas* (San José: DEI, 1991), p. 57].

12. Ibid., p. 62 (p. 57).

13. One can detect in this definition absolute Eurocentrism: "men" refers evidently to Spaniards, the Europeans, who do things the proper, commonly accepted way.

14. Acosta, *Comentarios Reales*, vol. 3, p. 62

15. José de Acosta, *De procuranda indorum salute*, in *Obras* (Madrid: BAE, 1954), p. 392. The first type barbarian establishes "stable republics with public laws and fortified cities, and to attempt to submit them to Christ by force of arms would only convert them into the firmest enemies of Christianity." In their case, one needs the method of *adaptation* of Ricci (in China) and Nobili (in India). However, in Latin America, Acosta recommends reliance on the force of arms . . . because the Indians lack fortified cities or firearms as in Eurasia.

16. Ibid. Both these views and K.-O. Apel's are false, as I will demonstrate in chapter 7.

17. Ibid., 393.

18. Regarding the evangelizing process in particular, see my introduction to the *Historia General de la Iglesia en América Latina*, vol. I/1, pp. 281–365: "La evangelización latinoamericana"; Fernando Mires, *La colonización de las almas. Misión y Conquista en Hispanoamérica* (San José: DEI, 1991); Luis Rivera Pagán, *Evangelización y violencia: La Conquista de América* (San Juan, Puerto Rico: Editorial CEMI, 1991); and Rodolfo de Roux, *Dos mundos enfrentados* (Bogotá: CINEP, 1990).

19. José Gaos, who is responsible for the recent appearance of *world* in Latin American philosophy, employed Heidegger's term in its precise existential meaning. *World* is connected with the later concept *culture*.

20. Germán Arciniegas, *Con América nace la nueva historia* (Bogotá: Third World Editors, 1990), p. 62.

21. Arciniegas repeats many times: "In 1493 Europeans began to establish their independence in the new world which they crossed the Atlantic to create" (ibid., 56). "We are the sons of the emigrants who left Europe to make a new world" (p. 64). "The voice of the children of

emigrants and of their emancipated natives continually resurfaces in American culture"(p. 66). "Discovery refers more to European self-discovery more than to an encounter with nude Indians"(p. 74). Arciniegas thus supports the theory of the *invention* of America espoused by O'Gorman and *criollos*.

22. Vieira taught that Africans were hell-bound because of their paganism and Satanic cults; only the purgatory of slavery in Brazil could purify them sufficiently to merit heaven in the next life. Arciniegas reproduces in secularized form the emancipatory myth of modernity.

23. Although Arciniegas explicitly criticizes Hegel (*Con América*, pp. 176ff: "Hegel y la Historia de América"), paradoxically he repeats his thesis. Arciniegas reproaches Hegel for ignoring that the European who left for America 1492 is a brother of equal worth with the European who remains. Hegel ignores the American brother, Arciniegas maintains, because his 1830 *Lectures on the Philosophy of Universal History* "erased the aborigines from the map" (ibid., p. 178). "The Washingtons, Bolívars, San Martíns, O'Higgins . . . and most recently the Martís derive from families as European as Hegel's" (ibid., p. 190). This fusion of the United States with Latin America in the reference to Washington represents the occult longing of the *criollos*. Because of this longing, they fail to give an account of their mestizo, hybrid, Latin American reality. Modernity ought not be understood as the expansion of the Same to Latin America, as if the European/North American particularity constituted the universality for understanding Latin American particularity.

24. Previously, Guillermo Correa wrote: "Se levanta la voz indígena para impugnar la celebración del V Centenario," in *Proceso* (Mexico), 516 (September 22): 44–47, in which he presented testimonies from Leopoldo Zea, Miguel León Portilla, Abelardo Villegas, Enrique Dussel, and others. The polemic began with Leopoldo Zea's article "¿Qué hacer con el V centenario?," to which Edmundo O'Gorman responded with "¿Qué hacer con Leopoldo Zea?," in *El Día–El Búho* (Mexico) (August 28, 1987). O'Gorman authored three earlier articles in *La Jornada–Semanal* (May 19, June 30, July 7, 1985) against León Portilla's idea of a meeting of cultures. León Portilla replied September 4 and 11, 1988, with "Las elucubraciones del inventor de la Invención de América," in *El Día–El Búho* (Mexico). The polemic turned personal: "The judgment and enraged condemnation of those who do not accept *Invención de*

América manifest Doctor Edmundo O'Gorman's belligerent attitude"(p. 1). O'Gorman published articles in the same paper on September 12 and 25, 1988 regarding the "Quinto Centenario del 12 de octubre de 1492. La visión del vencido," and he attacked León Portilla in his "¿Y, que hacer con Edmundo O'Gorman?" in *El Día–El Búho*, October 2, 1988. In "El capitán y la india," in *La Nación* (Buenos Aires), July 25, 1989, Germán Arciniegas plays with the relationship between Garcilaso de la Vega's mother and his father, a rather witless Spanish captain. "Reflexiones sobre el descubrimiento de América," in *La Jornada–Semanal* (Mexico), *Nueva época* 33 (January 28, 1990): 19–24, contains Silvio Zavala's comments on recent works regarding this theme. Other articles of Zavala, for example, "De las varias maneras de ser indigenista," in *Nueva época* (October 2, 1988), simply provide information. In "Estado de la cuestión del V Centenario" in *El Día–El Búho* (October 16, 1988), Zavala mediated between the polemicists. Leopoldo Zea readdressed the issue with his critical "¿Qué hacer con los quinientos años?" in *El Día–El Búho* (Mexico) (July 23, 1989): 19–21. My framework differs from all the above. I have taken up the Indian's perspective since my first historical works in 1966, including my doctoral thesis, "El episcopado hispanoamericano (1504–1620): Institución misionera defensora del indio" (Cuernavaca: CIDOC, 1969–1971), vols. 1–9, defended at the Sorbonne.

25. See my "Del descubrimiento al desencubrimiento (hacia un desagravio historico)," published in *El Día–El Búho* (December 9, 1984): 4–7, and in *Le Monde Diplomatique* 76 (April, 1985): 28–29. In my first works in 1964, I envisioned a total reconstruction of world history aimed at finding the place of Indian Latin America, the starting point of my interpretation. See my article "Amérique Latine et conscience chrétienne," in *Esprit* (July, 1965): 2–20. The Other provides the origin of a different interpretation of history. Levinas, my teacher during the 1960s, personally suggested the theme of the Indian as Other and spoke of the indigenous "holocaust." See my works *Para una ética de la liberación latinoamericana* (1973) and *Filosofía de la Liberación* (1976). When Tzvetan Todorov wrote *La conquista de América* after his sojourn in Mexico, I was delighted since he applied the hypothesis of Emmanuel Levinas's Other to the Indian. His impressive results resembled those of the philosophy of liberation, which had been using the same categories since the end of the 1960s.

Chapter 5: Critique of the Myth of Modernity

1. Aristotle, who defended slavery, Greco-centrism, and patriarchalism, inspired this obviously patriarchalist and sexist text.

2. Ginés de Sepúlveda's *De las justa causa de la guerra contra los indios* was published in Rome in 1550; my citations depend on the critical edition published by the Fondo de Cultura Económica, Mexico, 1987, p. 153.

3. See Appendix 2.

4. Kant's *Unmündigkeit* corresponds to Gines de Sepúlveda's *tarditas*, or slowness of understanding (Sepúlveda, *De la justa causa*, p. 81).

5. The ecological destruction of the planet earth indicates life's integration with the broader natural cycles of the atmosphere and the biosphere. The American native dwellers supported such cycles. One might ask how much the *quality of life* has developed? It is difficult to respond to this question qualitatively since the answer is a matter of degrees or, as Hegel would say, quantitative quality.

6. Once again, Kantian *Unmündigkeit* = *ruditas*.

7. Sepúlveda, *De la justa causa*, p. 109.

8. I recall Kant's discussion of laziness and cowardice (*Faulheit und Feigheit*) as qualities of culpable barbarity. They do not result from force or external oppression, but rather arise spontaneously (*volentes ac sponte sua*) as internal determinations of a *discouraged and servile soul*.

9. Sepúlveda, *De la justa causa*, pp. 109–11.

10. According to Hegel's philosophy of history, the will first appears as the tyrant's caprice, the only freedom that exists in Asia.

11. Sepúlveda, *De la justa causa*, p. 155.

12. See Appendix 2.

13. Following Aristotle ("the perfect should dominate the imperfect, the excellent its contrary," Sepúlveda, *De la justa causa*, p. 83) and the Scriptures (Proverbs: "The one who is stupid will serve the wise," p. 85), Sepúlveda concludes: "It is perfectly right for the Spaniards to exercise empire over these barbarians living in the New World and adjacent islands. These barbarians are as inferior to the Spanish in prudence, talent, virtue, and humanity *as children to adults or as women to men*[!].

Barbarians and Spaniards differ as much as do wild, cruel peoples from the most clement peoples" (p. 101).

14. "How fitting and salutary that these scarcely human barbarians submit to the empire of those who by their prudence, virtue, and religion will convert them from barbarity into civility" (ibid., p. 133).

15. "For very serious reasons, these barbarians ought to accept Spanish governance . . . which is to their advantage more than to the Spaniards'. . . . Should they refuse our governance (*imperium*), we may employ arms to compel them to accept it. Such a war will be just according to the law of nature and the authority of the great philosophers and theologians" (ibid., p. 135).

16. Regarding indigenous culpability, Sepúlveda comments: "The second alleged reason [for the conquest] concerns their crimes against nature, their abominable lewdness and the portentous devouring of human flesh. By persisting in these crimes, they continue worshiping demons instead of God. Their monstrous rites and human immolations provoke *the divine wrath* in the highest degree" (ibid., p. 155).

17. "Undoubtedly, those who wander outside Christianity err and infallibly approach the precipice; we should not hesitate to draw them back from it by any means and even against their will. If we do not, we will fulfill neither natural law nor Christ's precept" (ibid., p. 137).

18. In the Prologue to my *Philosophy of Liberation* (1976), I classified philosophy of liberation as postmodern. In that time prior to the postmodern movement, I was pointing out the need to overcome modernity. Since I now wish to distinguish myself from postmodernity, I propose a transmodernity.

19. The project G of the scheme of Appendix 2 ought to be affirmed, as opposed to project F.

20. In my work *El último Marx*, chapter 7, I traced how the mature Marx changed in response to the Russian populists' objections and began to think from the Russian periphery.

21. Sepúlveda, *De la justa causa*, pp. 143–45.

22. Ibid., p. 175. Here Sepúlveda utilizes las Casas's arguments in *De único modo*.

23. See the work of John L. Phelan, *The Millenial Kingdom of the*

Franciscans in the New World (Berkeley: University of California Press, 1956); Mario Cayota, *Siembras entre brumas: Utopía franciscana y humanismo renacentista, una alternativa a la conquista* (Montevideo, 1990). This book explains the influence of Joachinism and the spirituals in the spiritual conquest of Mexico.

24. Joachim de Fiore (died in 1202) predicted the commencement of the kingdom of the Holy Spirit in 1260, as the reign of evangelical poverty among Christ's authentic followers. The spiritual church, announced as the fulfillment of the millennium in the *Apocalypse*, was to replace the church of the pope. Hegel, too, betrayed Joachinist leanings in his idea of the "kingdom of the Father, the Son, and the Holy Spirit." Joachinism even influenced Marx; see my *Las metáforas teológicas de Marx* (Estella: Editorial Verbo Divino, 1993).

25. See Phelan, *Millenial Kingdom*, pp. 28 ff.

26. In Mendieta's interpretation of the parable, the three groups invited by the Lord refer to Jews, Muslims, and pagans. Then the Lord finally exclaims: "Go out into the roads and pathways and compel [Latin: *compellere*] them until they enter and and fill my house" (verse 23). As regards the central question of the legitimacy of this coaction, Mendieta, Motolina, and the other Franciscans concur with Sepúlveda.

27. In this point they demonstrate a militant anti-Lutheran optimism.

28. Phelan, *Millenial Kingdom*, pp. 42 ff.

29. Philip II reorganized Mexico's vice regency, named the new vice regent and lower authorities, and proposed to invade the republic of the Indians and convert it into a Spanish tributary.

30. Francisco de Vitoria favored waging war against indigenous people only if they resisted the preaching of the gospel. Las Casas did not find even this reason convincing.

31. In his immense *Apologética historia*, las Casas endeavored not simply to describe ancient indigenous customs, as did Sahagún, but also to demonstrate their rationality, dignity, and anthropological consistency. While Sahagún sought knowledge of the old world in order to destroy it, las Casas hoped to improve and develop the ancient traditions of indigenous cultures. Las Casas presented solid argumentation to prove that those who thought it a sublime, divine task to obliterate these traditions through tabula rasa only produced a greater evil.

32. Bartolomé de las Casas, "Argumento de toda ella" in *Obras escogidas* (Madrid: BAE, 1958), vol. 3, p. 3. Later he wrote: "Given all this discussion about the barbarians, one needs to make this distinction. . . . One will understand the character of these Indian nations, if one makes proper distinctions, *arguing negatively*" (ibid., vol. 4, pp. 444–45). Las Casas does not produce neutral anthropology or history, but bolsters the dignity and innocence of indigenous peoples and discredits every justification of war against them.

33. Prologue to Bernardino de Sahagún, *Historia Genral de las cosas de Nueva España* (Mexico: Porrúa, 1975), p. 17. Sahagún studies Náhuatl culture in order to destroy it more systematically, wheras las Casas does so in order to reveal its dignity, rationality, and high, moral, cultural, political, and religious development.

34. Bartolomé de las Casas, *De único Modo de atraer a todos los pueblos a la verdadera religión (1536)*, chap. 5:1 (Mexico: FCE, 1975), p. 65.

35. Ibid., pp. 65–66.

36. Ibid., chap 5:2, p. 71.

37. Ibid., chap. 6:1, p. 343.

38. Ibid.

39. Ibid., chap. 6:1, pp. 343–44. Las Casas displays renowned rhetoric in depicting the cruel terrors of the war in the Caribbean, Mexico, and Central America. These prophetic pages warn about the brutal violence that modernity will scatter throughout the peripheral, colonial world, only recently called the Third World. Las Casas would not be surprised to see the desolation of Iraq's poor, suffering people.

40. Ibid., chap. 6:2, p. 431.

41. See Appendix 2.

42. Ibid., chap. 6:3, p. 446. For las Casas, the kings, bishops, captains, counselors, and soldiers are all responsible. He conducts a Nuremburg trial of modern culture for its crimes in the holocaust of the conquest, and anticipates the history of violence to occur over the next four centuries.

Chapter 6: Amerindia in a Non-Eurocentric Vision of World History

1. The *fundament* for Aztecs and Mayans is the place where one finds help, rests, sits down, and allows things to *stand forth*. Similarly, human-

ity is the word, but its word dwells in the great originary father before the creation (opening-of-the-self-in-flower) of the universe.

2. *Open-in-flower* means to create.

3. *Heavenly being* is the divinity.

4. Among the Avá-Chiripa the *oporaiva* was the *singer*. In song, humanity expressed itself most fully and united the divine and the human, the individual and community, past and future, and heaven and earth. In song, the Tupi-Guaranís fully realized their being.

5. Túpac Amaru referred to the Spaniards as *Europeans*. See Boleslao Lewin, *La rebelión de Tupac Amaru* (Buenos Aires: SELA, 1967), p. 421. Years ago, I described Europe's violence as an *intrusion*, but indigenous assemblies at the end of the 1980s impressed upon me the idea of the *invasion* of the continent.

6. In a televised interview years ago, Edmundo O'Gorman argued that Indians did not discover America, because they lacked information about the continent as such and never grasped it as a totality. Their immersion in their regional, telluric experience hindered any global perspective from arising. But this argument ignores that the Indians first interpreted these American lands with their own cultural resources. The European discovery came on the scene later and superimposed itself upon that first indigenous experience. Heidegger permits a decription of the indigenous world which the European discoverers met.

7. While writing these lines, here in Zijhuatenejo in Guerrero (Mexico), I hear the cadenced crashing of the waves of the Greeks' great sea, of Martellus's and Columbus's *Sinus Magnus*, of Balboa's sea of the south, of the Pacific Ocean. It is highly appropriate to begin the second part of this book beside this ocean.

8. The plumes of the marvelously beautiful *quetzal* bird in Central America signified the divinity. *Cóatl* denoted the duality, the universe's two principles. *Quetzal-cóatl*, represented as a serpent by the Aztecs, was the supreme divinity, the dual principle of the universe.

9. See Leopoldo Zea, *América en la historia* (Mexico: FCE, 1957). Zea contends that in that epoch the *western culture* took on worldwide importance (pp. 88 ff.) and became synonymous with the United States on whose margins even Europe lies (p. 155). As in his earlier works [for example, in *América como conciencia* (Mexico: Cuadernos Americanos, 1953) or in *La essencia de lo americano* (Buenos Aires: Pleamar, 1971)],

Zea uses *occidental culture* as his interpretive key. Later, in a meeting on *philosophy of liberation* in San Miguel, with Salazar Bondy present, Zea adopts *dependence* as his key [see, for example, *Filosofía de la Historia Americana* (Mexico: FCE, 1978)]. He asseı ȝ that there is an Iberian colonizing project (pp. 103 ff.) and an occidental, North American one (pp. 133 ff.). Three counter projects oppose forms of dependency: the libertarian (pp. 188 ff.), conservative (pp. 211 ff.), and liberal/civilizing (pp. 244 ff.). These three projects pertain to an *assumptive project* (pp. 269 ff.) seeking to synthesize the past with the future after the pattern of Simón Bolívar and Martí. Zea, who never mentions the projects of Amerindians or subordinated classes, has not yet imagined a project of liberation that would suit the oppressed, exploited, and impoverished Latin American people.

10. I have discussed this theme extensively. In *Hipótesis para el estudio de Latinoamérica en la Historia Universal* [Resistencia (Argentina): Universidad del Nordeste, 1966], vol. 1, p. 268, I provide a thorough bibliography. Also see the Introduction to the *Historia General de la Iglesia en América Latina* (Salamanca: Sígueme, 1983), pp. 108 ff.; *El humanismo helénico* (Buenos Aires: EUDEBA, 1975); *El humanismo semita* (Buenos Aires: EUDEBA, 1969). Especially important is "Iberoamérica en la Historia Universal" in *Revista de Occidente* (Madrid) 25 (1965), pp. 85–95. Here I proposed the hypothesis developed in this book.

11. For Oswald Spengler they were the Egyptian, Babylonian, Indian, Chinese, Greco-Roman, Arab, Mexican, and Western [*La decadencia de Occidente* (Madrid: Ed. Calpe, 1923–1927), vols. 1–4]. Clearly by excluding some cultures he interprets world history Eurocentrically. In my account, I refer to only the first and most fundamental neolithic cultures in each macroregion. Arnold Toynbee [*A Study of History* (London: Oxford University Press, 1934–1959), vols. 1–12] excludes the Indic from his six primary civilizations: Egyptian, Sumerian, Minoic, Sinic, Mayan, and Andean. Alfred Weber describes "the history of the great cultures, Egyptian, Sumerian-Acadian-Babylonian, Chinese, and Indostanic, the four pillars of history" [*Kulturgeschichte als Kultursoziologie* (Munich: Piper, 1963), translation in Spanish (Mexico: FCE, 1960), p. 12]. Even though all Weber's Eurocentric explanations eliminate Latin America, I will borrow from him the idea of the *Primäre Hochkulturen* (the great first cultures). Karl Jaspers [in *Vom Ursprung and Ziel der Geschichte* (Munich: Piper, 1963)] emphasizes the importance of the

Achzenzeit (axis-time) in which the following figures and literary products simultaneously appeared: Confucius and Lao-tse in China, the Upan-
ishads of India, the Buddha in Nepal and the north of India, Zarathustra
in Iran, the first great prophets in Israel (Elijah, Isaiah), and the first pre-
Socratic philosophers in Greece. "The mystical epoch had come to an
end, and with it its tranquil placidity and its genius" (p. 21). Since this
axis time culminates the neolithic-urban revolution, once more Latin
America remains outside. Jaspers knows nothing of *Tlamitinime* critical
wisdom, Nezahualcoyotl in Mexico, or the Incan *amautas*. For Toynbee,
in contrast, the *amautas* had achieved a critical, universal level of thought
with their *viracochinism*, that is, the theological vision of Viracocha, the
originary Maker of the universe. In Jaspers's opinion, Mesopotamia,
Egypt, the Indus, the Huang-Ho, and later the Mediterranean, Indian,
and Chinese cultures excelled and anticipated the axis time. I have inte-
grated the idea of *contact zones* proposed by the *Saeculum Weltgeschichte* [edited by H. de Franke, H. Hoffmann, and H. Jedin (Freiburg:
Herder, 1965), vol. 1] into my account of the role of the Euroasian
steppes and the Pacific Ocean.

12. Darcy Ribeiro, in his work *El proceso civilizatorio* (Caracas: Universidad Central de Venezuela, 1970), writes: "By rural, artesan states we
intend . . . the city states inaugurating urban life based on irrigation agriculture within collectivist socioeconomic systems. Examples of such city
states can be found before 4000 B.C.E. in Egypt (Memphis, Mesopotamia,
Halaf); between 4000 and 3000 B.C.E. in Egypt (Memphis, Thebes); in
India (Mohnejo-Daro) around 2800 B.C.E.; before 2000 B.C.E. in China
(Yang-Shao, Hsia); and much later . . . in the Andean Plateau (Salinar and
Galinazo, 700 B.C.E., and Mochica, 200 C.E.); in Colombia (Chibcha,
1000 C.E.)"(p. 61). Ribeiro overlooks the Mesoamerican world, where,
for example, Zacatenco-Copilco flourished in 2000 B.C.E. in proximity to
Lake Tezcoco in the suburbs of Mexico. During Mesoamerica's classical
epoch, between 300 and 900 C.E., Teotihuacán III prospered in the
Yucatán-Aztec, area as did Tiahuanaco in the Bolivian Titicaca from 400
to 800 C.E.

13. The arrows do not indicate *direct* contacts between cultures but
show spatial movements and temporal sequences. In some cases, direct
contacts occurred, as between the Polynesian and Amerindian cultures.

14. See D.-O. Edzard, "Im Zweistromland," in *Saeculum Weltgeschichte*, 1, pp. 239–81, and in many other places of this work; C. L.

Wolley, *Ur, la ciudad de los Caldeos,* Spanish translation (Mexico: FCE, 1953); idem, *The Sumerians* (London: Oxford University Press, 1928); André Parrot, *Archeologie Mesopotamienne* (Paris, 1946); *Cambridge Ancient History* (Cambridge University Press), diverse editions.

15. Gordon Childe, *Los origenes de la civilización* (Mexico: FCE, 1959), p. 174.

16. Jouget-Dhorme, *Les premiers civilisations* (Paris: PUF, 1950), p. 115.

17. See E. Burrows, "Some Cosmological Patterns in Babylonian Religion," in *The Labyrinth* (London, 1950), pp. 45–70.

18. *Mitologías. Lo crudo y lo cocido I,* Spanish translation (Mexico: FCE, 1986), vol. 1, p. 21. Lévi-Strauss's own ethnographic language interpreting these myths constitutes a third code. This metalanguage differs "from philosophical reflection, which seeks to return to its origin, since my reflections appear as rays lacking any complete focus . . . they postulate, however, a common origin, an ideal point on which wandering rays converge when one considers the myth's structure" (ibid., p. 15). While ethnology's interpretive metalanguage may not be a philosophic metalanguage, myths cannot be dismissed as naive, uncritical language. They signify a rationalization process occupying humanity for hundreds of thousands of years since the time of *homo habilis,* and for tens of thousands of years during the era *homo sapiens.*

19. The ethical principle of *exteriority* or alterity (concern for the orphan, the widow, the stranger, the poor) surpasses Kohlberg's fifth and sixth ethical levels, since it places in question the universality of the life world. Kohlberg remains bound to this universality, as does John Rawls, whose two principles spring from the limited liberalism of the modern world.

20. See E. Otto, "Im Niltal. Aegypten," in *Saeculum Weltgeschichte,* 1, pp. 282 ff.; E. Drioton and J. Vanider, *L'Egypte* (Paris: Clio, PUF, 1952); John Wilson, *La cultura egipcia* (Mexico: FCE, 1958); Jouget-Dhorme-Vandier, *Les primières civilisations,* in *Peuples et civilisations,* vol. 1, pp. 21–300.

21. The Bantu cultures of black Africa originated the worship of Osiris, the god of the resurrection of the flesh and foundation of the Nile culture, with its pyramids sheltering the dead who awaited resurrection.

In this manner, these cultures enter world history—from which Hegel had excluded them.

22. The Egyptian pharaoh wore two crowns; the black Bantu crown faced south.

23. *Papiro ñu*, trans Juan Bergua (Madrid: 1962), pp. 181–82.

24. I argued this point in my earliest works, *El humanismo semita* and *El dualismo en la antropología de la Cristiandad: La antropología desde el origen del cristianismo hasta el descubrimiento de América* (Buenos Aires: Guadalupe, 1974). I have located the philosophy of liberation with respect to its most distant antecedents in world history, as is necessary. Arturo Roig's and Leopoldo Zea's reproach that I have ignored history seems out of place. In "Dependencia y liberación en la filosofía latinoamericana," *Filosofía y Cultura latinoamericana* (Caracas: Centro Rómulo Gallegos, 1976), pp. 211ff, Zea argues: "Alberdi's generation has offered interesting reactions to the philosophy of liberation. Another Argentine . . . Enrique Dussel, endeavors to erase our wicked past and not to assimilate it in order to begin once again from zero." Zea overlooks that I was criticizing restricted notions of philosophy such as the academic philosophy taught in universities, the scholastic philosophy of the colonial epoch, or present-day "founders'" philosophy begun in 1920 for what F. Romero called *normalization* purposes. Even though Zea criticizes me for denying all previous Latin American *thought* (Bolívar, Alberdi, Sarmiento, Barreda), I have never denied previous Latin American history, but have written books about it. Moreover, in order to show Latin American philosophy of liberation's indebtedness, as well as its uniqueness, I have exposed its roots in the Greeks and Semites, in the medievals and moderns, and throughout Latin American history. In contrast, the university philosophy practiced in Latin America to this day remains imitative and uncreative. My project of liberation, assumptive like Zea's, also assumes popular, oppressed viewpoints.

25. The founder of Christianity coincides (Matthew 25) with Friedrich Engels in *The Origin of the Family*. Ethics must treat economics.

26. Consult entries about India in the already suggested world histories; E. Mackay, *The Indus Civilization* (London, 1935); M. Wheeler, *The Indus Civilization* in *Cambridge History of India* (Cambridge University Press, 1953).

27. In addition to the corresponding chapter in world histories, see Marcel Granet, *La civilización china*, in *La Evolución de la Humanidad*, vol. 29; idem, *El pensamiento chino*, in the same collection, vol. 30, 1959. I have set aside any discussion of the mythic Hsia dynasty.

28. *Tao-Te Ching* 37:1; edition of Lin-Yutang, translated into Spanish by F. Mazia (Buenos Aires: Sudamericana, 1959), pp. 167–68.

29. Gustavo Vargas in *América en un mapa de 1489* (p. 67) states: "Since it lies near 8. 3 degrees southern latitude and since the details fit with Columbus's sketch and the Munster map, this city would be located on the northern Peruvian coast. It could easily be Chan Chan, as some, such as Jacques Mahieu, believe" ["El imperio vikingo de Tiahuanacua: América antes de Colón," in *El Laberinto* (Barcelona) 15 (1985), p. 36].

30. In Náhuatl, *anáhuac* means the ring of water surrounding the earth, and the Aztecs conceived the Atlantic and Pacific oceans surrounding Mexico to be part of one great sea, *teoatl*, or divine water, *ilhuica-atl*. The Aztecs called the totality of the world *Cemanáhuac* [see the magnificent work of Miguel León Portilla, *La Filosofía Náhuatl* (Mexico: UNAM, 1979), pp. 113, 150]. Panama's Cunas dubbed the earth *Abia Yala*, and the Incas called it *Tahuantisuyo*. Each indigenous language bestows its own autochthonous name on the earth known to it users, the American continent. See Aiban Wagua, "Medio Milenio! Algunas consecuencias actuales de la invasión european a *Abia Yala*. Visión indigena" (Ustupu, Kuna Yala [Panama]: 1990): "The Cunas, before the Europeans ever arrived, knew this world as *Abia Yala*, which means: mature earth, earth great mother, earth of blood. At present, an Italian name, America, has been imposed upon us" (p. 14). Felipe Poma de Ayala (Waman Puma), in his *El primer nueva Crónica y Buen Gobierno* (Mexico: Siglo XXI, 1980), vol. 3, pp. 913–16, discusses a beautiful and illustrated "map of the World of the kingdom of the Indies. The kingdom of Antisuio lies toward the right of the sea of the north [the Caribbean] and Colla-suio is located where the sun rises. Conde-suio is near the sea of the south [the Pacific Ocean], and Chincai-suio designates the Incan 'world earth.' These four parts form a 'cross,' whether in the Chinese theogonies or in the Pacific Polynesian, Aztec, Mayan, Chibcha, or Incan cultures."

31. Crete maintained contacts with the Aegean coasts, the delta of the Nile, Cyprus, and such cities as Gaza, Gezer, Megiddo, Tyre, Biblos, Alepo, Charchemish. This permitted interconnections between the

Hittites, Egyptians, Acadians, Babylonians, and Phoenicians. See G. Glotz, *La civilización egea*, in *La evolución de la humanidad*, vol. 10, 1956, pp. 211ff; Wolfgang Helck, "Der Ostmittelmerraum," in *Saeculum Weltgeschichte*, vol. 1, pp. 451–550.

32. Consult already cited world histories, and see especially Karl Narr, "Exkurs über die frühe Pferdehaltung," in *Saeculum Weltgeschichte*, vol. 1, pp. 578–81; W. M. McGovern, *The Early Empire of Central Asia*, London, 1939.

33. Political-military leaders in this region were entitled "Kan." In his 1489 map, Martellus denominated an area in northwest China *tartaria per totum*. Thus Columbus sought contact with the "Great Kan" in his first voyage in 1492.

34. O'Gorman correctly observes that they did not grasp the continent as a totality, but they did discover it region by region, valley and mountain, one after another from Alaska to the Tierra del Fuego. While not discovering America as the Europeans, the indigenous peoples performed the more important function of humanizing a terrain previously uninhabited. The conquest came to grips with this previous humanization by dominating the *cultures* that had humanized *nature*.

35. The prefix "pre-" frequently suggests Eurocentrism, as if history only occurred when written down or as if language were not the essential rational moment prior to its rational encoding. See J. Beaglehole, *The Exploration of the Pacific* (London, 1947); F. Keesing, *Native Peoples of the Pacific* (New York, 1946); Paul Rivet, *Los origenes del hombre americano* (Mexico: FCE, 1960); Hinz Kelm, "Frühe Beziehungen Amerikas zu Asien und Polynesien" in *Saeculum Weltgeschichte*, vol. 1, pp. 610–37 and 663–68; Hans Nevermann, "Die polynesische Hochkultur," in op. cit., pp. 355–78; Canals Frau, *Prehistoria de América* (Buenos Aires: Sudamericana, 1950).

36. In August 1990, attending a seminar on 1492, I inquired of some Araucanian/Mapuche chiefs the significance of *toki*. They explained that the matrilineal but polygamous Mapuche clans in war time elected a leader from among its most valiant, strong, and intelligent individuals. Like the Roman dictatorship, this institution permitted concerted action in warfare. Afterward, the *toki* (military chief) returned to his earlier activites, and the chiefs resumed governance of their clan. Thus, a military institution original to the Polynesians and wielded by the Mapuches

impeded the Spaniards during the entire colonial epoch from ever conquering southern Chile.

37. J. Imbelloni, *La segunda esfinge indiana* (Buenos Aires, 1942), p. 391. From the same author, "La première chaîne isoglosématique océano-américaine, le nom des haches lithiques," in *Festschrift W. Schmidt* (Vienna: Modling, 1928), pp. 324–35.

38. S. Canals Frau, *Prehistoria de América*, p. 425. This same author offers other parallels: "man" (*tama*) in Polynesian corresponds to the same word among the American Hokas; "nose," *ihu*, occurs in both; "head": *upoko* and *epoko*; "sun": *laa* and *ala*; "canoe": *matoi* and *mato*.

39. A Guaraní expression to be explained later.

40. See W. Krickeberg, H. Trimbron, W. Müller, and O. Zerries, *Die Religionen des alten Amerika* (Stuttgart: Kohlhammer, 1961); W. Schmidt, *Der Ursprung der Gottesidee* (Münster: 1926–1955), vols. 1–10. Although this book proposes that monotheism is humanity's original belief, it only demonstrates that *enotheism* without any duality is primordial. Idem, *Ursprung und Werden der Religion* (Münster, 1930); J. Comas, *Ensayos sobre indigenismo* (Mexico, 1953); S. Canals Frau, *Las civilizaciones prehispánicas*, already cited.

41. This group encompasses the Magallanic Indians, the Pampas of Gran Chaco, and tribes of eastern Brazil. See *Hipótesis para el estudio de Latinoamérica en la Historia Universal*, pp. 130 ff. ; *Introducción a la Historia General de la Iglesia en América Latina*, vol. 1/1, pp. 129 ff., especially the detailed map. See also Otto Zerries, "Die Religionen der Naturvölker Südamerikas und Westindiens," in W. Krickeberg and others, op. cit., pp. 269 ff.

42. The Californians, Shoshonis, Canadian Algonquins, Athabaskens, and Eskimos fall under this classification. See Werner Müller, "Die Religionen der Indianervölker Nordamerikas," in W. Krickeberg and others, *Die Religionen*, 171 ff.

43. "The Guaraní belong to the forests. . . . Their life is rapid, fleeting, and desperate. They struggle constantly for light and food in a flooded world" [León Cadogan, *La literatura de los Guaraníes* (Mexico: Joaquín Martiz, 1970), pp. 11–12]. The Guaranís left behind very few objects for museums and archeologists. Their technology, forms of local governance, textiles, and pottery were not very developed.

44. "The third class . . . includes savages similar to wild beasts, without human feeling, law, kings, pacts, magistrates, and the practices of a republic. They move their dwellings, or settle for stable habitats similar to wild animals' caves or animals' gardens. . . . The greater part of those in Brazil live like this . . . they are nude, timid, and prone to shameful pleasures and sodomy" [*De procuranda Indorum salute* (Madrid: Proemio, BAE, 1954), p. 393]. This definition moreover pertains precisely to the Guaranís.

45. The Guaranís sang this poetic song at the communal festive ritual and accompanied it with dancing and other rhythmic movements This feast was a central act of Guaraní existence.

46. "Opening-oneself-as-a-flower," as we have said, involves a creative, productive action, going beyond oneself.

47. "Heavenly being," as we have said, is the divine, the eternal.

48. Bartomeu Melía, *El Guaraní, experiencia religiosa* (Asunción: Biblioteca Paraguaya de Antropología, 1991), pp. 29–30; León Codogan, *La literatura de los Guaranís*, pp. 53–57.

49. Melía, *El Guaraní*, p. 34.

50. Freud rationalized the oneiric alluded to here.

51. "To-keep-oneself-standing" entails knowing that one is founded and supported, as it did among the Aztecs.

52. León Codogan, *Ayvu rapyta: Textos míticos de los Mbya-Guaraní del Guairá* (Universidad de São Paulo, 1959), p. 40. See the same author's *Ywyra ñe'ery; fluye del árbol la palabra* (Asunción: Centro de Estudios Antropológicos, 1971); B. Melía, *Die schönen Ur-Worte: die Kunst des Wortes bei den Guaraní* (Frankfurt: Museum fur Völkerkunde, 1988). "The word, the name, the prayer, the song, the medicinal invocation, prophecy, the political-religious exhortation—all these forms of *saying: ñembo'e*, are the privileged forms of Guaraní religion. The Guaraní behaves religiously by becoming the word and thus participating in the being of the first fathers, the fathers of words-souls" (Melía, *El Guaraní*, pp. 41–42). 53. *Teko* means what *ethos* meant for the Greeks: a mode of being and the place where one dwells. *Tekoha* meant the *place* to establish the Guaraní mode of being: "The *tekoha* signifies and produces at the same time the economic relationships, social relationships, and political-religious organizations essential for the Guaraní life. However redundant it

might appear, one must agree with the Guaraní leaders that without *tekoha* there is no *teko*" (ibid., p. 64).

54. Ibid., pp. 44–45.

55. The *clearing* illuminates in Heidegger, who thinks of the Black Forest and not the Amazon-Paraguayan forest.

56. Melía, *El Guaraní*, pp. 45–46. In the *socialist* reductions of Paraguay, the Jesuits intuitively preserved this originary communal and economic reciprocity on the basis of the word. Although not really socialists, their economy contained only use values, and no exchange values. Those living in the reductions preexisted class formations and their clan existence would have seemed utopic. For Marx human societies exemplified communitarian relationship prior to modern, capitalist individuality. Marx extrapolated beyond such relationships to the utopian communitarianism of the full individual in the full community [see the *Grundrisse* and my study of it: *La producción teórica de Marx* (Mexico: Siglo XXI, 1985); *Hacia el Marx desconocido* (Mexico: Siglo XXI, 1988); *El último Marx* (Mexico: Siglo XXI, 1990). These books render Marx all the more relevant even after the formal disappearance of the Soviet Union on December 26, 1991.

57. Hence, by inviting the the Spaniards to their *feasts*, the Guaranís believed that they confirmed a contract of eternal giving-receiving. How surprising it would have seemed that the Spaniards neither collaborated in preparations for the proximate feasts nor invited the Guaranís to their feasts. The Europeans would have seemed treacherous, demoniacal, perverse, and culpable of an unpardonable offense against the first father.

58. Melía, *El Guaraní*, p. 77.

59. Ibid., p. 84.

60. From *homo habilis*, four million years ago, until the Guaranís, humanity had achieved the essence of human development. These human beings barely differ from modern humanity when it comes to the use of language, an ethical sense, and appreciation of the dignity and meaning of life.

61. See R. and M. Cornevin, *Histoire de l'Afrique* (Paris: PUF, 1964), pp. 145ff.

62. See Samir Amin, *Eurocentrism* (New York: Monthly Review Press, 1989).

63. See Appendix 1.

64. Europe always expands from its margins, such as Russia, Spain, and later England. See Leopoldo Zea, *Discurso desde la marginación y la barbarie* (Madrid: Anthropos, 1988).

Part 3

1. See Paul Ricoeur's account of the rich meaning of *metaphor* in *La métaphore vive* (Paris: Seuil, 1975).

Chapter 7: From the Parousia of the Gods to the Invasion

1. The ancient God Omoteótl contained the dual principles of mother and father, as did the Mayan Alom-Qaholom. See *Popol Vuh* (Mexico: FCE, 1990), pp. 23 and 164. This originary divine duality resembles the twin deities of all other American cultures in the North American plains, the Carribean, the Amazon, and as far south as Tierra del Fuego. Heraclitus too espoused a dual principle.

2. Metaphors such as *being spread out, resting, lying* describe the absolute as the fundament beneath, founding and being the ultimate reference in the same sense as *Grund* in Hegel's greater and lesser *Logics*. To *lie* (όνοc) as the fundament of universe is to give it its *truth*.

3. This means the same as *in itself* (*in sich*).

4. The ocean, the seas to the north and south of the Aztec empire.

5. Although the heavens stand *above* the waters *below*, they are continuous with each other.

6. The kingdom below completes the trinity of heaven-earth-Hades, as in Mesopotamian cults. This below (*topan michtlan*) formed the region of the dead in contrast to *Tilocan*, the paradise of the just.

7. Cited from Miguel León Portilla, *La Filosofía Náhuatl* (Mexico: UNAM, 1979), p. 93.

8. With Karl-Otto Apel in Mexico in 1991, I discussed the presence of philosophy in America's protohistory and the possibility of an *Enlightenment* (*Aufklärung*) in the Jasperian sense of axis time (*Achsenzeit*).

9. In the Greek sense of "lover of wisdom," who in this context would have been a philosopher-theologian since Christianity later secularized the philosopher in the third century C.E.

10. Bk. 2, chap. 2 (Lima: Editorial Universo, 1967) vol. 1, p. 74. The Inca Garcilaso adds: "This is to say that the Christian God and Pachacá-mac were one and the same" (ibid., p. 75). He criticizes Pedro de Cieza, who "because he is Spanish does not understand the language as well as I, who am an Incan" (ibid., p. 74).

11. From *mati*: "he knows, is familiar with"; *tla*: "thing or some-thing"; *ni*, "giving the substantive character": *the one who knows. Tla-matini*: "he who knows something."

12. Chap. 7 (Mexico: Ed. Porrúa, 1975), p. 555. By painting the sacred codices, the painter became a principal official, as did the singer who intoned the ritual *song*. The splendor of Aztec ritual song exceeded that of the poor Guaranís of the tropical forests.

13. *Obras históricas* (Mexico: 1892), vol. 2, p. 18. *Coloquios y Doct-rina Cristiana* [*Sterbende Götter und Christliche Heilsbotschaft*, ed. W. Lehmann (Suttgart: 1949), pp. 96–97] mentions another social function after that of governors, priests, and astronomers: "Those who watch, give an account, turn noisily the codices' pages, and command the black and red ink of our painting are the ones who carry us, guide us, point out the way." They are the *tlamatinime*.

14. I stress this point to prove the existence of an Aztec philosophy.

15. If one does not smoke something up, it is clear, transparent, lucid.

16. The gods looked upon the earth through a needle hole, just as the astronomers looked at the heavens through a pierced object. One who is "perforated from both sides" understands the meaning of humanity from the gods' viewpoint and the meaning of the deity from the human view-point.

17. Truth: *Neltiliztli*, from the root *nelhuáyotl*: "cement, fundament" (as the Guaraní *fundament of the word*); and also from *tla-nél-huatl*: "foot." "The Náhuatl concern whether something *were true or was standing* [as among the Guaranís] aimed at knowing if it were fixed and well cemented, if it would *only slightly incline* toward the vanity of earthly *(tlaltícpac)*, dreamlike things" (León Portilla, op. cit., p. 61). Once again the question of fundament arises. "By chance is humanity the truth? Then our song would not be *truth*. What by chance *is standing*?" (Ms. "Cantares Mexicanos," folio 10, v; León Portilla, *La Filosofía Náhuatl*, p. 327).

18. *Teixtlamachtiani*: "he or she who makes another rich or communicates something to the other." *Ix* (from *ixtli*): "face, visage"; *te*: "the Other." The *visage* or *face* represents the being of the other. The even more powerful expression *teixicuitiani* commands one to take on the *visage* of others, thereby personalizing them and individualizing them. Finally, *teixtomani*, entails helping the other's visage develop. Someone *without visage* is ignorant, drifts, and finds no meaning in anything or in one's self. The educated person *has a visage* and thus can discover critical meanings transcending whatever is merely earthly (*tlaltícpac*), ephemeral, phenomenal, or platonically doxical, "as if it were a dream." All wisdom surpasses the *tlaltícpac* to reach "that which surpasses us" (*topa mictian*), the transcendent. This explicit enlightenment (*Aufklärung*) achieves the level of Parmenides' poems and Heraclitus' oracles and exemplifies a kind of Jaspersian axis time similar to that among the pre-Socratics. The limitations of space prevent me from presenting here León Portilla's profound and detailed arguments about Aztec culture.

19. *Tetezcaviani* derives from from *tezcatl* and *tezcavia*, which means "to place a mirror before others." The *mirror* symbolizes critical, speculative reflection by which one looks at oneself and overcomes meaninglessness. The *tlamatini* places a mirror before the other's visage and enables self-discovery, self-reconstruction, and self-development.

20. The basic concept of world, *cemanáhuac*, indicates the complete ring of water and derives from *cem*: "entirely, all"; *a(tl)*: "water"; *nahuac*: "ring." The sea of the North (the Caribbean, Atlantic) and the sea of the South (Pacific) encompass Mexico's world. The waters of this one divine ocean (*teóatl*) are continuous with those of heaven (*ilhuicaatl*). See Eduard Seler, *Gesammelte Abhandlungen zur Amerikanischen Sprach- und Altertumskunde* (Berlin: Ascher and Behren, 1923), vol. 4, p. 3. *One applies one's light to the world* signifies that one observes and discovers with the light of one's intelligence the world's mysterious aspect. *Tla-ix-imantini* means "one who knows things by one's visage."

21. *Itech netlacaneco* comes from *ne-tlaca-neco*: *-neco*: "he is desired"; *tlacatl*: "human being"; *ne-*: impersonal prefix. *Itech netlacaneco* means "the people are humanly desired" thanks to him (*itech*). He humanizes, civilizes, educates, and supports love and desire. This text, the product of a delicate subjectivity, recommends patient, humble, profound, solidary action.

22. León Portilla, *La Filosofía Náhuatl*, pp. 65–74.

23. For instance, the *magician who turns the other's face* (*teixcuepani*) refers to one who shows the other the nape of the neck instead of the face with its power to promote self-realization. The Europeans discovering America could only see *a face turned toward the back* (*en-cubierto*). The magician also *makes others lose their face* (*teixpoloa*) (Ibid., p. 73).

24. "All these songs consist in *some metaphors* so obscure that no one can understand them unless they carefully study and discuss them in search of their meaning. Even though I have listened carefully to their singing and immersed myself in their words and metaphoric terms, I found their songs baffling. After much conferring, I have come to see that these songs express *admirable opinions* of divine prophecy and human feeling" [Diego Durán, *Historia de las Indias de Nueva España e Islas de Tierra Firma* (Mexico: Porrúa, 1967), vol. 1, p. 21].

25. "They rose at four to clean the house. . . . They cook food in the Calmécac house. . . . Every midnight they all wake up to pray, and they punish those who sleep through prayer by pricking their ears, chest, muscles, and legs" [B. de Sahagún, *Historia General de las cosas de Nueva España* (Mexico: 1829), vol. 1, p. 327].

26. Náhuatl philosophical treatises involved dialogues or conversations similar to Platonic dialogues, only they focused on the divinity and were known as *Teulatolli*. These discourses followed their own rules and patterns for argumentation.

27. Much more than poetic work, it expressed wisdom, an intercommunication between divine and human. It crowned Náhuatl culture in a more elaborate way than the word for the Guaranís.

28. "They were taught the *tonalphualli* with its book of dreams (*temicamatl*) and book of years (*xiuhámatl*)" (*Códice Florentino*, book 3, p. 65, in León Portilla, *La Filosofía Náhuatl*, p. 228). The dream was the privileged locus of divine revelation, as was the case among the the Guaranís and the rest of the Amerindian peoples.

29. Clavigero recovered these traditions and evaluated them as philosophy in eighteenth-century Mexico during the Spanish enlightenment. [See Bernabé Navarro, *La Introducción de la Filosofía Moderna en México* (Mexico: El Colegio de Mexico, 1948); Jean Sarrailh, *La España Ilustrada de la segunda mitad del siglo XVIII* (Mexico: FCE, 1974)].

30. The *Popol Vuh* of the Mayas posited four types of humanity preceding the Mayans. The Toltecs, who preceded the Aztecs as the Greeks the Romans, espoused Tlacaélel's sacrificial vision and believed that they were living a fifth age, which possessed its own distinct sun, as had the previous four ages.

31. Plato (in the *Parmenides*), Plotinus (in the *Enneads*), Hindu thought, and Chinese Taoism all inquired how the *One* could issue in a *plurality*.

32. Unlike Aristotle who believed in sixty heavenly spheres, the Aztecs claimed thirteen spheres beginning with the moon's, then the stars' (the Greeks' ultimate spheres), and then the sun's until the thirteenth heaven where Omeoteótl dwelt.

33. "The foundational god and his co-principle dwell there" (León Portilla, *La Filosofía Náhuatl*, p. 151). The ancient God always appeared with a co-principle.

34. The metaphor is not now simply mythic, but also conceptual.

35. This is said in many ways: *Omecíhuatl* (dual woman), *Ometecuhtli* (dual lord), *Tonacacíhuatl* (woman of our flesh), *Tonacatecuhtli* (lord of our flesh), *in teteu inan* (mother of the gods), and *in teteu ita* (father of the gods).

36. Gerónimo de Mendieta, *Historia Eclesiástica Indiana* (Mexico: 1945), vol. 1, p. 95.

37. The absolute self-production occurs through thought. *Yucoya* signifies "to produce by thought."

38. In the originary night, everything is invisible and mysterious, and in the originary wind everything is impalpable, imperceptible, supersensible, and absolutely transcendental.

39. Duality constitutes perhaps Ometeótl's most extraordinary quality. *Tloc*: "near"; *náhuac*: "surround like a ring"; the termination *-e* indicates the abstract (such as *-dad* in Spanish or *-heit* in German): "nearness-surrounding." We live in this originary divine duality, Ometeótl, who is near and surrounds us. In his presence, the *tlamatinime* partake of the mystical-ontological experience typical of great contemplatives in all great civilizations in their axis time. Augustine describes the Christian God similarly as one "in whom we live and are."

40. No Hegelian *Entzweiung* ("self-bifurcation") takes place here, since from the origin there are two; any splitting would result in an *Entvierung* ("a making of four out of oneself"). Hegel wrote: "The absolute is both the night and the light anterior to the night, as well as the the difference between both" [*Differenz des Ficht'schen und Schelling'schen Systems der Philosophie* (Hamburg: Lasson, 1962), p. 65; see my *Método para una filosofía de la liberación* (Salamanca: Sígueme, 1974), pp. 89 ff.]. The metaphors (night, light) are identical. Further reflection on Náhuatl ontology would illustrate to sceptics the *formal, explicit beginning of philosophy* in Latin American's protohistory prior to 1492.

41. *Historia de los Mexicanos por sus pinturas*, in J. Garcia Icazbalceta, *Nueva Colección de Documentos para la Historia de México* (Mexico: 1890), vol. 3, pp. 228 ff.

42. A smoked mirror would not reflect and so would be invisible at night. It would differ from *Tezcatlanextia*, the "mirror that makes things appear" and manifests Ometeótl, who produces things as his reflection. The mirror symbolizes the turning on self typical of reflection, whether it is the divinity who reflects or the philosophical *tlamatini*: "who dialogues with his own heart" (*mavolnonotzani*).

43. León Portilla, *La Filosofía Náhuatl*, pp. 103 and 333.

44. Life implies mobility (*Bewegenheit*), as Marcuse proved in his study of Being in Hegel. Likewise, life meant mobility for the Aztecs, and the heart was the moving organ. In heaven, the sun moved itself, following its path (*Iohtlatoquiliz*) and setting in motion or vitalizing all living beings that moved themselves. These living beings owed their lives in sacrifice to maintain the sun's life. This vital-sacrificial circle resembles Marx's metaphors in his discussion of *capital*.

45. The phrase means "those deserved" by Quetzalcóatl who had raised them from the dead by "pouring out his blood" for them. (*Manuscrito de 1558*; León Portilla, *La Filosofía Náhuatl*, p. 184). *Mazenhualtin* refers to those whom the god deserved because of the his bloody self-sacrifice. All humanity is born with a debt of blood to Quetzalcóatl, a divine and unchained Prometheus or a bloodied Christus.

46. *Moyocoia* indicates that the divinity's plans achieve their goal, as in Judaeo-Christian notions of providence.

47. *Códice Florentino*, bk. 6, fol. 43v; León Portilla, *La Filosofía Náhuatl*, pp. 199–200 and 349.

48. *Iohtlatoquiliz* means "advance through heavenly paths." The path (*ohtli*) is necessary, and all persons follow equally their own paths. From birth, their astrologically chosen names depend on the day's omens and mark out a future destiny.

49. The *Anahuac*, the land surrounded by the ocean, *teoatl*, formed the known world (*cemanánuac*) and rested on its foundation, the earth's navel (*tlaxicco*), under which Ometeótl lay (*ónoc*).

50. *Nelli* (truth) has a particular meaning in Náhuatl: that which is founded as eternally permanent. The question has the following meaning: By chance do people possess in their being something firm, something well-rooted? It would be, for Hegel, the question of the essence (fundament) in its dialectic-ontological meaning, and not in its ontic or traditional metaphysical meaning.

51. To be *founded* in Ometeótl, the absolute, approaches what the Guaranís meant by "to be standing."

52. *Ms. Cantares Mexicanos*, fol. 10v; León Portilla, *La Filosofía Náhuatl*, p. 61.

53. Ibid., fol. 9 v; p. 142.

54. At the end of an Aztec century, which lasted fifty-two years (4 x 13), they superimposed a new floor on all the old temple floors and burnt the *new fire*.

55. This year was celebrated every sixty-five solar years.

56. Sahagún announces the theme of second book: "Which treats of the calendar, feasts and ceremonies, sacrifices and solemnities" (*Historia General de las cosas de la Nueva España*, ed. cit., pp. 73 ff.).

57. "On judiciary astology and the art of prophesying" (ibid., bk. 4, pp. 221 ff.). When deciding about births or other temporal events, the Aztecs relied on astrological revelations about each day, year, or period of years, and they considered these revelations to be valid forever.

58. "Which treats of auguries and almanacs, the natural things taken from birds, animals, and insects to prophesy the future" (ibid., bk. 5, pp. 267 ff.). Sahagún speaks inexactly here since the auguries and almanacs looked upon events completed in the present as capable of being predicted from their past, and thus did not strictly predict the future. In addition, these temporal doctrines tended to conflate the present looking to the future, the present of the present, and the present of the past. This lack

of any historical meaning distinguished Moctezuma's tragic, Promethean consciousness from Cortés's dramatic Christian, modern consciousness. See Paul Ricoeur's *The Symbolism of Evil*, and my *El humanismo semita*.

59. *El Códice Florentino* (bk. 6, chap. 2) mentions the names of the Aztecs who approached the ships: Pintol Huasteco, Yoatzin de Nuchtlancuauhtla of Teuciniyocan, and the guides Cuitlapíltoc and Téntitl. The other side's history had its real names and persons.

60. Indigenous informers of Sahagún, *Códice Florentino*, bk. 4, chap. 2 [cit. M. León Portilla, *El reverso de la conquista* (Mexico: Joaquin Mortiz, 1978), pp. 32–33].

61. This analysis relies on the plausible tradition that Moctezuma believed that Cortés was Quetzalcóatl. James Lockhart [see from this author: *Nahuas and Spaniards: Postconquest Central Mexican History and Philology* (Stanford: Stanford University Press, 1991); other works of the same author are in ibid., pp. 301–2] and Susan Gillespie [*The Aztec Kings. The Construction of Rulership in Mexican History* (Tucson: University of Arizona Press, 1989)] point out that chroniclers incorporated this belief in a Quetzalcóatl redivivus decades after the events. For example, nothing appears on this subject in Náhuatl texts produced even after 1540. Such information does not prove that this belief did not exist, since it is plausible that the belief was recorded well after its currency.

62. Tzevan Todorov, in *La conquista de America*, referring to "Moctezuma and the signs (pp. 70 ff.)," concurs with me, but he attributes Moctezuma's apparent hesitancy to the Aztecs' different communication modes. This book, though, fails to take advantage of its own recognition that everything had been arranged from all time. Tzvetan Todorov and Georges Baudot have published a collection of *Récits aztèques de la Conquête* (Paris: Seuil, 1983) [with an excellent Italian edition, *Racconti aztechi della Conquista* (Turin: Einaudi, 1988)], which includes the *Códice Florentino*, *Anales históricos de Tlatelolco*, *Códice Aubin* in Náhuatl; for Spanish, consult Diego Muñoz Camargo's *Códice Ramírez*, *Historia de Talxcala* and Diego Durán's *Historia*.

63. N. Wachtel, the author of *La vision des vaincus*, p. 45, wonders why Moctezuma received "*les Blancs comme des dieux.*"

64. Miguel León Portilla, *El reverso de la conquista*, p. 20, indicates the possibilities Moctezuma ponders without explaining the rationality of his decisions.

65. Octavio Paz, *El laberinto de la soledad* (Mexico: FCE, 1976), p. 85: "Moctezuma interpreted the Spaniards' arrival in the beginning not as an *exterior* danger, but rather as a harrassment internal to a cosmic era." At first, Moctezuma did not confront the end of the world as a distinct third possibility. *Posdata* (Mexico: Siglo XXI, 1970) pursues the discussion (pp. 126–43) without delineating the possibilities as I have.

66. In J. Lafaye's *Quetzalcóatl y Guadalupe: La Formación de la conciencia nacional en México* (Mexico: FCE, 1977), pp. 219–24, the situation is not clarified at all.

67. León Portilla, *El Reverso*, pp. 38–39. Náhuatl etiquette promoted the rhetorical formulas *you* and *your* evident to this day in the Mexican expression, "*My house is your house. (mi casa es su casa)*".

68. In the sense of Heidegger's *Möglichkeit* [see my *Para una ética de la liberación latinoamericana* (Buenos Aires: Siglo XXI, 1973), vol. 1, pp. 65ff: "The ontic possibilities"] or of N. Luhmann's self-referential and auto-poetic mechanisms in *Systemlehre* (Frankfurt: Suhrkamp, 1987).

69. Based on key Náhuatl texts and their plausibility for supporting Lockhart's hypotheses, I would include the following as resources: (1) To listen to the judgment of the warriors in the Tlacaélel tradition who were poised to act once they realized an invasion was occurring. (2) Ask the judgment of the *tlamatinime* philosophers. (3) Consult the astrologers, who predicted Quetzalcóatl's return on a *ce-acatl*, a date on which the Spaniards arrived. (4) Follow the auguries or predictions that indicated unavoidable future fatalities on the bases of eight signs referring to the four elements of the Aztecs and pre-Socratics: earth, air, fire, and water. See León Portilla's discussion of eight "fatal presages" in *El reverso de la conquista*, pp. 29ff.

70. *Abnormalities* (such as birth defects) were either eliminated (as among the Spartans) or divinized (as among the Zapotecans who elevated their sick to the pantheon of gods on Mount Alban). No one anticipated the least probable abnormality that human beings would appear on the great ocean.

71. The possibility that they were human could have seemed least dangerous, since their small numbers posed no military danger, even with their military technology. Moreover, in the strategic interest of eliminating other possibilities, Moctezuma postponed consideration of the inva-

sion possibility. That the Spaniards were only human could not as yet have made *sense* to someone with Moctezuma's interpretive framework.

72. The cultured Toltecs were to the Aztecs what the Greeks were to the Romans, and one could even claim that the Aztec exemplified *toltecavotl* ("Toltequidad," like *Romanitas* for the Romans, or *Christianity* for the Christians, or *Deutschtum* for the Germans). The historical figure Quetzalcóatl was actually the wise priest *Ce Acatl Topilzin* (around eleventh century B.C.E.), *the one born in day 1—Caña, our prince.* [See Walter Lehmann, "Geschichte der Königreiche von Colhuacan und Mexiko," in *Quellenwerke zur alten Geschichte Amerikas* (Stuttgart: 1938)]. As a young, single man in the environs of Tulancingo, he had been sought out to be king of Tula. A strong thinker and formulator of the ontology of Ometeótl, he opposed ideas that would later make up the Tlacaelel vision: "It is said that when Quetzalcóatl lived here, the sorcerers often wished to deceive him into making human sacrifices. But he never wanted to do so, because he loved his own Toltec people very much" (*Anales de Cuauhtitlán*, Códice Chimalpopoca, fol. 5; León Portilla, *La Filosofía Náhuatl*, pp. 307–8). Upon being unjustly expelled, he promised to return. The Aztecs, and Moctezuma in particular, had much to fear, since they had shed much Toltec blood, since the sacrificial myth of Huitzilopochtli contradicted Quetzalcóatl's convictions, and since the exiled Quetzalcóatl would have every right to seize Moctezuma's throne (as Moctezuma knew full well when he faced Cortés). When Cortés counseled Moctezuma not "to sacrifice human beings, Moctezuma summoned his chief priest the next day and ordered him to refrain from human sacrifice for some days in order to placate the Spaniards" (Torquemada, *Monarquía Indiana*, 4, chap. 40; ed. cit., vol. 2, p. 173). Such behavior reveals Moctezuma's identification of Cortés with Quetzalcóatl, the wise priest of Tula.

73. The fifth sun, one reads, "was the sun of our chief in Tula, Quetzalcóatl" (*Documento de 1558*; León Portilla, *La Filosofía Náhuatl*, p. 103). The almanacs predicting *movement of the earth and a hunger from which we will perish* (ibid.) foretold the demise of the fifth sun.

74. Paz (*El laberinto*, p. 85) mistakenly believes that Moctezuma first faced the possibility of the end of the fifth sun.

75. *Informantes de Sahagún*, in Miguel Leon Portilla, *La Filosofía Náhuatl*, p. 35.

76. The Aztec subjects never cooperated completely with Cortés, since if the Aztecs defeated Cortés they would have wreaked vengeance on unfaithful subjects. The same thing happened in Atahualpa among the Incas.

77. The most hopeful possibility for Moctezuma was that the newcomers were human since his warriors, faithful as ever to Huitzilopochtli, would have crushed Cortés's small number of troops. But Moctezuma first had to test rationally the other weightier and more negative possibilities.

78. In his offer to Cortés, Moctezuma manifested the *ethos* of a Calmécac hero and wise man: "Five or ten days ago I felt anxiety and fixed my eyes on the region of the dead until you came among the clouds and mist." The *tlamatini* contemplated the transcendent (*topan mictlan*) beyond the merely earthly (*in tlaltícpac*) and resolved like Quetzalcóatl to *love his people very much*. Thus, he "caviled about what was going to happen to the city" and renounced his throne to avoid greater suffering for his people. Like Quetzalcóatl in Tula, this new Mexican Quetzalcóatl stood aside, renounced his power, and suffered personal immolation. Cortés, the adept soldier and cunning politician, lacked such moral stature and so could not have grasped the immense ethical greatness of the man before him!

79. One would have to resort to another and more difficult argument for the Cortés/Quetzalcóatl identification if Lockhart's denial of the identification were substantiated. What is evident is that for some strange reason the Náhuatl chroniclers omitted mentioning this identification in texts around the time of the conquest in 1520.

80. Following E. O'Gorman's fruitful hypothesis that Columbus *was unable to discover America*, I can also say that Moctezuma "was unable to discover an invasion" until Pánfilo Narváez's arrival.

81. Torquemada, *Monarquía Indiana*, chap. 59, p. 184.

82. They witnessed the death of horses and Spanish soldiers, spent long weeks in the company of the Spaniards, and observed no other extraordinary signs.

83. Moctezuma had committed an *a posteriori* error, and not an *a priori* one.

84. Modern humanity fails to understand the *reasons of the Other*.

See the contribution to the dialogue with Karl-Otto Apel in Mexico entitled: "La razón del Otro. La *interpelación* como acto-de-habla."

85. Cortés should have left Mexico City immediately after his return from the coast with the reinforcements gained from the defeat of Narváez. Instead, with little understanding of Moctezuma's reasons, he believed that he could continue using him. Meanwhile Moctezuma had allowed himself to be used as part of his testing procedure for the possibilities facing him. Alvarado erroneously thought that a show of aggression would strengthen his hand and overlooked that it was not Spanish bravery but the Mexican *tlamatinime* world vision (Weltanschauung) that was protecting him. Once this vision had proved faulty, the logic of war replaced it, and Alvarado found himself endangered.

86. Theoretically he resembled the Hegel of the *Philosophy of Right*, but even more so the theoretician of war Clausewitz and the politician Bismarck. Even though he did not wish to be king over the empire, he ended up protecting four other kings.

87. Fernando Alvarado Tezózomoc, *Crónica Mexicáyotl* (Mexico: UNAM, 1949), p. 121. About Tlacaélel see León Portilla, *La Filosofía Náhuatl*, pp. 249 ff.; and from the same author, *Los antiguos mexicanos* (Mexico: FCE, 1990), pp. 46 ff; pp. 92 ff.

88. Durán, *Historia de las Indias*, p. 95.

89. *Documento de 1558*, already cited (León Portilla, *La Filosofía Náhuatl*, pp. 103–9).

90. *Ms. Cantares Mexicanos*, fol. 20v (León Portilla, *La Filosofía Náhuatl*, p. 257). Karl Marx's theological metaphors (see my *Las metáforas teológicas de Marx*), inspired by Semitic-biblical Judaeo-Christian texts, portray capital as the new Moloch who lives off the oppressed by sucking their blood. The circulation of value is *Blutzirkulation* (circulation of blood).

91. *Ms. Anónimo de Tlatelolco* (1528) (see León Portilla, *El reverso*, p. 43).

92. The Spaniards attributed their salvation to the Virgin of Remedies. Again, in 1810, Hidalgo hoisted the standard of the Virgin of Guadalupe as the flag of the Americans, and the Spaniards (*gachupines*), the banner of the remedies. The struggle of virgins, the struggle of gods, the struggle of classes! See my "Christliche Kunst des Unterdrückten in

Lateinamerika. Eine Hypothese zur Kennzeichnung einer Aesthetik," in *Concilium* 152 (1980): 106–14.

93. *Ms. Anónimo de Tlatelolco*, in León Portilla, *El reverso*, p. 53.

94. This question was essential: Does the destruction of the empire show that the gods abandoned us? This profound and tragic question announces the consummation of the fifth sun.

95. *Cantares Mexicanos* (León Portilla, *La Filosofía Náhuatl*, p. 62). Do not think that the indigenous people resisted the invasion minimally. Their resistance was heroic and constant.

Chapter 8: From the Resistance to the End of the World and the Sixth Sun

1. Gerónimo le Medieta, *Historia Ecclesiástica Indiana*, bk. 3, chap. 49 (Mexico: Ed. Chávez Hyhoe, 1945), vol. 2, p. 161.

2. Alonso de Góngora Marmolejo, *Historia de Chile* (Santiago: Ed. Universitaria, 1970), p. 71.

3. Josefina Oliva de Coll, *La resistencia indígena ante la conquista* (Mexico: Siglo XXI, 1991), pp. 9–10. See M. T. Huerta and P. Palacios, *Rebeliones indígenas de la época colonial* (Mexico: 1976); J. de Vos, *Tierra y Libertad. Panorama de cuatro rebeliones indígenas en Chiapas* (Chiapas: n.d.); Segundo Moreno Yañez, *Sublevaciones indígenas en la Audiencia de Quito* (Quito: 1978); B. Lewin, *La rebelión de Túpac Amaru* (Buenos Aires: 1967). In my Sorbonne doctoral thesis in history, "El episcopado hispanoamericano y la defensa del indio (1504–1620)" (Cuernavaca: CIDOC, 1969–1971), vols. 1–9, I took more than two thousand pages to describe the oppression and resistance of the Indians throughout sixteenth–century Latin America. These descriptions drew on mostly unpublished documents in the Archivo General de Indias in Seville.

4. Bartolomé de las Casas's entire work attempts to recover this valiant resistance. His most famous works, *Brevísima relación de la destrucción de las Indias* [in *Obras escogidas* (Madrid: BAE, 1958), vol. 5, pp. 134 ff.] and the *Historia de las Indias*, orchestrate apologias on behalf of the brave, indigenous resistance.

5. The laws of apartheid in South Africa, demanding that Africans over seventeen carry a pass, provoked the protest resulting in the

Sharpeville slaughter. Modernity's first apartheid took place in late fifteenth-century Santo Domingo.

6. See Oliva de Coll, *La resistencia*, pp. 38 ff.

7. Ibid., p. 45.

8. Ibid., p. 52.

9. Ibid., p. 72 ff.

10. Ibid., p. 77 ff.

11. "Many things occurring in this circle [of Mexico City], were recorded and pondered over generations, especially regarding the Temistitán women. It was marvelous and awesome to witness the swift and constant service afforded their husbands as they cured wounds, carved rocks for slings, and performed other tasks one thought excessive for women" (ibid., p. 95).

12. Ibid., pp. 113 ff. The Mayas' political organization, less unified than the Aztec, impeded the Spaniards and the later Mexican state from dominating them.

13. Ibid., pp. 129 ff.

14. Ibid., pp. 148 ff.

15. Ibid., pp. 171 ff.

16. Ibid., pp. 182 ff.

17. Ibid., pp. 195 ff.

18. "Because of outcry that has reached up to heaven and in the name of the all-powerful God, we order and demand that no one pay or obey in any way the *intrusive European* ministers [*sic*]" (an edict in the pocket of Túpac Amaru at the time of his death in 1781; the text cited above comes from Lewin, *La rebelión de Túpac Amaru*, p. 421). The Amerindians interpreted and named the European invaders as *intrusive*, from Columbus to the United States marine incursion into Panama which occurred in 1990.

19. Ibid., pp. 241 ff.

20. Ibid., pp. 254 ff.

21. *Informantes de Sahagún*, Códice Florentino, bk. 12, chap. 9, in León Portilla, *El reverso*, p. 35.

22. *Anales de Cuauhtitlán*, ed. W. Lehmann, p. 62 (León Portilla, *La Filosofía Náhuatl*, p. 103).

23. Since the Aztecs considered the end of the empire and the fifth sun identical, the subsequent Spanish domination announced the arrival of a new sun. Astronomical and political concepts coincided in their *cosmo-politics*, as among the Hellenists and Romans. In fact, all empires involve the gods and the universe in their destiny, as is the case in the North American empire where Ronald Reagan's apocalyptic ideology flourished.

24. *Pacha*: "universe"; *kuti*: "commotion, revolution, final agony."

25. León Portilla, *La Filosofía Náhuatl*, p. 126.

26. Bartomeu Melía, *El guaraní: Experiencia religiosa* (Asunción: Biblioteca Paraguaya de Anthropología, 1991), p. 76.

27. The conquistadores trained dogs for warlike tasks such as beastially devouring the wise men.

28. The Aztecs painted their manuscripts with illustrations in black, for the mystery of the originary night, and red, for the clarity of day, love, life, and blood.

29. From *Ms. Anónimo de tlatelolco* (León Portilla, *El reverso*, p. 61).

30. The Aztecs hoped that the Europeans would seize their codices and ingest their meaning before destroying them, just as the Aztecs had done with the codices of Azcapotzalco and other dominated peoples. In this way, at least, the destroyed codices would have survived as subsumed within the history and theory of the conqueror.

31. I cite constantly the text given by Walter Lehmann in *Sterbende Götter und Christliche Heilsbotschaft* (Stuttgart: 1949) and in Náhuatl and Spanish by M. León Portilla, *La Filosofía Náhuatl* pp. 129–36. The Náhuatl text was recorded afterward in the College of Tlatelolco, founded by the Franciscans for the children of the chiefs. One editor, Antonio Valeriano, a neighbor of Azcapotzalco, was responsible for the texts on the tradition of the virgin of Guadalupe. The text at Tlatelolco discussed in thirty chapters "all the conversations, confabulations, and sermons exchanged between the twelve religious and the principal leaders and lords and satraps" (Lehmann, p. 52) in Mexico in 1524. Three years before the ancient metropolis had been destroyed.

32. According to León Portilla's numeration: (1) Rhetorical introduction (numbers 872–912). (2) Preparation of the response to the friars' proposal (913–932). (3) Central statement of the question to be debated (933–938). (4) Arguments proving the *tlamatinime's* conclusion (939–1004): (a) from authority (943–961), (b) from existential coherence (962–988), (c) from antiquity (989–1004), (5) Conclusion: we cannot abandon our norms (1005–1043). (6) Corollary: Do with us what you like (1044–1060).

33. Their manner of approach resembles Moctezuma's reception of Cortés, one respects the Other, one gives way before the Other in order to establish first the pragmatic or illocutionary moment of communicative rationality. Mexican culture continues this tradition, since one never proceeds immediately to the subject of conversation and its propositional content. Such a roundabout procedure, so unstrategic in its rationality, appears unproductive to the capitalist.

34. *Timacevalti*: "ignorance" flows from wisdom according to Nezahualcoyotl: "By chance do we speak the *truth*, giver of life? We are only dreaming or awakening from a dream. No one here speaks the *truth*!" (*Ms. Cantares Mexicanos*, fol. 17r; León Portilla, *La Filosofía Náhuatl*, p. 60).

35. Unlike the *tlamatinime* who recognize cultural chasms, the recently arrived Franciscans operate with a simplistic modern optimism about teaching the Christian faith. Their honest, naïve, sincere, truthful, rationalist stance blinds them to patent distances *subtending* every future conversation and portending difficulties, incommensurabilities, and communicative pathologies. The modern conquerors strive to overcome such obstacles in the least time possible in order to arrive at the information of the propositional content. In contrast, for those who truly seek to communicate with the *reason (ratio Grund)* of the Other, the pragmatic-communicative moment protrudes with an unbearably weighty and nearly invincible priority.

36. Unavoidably, the translator for the Aztec wise men *could not function adequately*, since no one could have known both cultures sufficiently to express *fully* what each was saying. They carried on the supposed dialogue in Castillian, the hegemonic language of the conqueror. Since its consensus alone was valid, the Other had to *enter* into this community on its terms to be heard.

37. *Yn ihiio yn itietel.* This constant Náhuatl linkage of phrases, similar to "face to face," exemplifies *dephrasism* and occurs frequently in this highly refined rhetorical text.

38 *In tloque, navqued.* Ometeótl, according to Náhuatl mystical experience, penetrated each being's intimate core and surrounded humanity with a divine presence. How could those Franciscans, even though well-educated and imbued with Cisneros's mystical reforms, have understood that it would have taken *weeks* to dialogue adequately about this experience? One could no more easily race through an account of nirvana in a conversation with the Buddha.

39. These wise men displayed bravery, lucidity, and heroic magnanimity when faced with the tragic situation that Franciscans could not appreciate their holiness, and even less so the conquistadores.

40. *Tipoliuini timiquini,* the ethical apprehension that everything "earthly" (*in Tlaltícpac*) is merely finite, was also accessible in the realm that surpasses (*Topan mictian*) "this world, the region of the dead."

41. *Tel ca tetu in omicque* indicates that one's world has collapsed and life seems worthless. The Europeans, who could scarcely suspect the tragedy of these living-dead ones, should have included indigenous culture in an emergent authentic new world, but they were unable.

42. *In top in ipetlacal,* another dephrasism, refers to what is hidden and cannot be revealed, because it would not be received as pertaining to the ark of security. In this pragmatic speech moment, it is evident that the internal richness of one culture is only communicable within a communitarian, historical praxis. People must live together a long time to be able to receive a revelation (as I have pointed out repeated in my *Filosofía de la Liberación,* in *Para una ética de la liberación latinoamericana,* vol. 1, chap. 3, and in my discussion with K.-O. Apel, "La *interpelación* como acto-de-habla"). The meaning of *reveal* (*Offenbarung*) differs in this respect from the manifesting or appearing (*Erscheinung*) of the phenomenon, which by the time it is expressed propositionally seems already known.

43. *In ilhuicaya in tlalticpaque,* another dephrasism, highlights the beyond and accentuates that the earth is perishable.

44. See J. Glotz, "L'Evolution de la religion," in *Histoire des Religions* (Paris: Bloud et Gav., 1964).

45. The Franciscans could never have demonstrated the rational truth of the trinity or the incarnation of the word in Jesus Christ, since such doctrines constitute part of the consensus of the community of believers. The *tlamatinime* make just this case.

46. *Informantes de Sahagún, Códice Florentino*, bk. 12, chap. 9 (cited by León Portilla in *El reverso*, p. 35).

47. *Intlamanitiliz*, meant the ethos of the life world, reflexively perfected in the *Calmécac*.

48. *Quineltocatiui*: "the true" is that which is founded forever in the gods, and outside it everything is passing, changeable, and perishing.

49. *Techmaceuhque*: "with their sacrifice they gave us life."

50. In the night before the daylight of the fifth sun.

51. As members of the Aztec ruling class, they recognize clearly that their political power has passed to the hands of modern Spaniards and the fifth sun has gone into eclipse.

52. Karl Marx, *Capital* (London: Lawrence and Wishart, 1977), I, chap. 31 (vol. 1, p. 712).

53. "The second prophetic wheel of a doublet of katuns," *Ahau 2* (Mexico: FCE, 1991), p. 68.

54. Ibid., "First wheel of prophecies," pp. 49–50.

55. Ibid., "Second wheel of prophecies," *Ahau 9*, p. 71.

56. In "Los testimonios mayas de la conquista," in León Portilla, *El reverso*, p. 84.

57. *Ms. Anónimo de Tlatelolco* in León Portilla, *El reverso* , p. 60.

58. *El primer nueva Crónica y Buen Gobierno*, fol. 374; (Mexico: Ed. Siglo XXI, 1980), vol. 2, p. 347. He comments: "These first men braved death itself because of their interest in gold or silver. They belong too much to this world, these Spanish magistrates, priests, and farm-owners whose greed for gold and silver will lead them to hell" (ibid.).

59. See René Girard, *Le sacré et le profane* (Paris: Gallimard, 1965); idem, *La violence et le sacré* (Paris: Grasset, 1972); idem, *De choses cachées depuis la fondation du monde* (Paris: Grasset, 1978); idem, *Le Bouc émissaire* (Paris: Grasset, 1982). Hugo Assmann reflects on Girard's influence in Latin America in *René Girard com teólogo da libertaçao*

(Petrópolis: Vozes, 1991), as does Franz Hinkelammert in *Sacrificios humanos y sociedad occidental* (San José : Costa Rica: DEI, 1991).

60. See Michel, Aglietta-André Orléan, *La violence de la monnaie* (Paris: PUF, 1982).

61. Marx, *Capital*, I, chap. 10:1, p. 224. The modern myth hides the violence essential to it.

62. Ibid., I, chap. 31:1, p. 702.

63. Ibid., pp. 711–12.

64. See Appendix 2.

65. *Posdata* (Mexico: Siglo XXI, 1970), pp. 104 ff.

66. Marx, *Capital* I, chap. 26; 1, p. 668.

Epilogue:
The Multiple Visages of the One People and the Sixth Sun

1. See "The Popular Question," in my *La producción teórica de Marx*, pp. 400–413.

2. See John Collier, *Los Indios de las Américas* (Mexico: FCE, 1960); Ramiro Reynaga, *Tawantisuyu. Cinco siglos de guerra Qheswaymara contra España* (Mexico: Nueva Imagen, 1981); Charles Gibson, *The Aztecs under Spanish Rule 1519–1810* (Stanford: Stanford University Press, 1964); Thornton Russell, *American Indian Holocaust and Survival, a Population History since 1492* (Norman: University of Oklahoma Press, 1987); Walter Krickeberg, *Etnología de América* (Mexico: FCE, 1946); Ruth Barber, *Indian Labor in the Spanish Colonies* (Albuquerque: University of New Mexico Press, 1932); Silvio Zavala, *La encomienda indiana* (Mexico: Porrúa, 1973); Roberto MacLean, *Indios de América* (Mexico: UNAM, 1962). James Lockhart's studies and his recent *Nahuas and Spaniards* initiate a serious philological discussion about the postconquest life of the Náhuatls.

3. The Spanish organized the first reductions in the urban settings of Mexico, Guatemala, Eduador, Peru, and Bolivia in order to break large populations down into communities in which Christian doctrine could be imparted. As Lochhart shows (*Nahuas and Spaniards*, pp. 23 ff.), indigenous social and political structures underwent transformation under Viceroy Francisco de Toledo after the death of Viceroy Luis de Velasco in

1564 (see John L. Phelan, *The Millennial Kingdom of the Franciscans in the New World*, pp. 77 ff.). The Toledo era began what Gerónimo de Mendieta called the *Age of Silver*, the diabolic time of mammon. Furthermore, plagues of 1570 and 1595 diminished the indigenous population from more than five million—possibly as high as eighteen million according to other demographic studies—to less than two million.

4. *El Día* (Mexico) (February 12, 1988): 6.

5. Cited in *500 años de evangelización in México* (Mexico: CENAMI, 1987), p. 27.

6. This book might fulfill that desire.

7. *500 años*, p. 187.

8. Ibid., p. 197.

9. Ibid., p. 198.

10. Ibid., p. 199.

11. *Brevissima Relación de la destrucción de las Indias* (Madrid: BAE, 1957), vol. 5, p. 137.

12. See my article on racism toward Afro-Latin Americans: "Informe sobre la situación en América Latina," in *Concilium* 171 (1982), pp. 88–95. Consult also J. Saco, *Historia de la esclavitud de la raza negra en el Nuevo Mundo* (Havana, 1938); E. Vila Vilar, *Hispanoamérica y el comercio de esclavos* (Seville, 1977); R. Mellafe, *Breve historia de la esclavitud negra en América Latina* (Mexico: 1973); L. Rout, *The African Experience in Spanish America: 1502 to the Present* (Cambridge: 1976); L. Fonor, *Slavery in the New World* (Englewood Cliffs, N. J. : 1969).

13. What a euphemism for the commerce of African slaves in which Portugal, Holland, England, France, and even Denmark participated! Although slavery characterized many eras, and although Aristotle justified it in his *Politics*, it had never been carried out with such numbers and such systematization. In this slavery system peculiar to mercantile capitalism and its primitive accumulation of capital, African slaves objectivated their lives in the value of the tropical products sold in European markets. This system played a constitutive role in the birth of modernity; modernity accepted its invisible cruelty, barbarity, and irrational violence and justified it through *emancipative reason*. This history reveals the persistence of the sacrificial myth referred to throughout this book. I repeat, the brutal Roman Empire neither treated slaves so universally and so

objectively as *mechandise*, as *things for sale*, nor produced that absolute *Versachligung* of persons and *fetishism* proper to the modernity which Karl Marx critized with a clarity unequaled to this day. Karl-Otto Apel, in dialogue with me in Mexico in 1991, illustrated the superiority of the Enlightenment (*Aufklärung*) over other cultures' achievements by pointing to its ethical prohibition of cannibalism. I asked him why modernity seemed to overlook the most monstruous deed of slavery and the horrifying numbers of its victims. There was silence.

14. In addition to Hitler's cruel and violent holocaust of the Jews with its refined, systematic manner of murder, one should never forget the five million Africans who perished miserably in slave trading boats crossing the Atlantic. But the more than six million survivors of this middle passage *lived* long lives, bore sons and daughters, and suffered treatment appropriate only to animals. They endured a living death during the five centuries of modernity. Modernity's original racism prolonged itself even into the nineteenth century when France, Italy, and Germany took for granted the superiority of the white European race over the Indians, Africans, and Asians. Such racism thrives today in the European Common Market.

15. For example, those of Galam Bambouk, Bouré or Bit; see R. and M. Cornevin, *Histoire de l'Afrique* (Paris: Payot, 1964), pp. 176 ff.

16. It continues: "Concernant le Gouvernement, l'Administration de la Justicie, la Police, la Discipline et le Commerce de Negres dans les Colonies françaises" (Paris: Chez Parault, 1762).

17. According to a Zaire missionary, Africans bury a child's umbilical cord at birth to symbolize that earth has become the child's nutrient mother. Africans in foreign lands keep their umbilical cord in a little box and bury it in their homeland when they return. The slaves, strangers in Latin and North America, kept their umbilical cords in small boxes to signify their desire to return to Africa.

18. See Alexander Lipschutz, *El problema racial en la conquista de América y el mestizaje* (Mexico: Siglo XXI, 1975); Angel Rosenblat, *La población indígena y el mestizaje en América* (Buenos Aires: Ed. Nova, 1954); Harry Shapiro, *Race Mixture* (UNESCO, 1953); Claudio Esteva Fabregat, *El mestizaje en Iberoamérica* (Madrid: Alhambra, 1988); Magnus Morner, *Race Mixture in the History of Latin America* (Boston: Little Brown, 1967); José Pérez de Barradas, *Mestizos de América* (Madrid: Cultura clásica moderna, 1948).

19. Here Octavio Paz writes "Mexican," but I have changed it to *mestizo*, my topic.

20. Mexicans are accustomed to crying out with affirmation, "Viva México, hijos de la chingada" [Long live Mexico, sons of the violated one]; the *hijos de la chingada*, Paz observes, refers to enemies, but the term could refer as well to the Mexican people.

21. Octavio Paz, *El laberinto de la soledad* (Mexico: FCE, 1950), 1973 ed., pp. 78–79.

22. Octavio Paz writes: "In the liberal reform in the mid- nineteenth century, the mestizos [Mexicans] seemed to break with tradition and so with themselves, in a way. . . . The ideals of the state founded by Juárez (or Sarmiento) differed from those animating New Spain and the pre-Cortesian societies. The mestizo [Mexican] state proclaimed a universal and abstract conception of humanity. . . . The reform constituted the great rupture with mother" (op. cit., 79). The hegemonic politics of the late 1980s represented by Menem in Argentina, De Mello in Brasil, or Fujimori in Peru promoted modernization, privatization, and the dissolution of the welfare state, and produced new historical *ruptures.*

23. Pedro Morandé in *Cultura y modernización in América Latina* (Santiago: Cuadernos del Instituto de Sociología, Universidad Católica de Chile, 1983), p. 162, writes: "Our original cultural synthesis is Latin American, mestizo, and ritual." Popular culture is equivalent to mestizo culture. See the work of Néstor Garcia Canclini, below.

24. A Náhuatl name for the "Apparition of the Virgin of Guadalupe" (J. Lafaye, *Quetzalcóatl y Guadalupe, La formación de la conciencia nacional en México* [Mexico: FCE, 1977], with translation and commentaries by Clodomiro Siller [Mexico: CENAMI, 1980]).

25. "The faith bloomed as well as the knowledge of God, our root [this is now an expression of Náhuatl thought], the giver of life [another Náhuatl expression]. Saturday morning at dawn, as he arrived near the Tepeyac he heard singing above" (initial text of *Nican Mopohua*). The dawn represents new sun; the song above, a sacred event; and the flowers of Castilla at the narrative's end, the Aztec *flower and song.*

26. *Cordel*: bound prisoner; *escalerilla de tablas*: one walked upon, oppressed; *excremento*: depreciated, sinner (*tlaelcuani*); *hoja suelta*: dead man.

27. Paz, *El laberinto de la soledad*, pp. 76–77.

28. The mountain where the goddess Tonantzin appeared to Juan Diego and the site of the church of Maria Guadalupe.

29. Miguel Sánchez applied the Apocalypse chapter 12, which narrates that "a great sign appeared in heaven, a woman, clothed in the sun, with the moon beneath her feet." More importantly, it mentions that "two wings of a great eagle were given to the woman" who later had to struggle for water. Sánchez interprets these details as referring to the Virgin of Guadalupe and to Mexico, the land of the cactus, the eagle, the Náhuatl serpent, and desiccating lake Tezcoco. Sánchez interprets John's Apocalypse as referring explicitly to Mexico.

30. Fray Teresa Servando de Mier urged the emancipation of America on the basis of the tradition that St. Thomas the Apostle/Quetzalcóatl had preached the gospel in Mexico in the first century and predicted the Virgin of Guadalupe. The indigenous peoples were not indebted to Spaniards, foreigners, and invaders for their Christian faith.

31. In his war with the Spaniards, Miguel Hidalgo placed the Virgin of Guadalupe on his banners, as did Zapata, the peasant revolutionary of the twentieth century, even as he destroyed churches and seized temples. Photographs in the museum of the so-called *Casa de Cortés* in Cuernavaca record Zapata's deeds.

32. He writes on p. 209: "I have written this book for the fatherland, for my friends and my companions, and for the citizens of this new world."

33. Lafaye, *Quetzalcóatl y Guadalupe*, pp. 341–43.

34. Haiti gained liberation from France in 1804 under the African, Toussaint l'Ouverture, the first Latin American liberator. Bolívar took refuge in Afro-Caribbean Jamaica where he wrote his famous *Carta de Jamaica*.

35. The United Provinces of the Río de la Plata issued the first declaration of independence from Spain in the Congress of Tucumán, July 9, 1816, in Salta del Tucumán. The counterrevolution, in direct opposition to Hidalgo's project, reached its apex in 1821 when it named as its leader Iturbide, a military man of pure white racial origins.

36. With the *fico* of Joao I in 1822, Brazil became independent of Portugal and was known as the empire of Brazil until the founding of the republic in 1889.

37. "Articulo periodístico a la Gaceta Real de Jamaica," of September 28, 1815, in Kingston; see the text in *Doctrina del Libertador* (Caracas: Biblioteca Ayacucho, 1975), pp. 75 ff.

38. *Criollo* or mestizo controlling groups concoct libertarian, conservative, and civilizing projects which replace the Iberian project and favor occidental colonization. See Leopoldo Zea, *Filosofía de la Historia Americana*, pp. 188 ff., on the *libertarian project*, or pp. 108 ff., on the Iberian colonizing project.

39. Ibid., pp. 165 ff. ; pp. 269 ff.

40. See Pablo González Casanova, *Historia Política de los campesinos latinoamericanos* (Mexico: Siglo XXI, 1984), vols. 1–4; Steve Stern, *Resistance, Rebellion and Consciousness in the Andean Peasant* (Madison: University of Wisconsin, 1987); Rodolfo Stavenhagen, *Agrarian Problems and Peasant Movements in Latin America* (Garden City, N. Y. : Doubleday, 1970); David Lehmann and Hugo Zemelmann, *El campesinado* (Buenos Aires: Nueva Visión, 1972); Miguel Díaz Cerecer, *La condición campesina* (Mexico: UNAM/I, 1989).

41. Capitalism presented the northeasterners with the option of dying from hunger or destroying the forest. While the disappearance of the last great tropical forest would be an ecological catastrophe, it is imperative to do justice to the peasants impoverished by market capitalism and impelled to destroy the forests. The ecological movement frequently lacks economic consciousness and would profit from a reading of Marx's *Capital* to discover the close connections between relative surplus value and ecologically destructive technology. Capitalism increases productivity without concern for its antiecological effects or for the unemployment of hungry masses, such as the northeasterners. To reproduce their lives, these poor ones are compelled to destroy whole regions, without understanding that the forest's disappearance would quickly convert the Amazon area into a desert.

42. See Pablo González Casanova, *Historia del movimiento obrero en América Latina* (Mexico: Siglo XXI, 1984), vols. 1–4; Julio Gaudio, *El movimiento obrero en América Latina (1850–1910)* (Bogotá: Tercer Mundo, 1978); Anibal Quijano, *Clase obrera en América Latina* (San José: Ed. Universidad Centroamericana, 1982); Ricardo Melgar Bao, *El movimiento obrero latinoamericano. Historia de una clase subalterna* (Madrid: Alianza, 1988); Carlos Rama, *Historia del movimiento obrero*

y social latinoamericano contemporáneo (Barcelona: Laia, 1976); and Victor Alba, *Politics and the Labor Movement in Latin America* (Stanford: Stanford University Press, 1968).

43. And then only at certain locations, such as in Buenos Aires, São Paolo, and Mexico City, and later gradually in Montevideo, Santiago, Lima, Bogotá. The first conscienticized were anarchic-syndicalist worker groups and socialists, who would subsequently form populist workers' unions in Mexico, Argentina, and Brazil.

44. See my *Filosofía ética de la liberación*, vol. 3, in its introduction to the third part: "La histórica latinoamericana." Or see *Hacia un Marx desconocido*, chap. 15: "Los Manuscritos del 61–63 y el concepto de dependencia," pp. 312 ff. (English translation in *Latin American Perspectives* [Los Angeles], vol. 1, 1991). In these writings of the early 1990s, I examine the pertinence and the significance of the former *theory of dependence*. One needs to return to this theory to explain the increasing misery of peripheral, dependent capitalism in Latin America, Africa, and Asia—European modernity's ancient colonial world.

45. Mauro Marini, *Dialéctica de la Dependencia* (Mexico: Era, 1973).

46. The majority of the people in the named countries do not have the security of even a minimal salary. According to Franz Hinkelammert, to be exploited—that is, to receive a hunger wage and produce enormous surplus value—has become a privilege today in Latin America. The poor majority stand beyond whatever stable relationships may maintain between capital and labor.

47. The transference of value from periphery to center represents contemporary, worldwide, structural injustice, justified by the sacrificial myth of modernity and the free market. The history of this transference commences with a *first epoch* of monetary mercantilism (fifteenth–seventeenth centuries) and the Iberian hegemony. Under that hegemony, Latin America furnished gold and silver to Europe for its originary accumulation and never received compensation or interest for the credit it advanced. The *second epoch*, preparatory for later dependency, involved the first form of free exchange capitalism under the Bourbon reforms, which rendered Spain dependent on England and impeded Latin America's nascent industrial revolution. The *third epoch* witnessed a second, imperialistic style of capitalism, which built up credit indebtedness (for example, by the installation of railroads or ports) and imported Latin

American raw materials at below-value prices. The dependency characteristic of the *fourth epoch* entailed a transfer of value via competition between the diverse organic compositions of central and peripheral capitals. The *fifth epoch* of today consists of value transference through transnationals and international credits. Such mechanisms directly transfer capital in exchange for the payment of the highest interest rates ever heard of. I have described this long history of exploitation in other works.

48. Hegel, *Philosophy of Right,* pars. 246–48.

49. *Capital,* I, chap. 25:1, p. 576.

50. Ibid., p. 604.

51. See Franz Hinkelammert, *Crítica de la razón utópica* (San José: DEI, 1984). He argues in favor of some types of planned economy in contrast to Karl Popper who eliminates *all* planning on the basis of his critique of perfect planning. For Hinkelammert, the contradiction of a perfectly competitive market does not preclude versions of a partially planned market economies. Such planning, undertaken insofar as necessary, is possible but never perfect, and it avoids Stalinism.

52. See CEPAL, *Bibliografía sobre marginalidad social* (Santiago de Chile: CEPAL, 1973); Gino Germani, *Marginality* (New Brunswick: Transaction Books, 1980); Miguel Izard, *Marginados, fronterizos, rebeldes y oprimidos* (Barcelona: Serbal, 1985); Dióscoro Negretti, *El concepto de marginalidad: aplicación en el contexto latinoamericano* (Caracas: Universidad Central de Venezuela, 1987); José Nun, *Superpoblación relativa, ejército industrial de reserva y masa marginal* (Santiago de Chile: Centro Latinoamericano de Demografía, 1971); Esmeralda Ponce de León, *Marginalidad de la ciudad* (Mexico: Trillas, 1987); Fernando Serrano Migallón, *Marginalidad urbana y pobreza rural* (Mexico: Diana, 1990); Alberto Ruiz de la Peña, *La marginalidad social* (Mexico: UNAM, 1977).

53. Many attribute overpopulation to the demographic explosion of the Third World, but such explosions occurred in Europe also at the end of the Middle Ages and ever since the industrial revolution. The immense proportions of the Third World's present explosion warrants no cynical Malthusianism, however.

54. See the works of Néstor Garcia Canclini: *Arte popular y sociedad en América Latina* (Mexico: Grijalbo, 1977) bibliography, pp. 277 ff.;

Las culturas populares en el capitalismo (Mexico: Nueva Imagen, 1984); "Para una crítica a las teorías de la cultura," in *Temas de Cultura latinoamericana* (Mexico: UNAM, 1987).

55. On modernity as *modernization* see Robert Kurz, *Der Kollaps der Modernisierung* (Frankfurt: Eichborn Verlag, 1991), especially "Der Opfergang der Dritten Welt als Menetekel" (pp. 189 ff.).

56. Indicated by G in the schematization of Appendix 2.

Appendix 2: Two Paradigms of Modernity

1. Kant, *Was heisst Aufklärung?*, A, 481.

2. See Max Horkheimer and Theodor Adorno, *Dialektik der Aufklärung* (1944) (Frankfurt: Fischer, 1971) [English: *Dialectic of Enlightenment*, trans. John Cumming (New York: Herder and Herder, 1972)], and Jürgen Habermas, *Der philosophische Diskurs der Moderne* (Frankfurt: Suhrkamp, 1988), pp. 130 ff.: "Die Verschlingung von Mythos und Aufklärung"; [English: *The Philosophical Discourse of Modernity*, pp. 106 ff. : "The Entwinement of Myth and Enlightenment: Max Horkheimer and Theodor Adorno"]. Horkheimer and Adorno admit modernity's mythical aspects, which Habermas cannot accept. I locate modernity's myth not at an intra-European level, as do Horkheimer, Adorno, and Habermas, but rather at a world level, in the conflicts between the center and the periphery, the North and the South.

3. Kant, *Was heisst Aufklärung?*, speaks of *culpable* (*verschuldeten*) immaturity.

4. Francisco de Vitoria, professor of Salamanca, defends war against the indigenous peoples because they impeded the preaching of Christian doctrine. For Vitoria, war was permissible only to destroy these impediments.

5. For Kant, *unmündig*: "immature, untrained, uneducated."

6. My *Philosophy of Liberation* takes up the analectical character of the dialectical, subsumptive moment.

7. Tzevan Todorov, *Nosotros y los otros* (Paris: Seuil, 1989).

8. "Des Cannibales," in *Oeuvres Complètes* (Paris: Gallimard-Pléiade, 1967), p. 208.

CHRONOLOGY

700   Foundation of Tula (Mexico).

711   Muslim conquest of the Iberian peninsula.

718   Beginning with Covadonga, the Reconquest (718–1492).

900   Quetzalcóatl, wise Toltec priest.

1398   Tlacaélel is born in Mexico-Tenochtitlan.

1415   Conquest of Ceuta in north Africa.

1441   First African slaves sold by Portugal; caravel invented.

1460   Henry the Navigator, Portuguese prince, dies.

1485   Consecration of the greater temple in Mexico devoted to Huitzilopochtli.

1487   Slaughter of Muslims in Málaga. Díaz rounds the Cape of Good Hope and reaches the Islamic sea.

1489   Henry Martellus constructs in Rome the map of the fourth Asiatic peninsula.

1492   January: The Catholic kings defeat Sultan Boabdil and occupy Granada. Nebrija publishes a Spanish grammar.

THE INVENTION OF THE ASIATIC BEING OF THE ISLANDS
OF THE OCEANIC SEA

1492   October 12: Christopher Columbus arrives on some islands in the west of the Oceanic sea. The Atlantic (*sea of the North*) is born.

1493   Second voyage of Columbus.
1497   Third voyage of Columbus and exploration of the
        Orinoco, River of Paradise.
1502   Fourth voyage of Columbus.
1506   Columbus dies without discovering America.

THE DISCOVERY OF THE NEW WORLD

1502   Amerigo Vespucci returns from his voyage to the
        southern antipode and writes *Mundus Novus* (1503-1504).
1504   First African slaves arrive in Santo Domingo.
1507   The *Cosmographiae Introductio* published.
1511   Prophetic criticism of Antón de Montesinos in
        Hispañola; first cry of criticism against modernity's
        violence.
1513   Vasco Nuñez de Balboa discovers the *sea of the south*
        (the Pacific Ocean).
1520   Sebastián Elcano sails around the world, as the single
        survivor of the expedition of Magellan, and thus
        terminates the era of discoveries.

THE CONQUEST OF THE URBAN CULTURES FROM THE PAROUSIA OF THE GODS TO THE INVASION

1519   Hernán Cortés begins the Conquest of Mexico-
        Tenochtitlan.
1520   May 22: Slaughter of the Aztec warriors by Alvarado.
        June 24: Cortés vanquishes Pánfilo Narváez.
        June 30: The Sad Night (*noche triste*).
1521   Defeat of the *Comuneros*, the nascent Spanish
        bourgeoisie, in Villalar, Spain. On August
        13, Cortés occupies the last neighborhood in the
        environs of Mexico-Tenochtitlan.
1525   Cortés assassinates Cuahutemoc.
1545   The silver mine of Potosí (Peru) is discovered.
1546   The silver mine of Zacatecas (Mexico) is discovered.
1553   Battle of Fort Tucapel in Chile; the Mapuche Lautaro
        stops the Spanish in the south and puts an end to
        the conquest of urban cultures.

The Spiritual Conquest From the End of the World to the Sixth Sun

1524   The "Twelve Apostles" arrive, Franciscans, in Mexico; Mendieta's Golden Age: 1524–1564.

1536   Bartolomé de las Casas writes *De único Modo* in Guatemala.

1550   The philosophical-theological dispute over modernity between Ginés de Sepúulveda and Bartolomé de las Casas begins in Valladolid.

1552   Bartolomé de las Casas writes *La destrucción de las Indias*.

1568   Philip II convokes the Great Meeting (*Junta Magna*).

The Originary Constitution of the Modern Ontology Ends

1580   Montaigne begins his *Essais* (especially "Des Cannibales.")

1636   Descartes expresses the *ego cogito* in the *Discourse on Method*.

INDEX

1492, the year of, 12–13, 26, 28–30,
    50, 56–57, 61, 75, 85, 87–88, 90,
    93, 95, 116–17, 120, 122, 131–32,
    134, 138–39, 141, 146–47, 152–54,
    167–68, 179, 188, 201, 211
abstract figure (*gestalt*), 17, 27, 93, 149,
    162; abstraction, 17, 20, 84, 95, 98,
    116, 120, 124, 132, 187, 204
Acosta, José de, 52, 54, 85, 165–66
Adorno, Theodor W., 26, 151–52, 209
Africa, 11, 13, 17, 20–22, 24, 26,
    28–29, 31, 33, 35, 45, 48, 56, 75,
    78, 88, 90, 116–17, 123, 127,
    132–34, 139–41, 149, 152, 154,
    156, 163, 167, 176, 196, 203, 207,
    211; Bantu, 75, 116, 176; coast of,
    11, 123, 141, 152; North Africa,
    11, 28, 211
agriculture, 69, 75, 80–81, 84, 95,
    111, 120, 157, 175
alterity, 12, 26, 36, 66, 69–70, 72,
    132, 137–40, 156, 160, 176
Alva Ixlizóchitl, Fernando de, 96
Alvarado, Pedro, 44, 103, 108, 147,
    194, 212
America, invention of, 27, 31–32,
    154, 167
Amerindians, 10–12, 68, 73–74,
    78–81, 84–85, 106, 111, 115, 117,
    124, 140, 172, 174–75, 186, 196
    See also Indians; tribal cultures
Anadir valley, 79

Andalusia, 13, 160
Andes Mountains, 75–76, 84
anthropology, 52, 70, 78, 81, 171–72
Antilles, the, 84, 155
antiquity, 10, 23, 113–14, 135, 198
Apel, Karl-Otto, 12, 67, 112, 132,
    146, 166, 183, 194, 199, 203
Apologética Historia Sumaria (las
    Casas), 70
Arab world, 11, 33, 78, 88, 116,
    133–34, 155, 157, 174; Islam in,
    90, 134
Araucanians, 80, 99, 109, 115, 179
Arciniegas, Germán, 56, 166–68
Argentina, 13, 109, 147, 153, 158,
    174, 204, 207
Asia, 11, 17, 20–23, 29–31, 35, 45,
    75–76, 78–81, 88, 90, 93, 116,
    132–34, 139–40, 149, 152–55,
    157–58, 163, 169, 179, 207, 211;
    Minor, 135; southeast, 11; steppes
    of central, 75
astrology, 43, 100-101, 189, 191;
    stars, 99, 187
    See also sun
Atahualpa, 51–52, 105, 193
Atlantic, North, 28, 123, 155, 185, 211
Augustine, Saint, 67, 188
Ayvu Rapyta, 73, 85, 181
Aztec: calendar, 126, 160; culture, 26,
    39–41, 44–45, 48, 51–52, 54, 64,
    68, 70, 75, 79–81, 84, 93, 95–105,

108–11, 113, 117, 126, 147,
160–61, 172–73, 178, 181, 183–85,
187–93, 196–98, 200–201, 205,
212; empire, 40, 52, 160, 183
Balboa: *see* Núñez de Balboa
barbarianism, accusation of, 10, 13,
22, 35, 50, 54, 63–67, 70, 85, 87,
133, 136–37, 139, 158, 166,
169–70, 172, 183, 202
Bering Strait, 79, 81
Bernstein, Richard, 9, 145
blacks, 22
blood, 13, 47, 56, 102, 104–5, 110,
112, 116–17, 123, 178, 188–89,
192, 194, 197
Boabdil, 13, 31, 154, 211
Bolívar, Símon, 127–28, 174, 177, 205
Bolivia, 47, 68, 148, 164, 201
Brazil, 11, 33, 56, 76, 124, 127–29,
163, 167, 180–81, 206–7
*Brevissima relación de la Destrucción
de la India* (las Casas), 37
California, 68, 80, 165, 171
Calmécac community, 97
Canary Islands, 29
cannons, 42, 155
Caonabo, 107
Cape of Good Hope, 24, 29, 211
capitalism, 11, 25, 45, 47–48, 69, 77,
88, 116–17, 120, 122–23, 129–31,
133, 135, 140, 150, 157, 182, 188,
194, 198, 200–202, 206–9
Caribbean, the, 11, 38–39, 115,
123–25, 155, 172, 178, 185
Castillo, Bernal Díaz de, 43, 141,
161–63, 165
Catechism of Trent, 52
Catholicism, 13, 29, 31, 38, 42, 105,

126, 159–60, 162, 211; Franciscans,
51–52, 68–69, 108, 146, 152, 165,
171, 197–200, 202, 213; friars, 49,
52, 112, 198; Jesuits, 69, 87, 182;
Joachinists, 68; missionaries, 24, 35,
52–53, 55, 68–69, 111–12, 120–21,
152; the pope, 29, 50–51, 53, 121,
159, 171
See also Christianity; Christian God
Caturelli, Albert, 36, 156
Cempoalla, 42
CENAMI, 121, 202, 204
center, vs. periphery, 9–12, 17, 21–22,
25–26, 28, 31–33, 35, 45, 47, 76,
79, 81, 88, 90, 93, 107, 113,
116–17, 119–20, 125, 129–32,
134–35, 137–40, 145, 149–50,
152, 154–55, 158–60, 163, 170,
172, 207–9
Central America, 123, 125, 172–73
century, eighteenth, 20, 127, 134–35;
fifteenth, 17, 79, 85, 97, 129, 135,
150; seventeenth, 10–11, 109, 158;
sixteenth, 11, 64, 71, 79, 120-21,
134, 163; twentieth, 72, 108, 125,
128, 135, 205
Charles V, Emperor, 43, 47, 159
Chile, 52, 80–81, 109, 180, 195, 204,
208, 212
China, 11–13, 30–31, 33, 75, 77,
79–80, 88, 90, 116, 146, 152,
154–55, 157–58, 166, 175, 178–79
Christianity, 13, 23–24, 28–29, 42,
48–54, 67–69, 71–72, 111–12,
115, 122–23, 133–35, 146, 156,
159, 165–66, 170, 177, 183–84,
188, 190, 192, 198, 201, 205, 209;
Christendom, 39, 55, 111;

Christianity (*continued*)
    Christianizing, 123; cross, symbol
        of, 33, 39, 41, 178; doctrine of, 52,
        54, 112, 201, 209; Trinity, 151,
        171; vs. infidels, 71
Christmas Islands, 80
CIA, the, 134
Cipango, island of, 30
Codex of Hammurabi, 76
Colloquios y Doctrina Christiana , 111
Colombia, 124, 148, 175
colonialism, 25, 45, 47, 51, 109, 111,
        117, 120, 123, 125, 127–28, 131,
        134, 136–37, 140, 150, 159–60,
        165, 172, 177, 180, 195, 207
colonization, 11–12, 25, 27, 35, 37,
        45–48, 64, 69–70, 90, 97, 111,
        117, 119–20, 125, 130, 137, 159,
        166, 174, 206
Columbus, Christopher, 28–29, 68,
        211; voyages of, 28–31, 33,
        154–55, 179, 211–12
Columbus, Diego, 108
Comentarios reales de los Incas
        (Vega), 96, 166
commerce, 31, 33, 65, 77, 88, 90, 98,
        117, 119, 157, 202–3
"common good," concept of, 63–64
concept (*Begriff*), 12, 19–21, 26–27,
        33, 57, 65–66, 78, 97–98, 133–36,
        138, 149–50, 154, 160, 166, 185,
        187, 197, 204, 207–8
concubinage, 46
conquest, 11–13, 17, 25–27, 35,
        37–39, 41–46, 48–54, 56–57,
        63–66, 68, 74, 77, 88, 90, 97, 104,
        107, 109, 112, 117, 121, 126, 148,

152, 155, 159, 162, 164–65,
        170–72, 179–80, 193, 197–98,
        211–13; conqueror, 42, 45–46, 51,
        104, 197–98
contact zones, 75, 175
Cortés, Hernán, 26, 38–46, 50, 55,
        68, 76, 97, 100–105, 109, 124–25,
        131, 147, 157, 159–60, 162–63,
        190, 192–94, 198, 205, 212
Cosmographiae Introductio (Ring-
        mann & Waldseemüller), 34, 212
cosmos, 34, 104, 106, 110, 176, 191,
        197, 212
Costa Rica, 13, 201
covering over (*encubierto*), 12, 85, 119
criollo, 47, 55–56, 109, 119–20,
        124–28, 131, 134, 157, 167, 206
"Crítica de la Pirámide" (Paz), 117
Cuahutemoc (Guatemuz), Emperor, 43,
        108, 212
culture: and economics, 11, 45, 48,
        125, 148; and history, 12, 48, 56,
        70, 75, 120, 124, 131, 154, 156,
        159, 166, 174, 177, 199, 204; and
        religion, 13, 84, 112, 124, 172;
        culture and technology, 11, 39;
        cultural re-education, 49; inter-
        cultural communication, 12; inter-
        cultural dialogue, 12, 95, 132
cultures: Afro-American, 124; Afro-
        Brazilian, 123–24; Afro-
        Caribbean, 123, 205; diverse, 12,
        128; other, 10, 24, 32–33, 35, 39,
        52, 55, 65–66, 75, 146, 183, 203
        See also: Aztec culture
*De la justa causa de la guerra contra
        los indios* (Sepúlveda), 63, 169

De Unico Modo (las Casas), 70
de Medici, Lorenzo, 28, 33, 52, 181
Der philosophische Diskurs der Moderne (Habermas), 145, 151, 209
Descartes, René, 17, 48, 50, 74, 148, 213
development (*Entwicklung*), 11, 20, 22, 24–26, 66, 84–85, 112, 126, 131, 136, 146, 148–49, 151, 172, 182; developmentalist fallacy, 19, 26, 66, 135–37, 148, 157
dialectic, 20, 25, 145, 151, 209
discovery (*des-cubierto*), concept of, 10–13, 23–25, 27–37, 39, 47, 50, 57, 75, 78–79, 85, 87–88, 91, 93, 103–4, 107, 116, 119, 121–22, 134, 137, 139, 141, 146, 148, 150–52, 154, 156, 162, 164, 167, 173, 179, 185–86, 193, 206, 212
domination, 9, 12, 24, 26, 34–36, 38–39, 42, 45–46, 51, 54–56, 64–66, 70, 79, 90, 97, 99, 104, 107, 114, 119–20, 124, 126–28, 136, 140, 153–54, 157–60, 164, 169, 179, 196–97
earth, the, 9, 32–35, 44–45, 73, 76, 95–96, 99, 110–11, 115–16, 124, 126, 137, 161, 169, 173, 178, 184, 189, 191, 193, 199, 203
earthly, the (*tlaltípac*), 28, 48, 51, 86, 97–99, 107, 153, 184–85, 193, 199
East, the, 22, 41, 98–99, 115, 149
Easter Island, 80–81
economics, and technology, 11
    See also technology
Ecuador, 124, 141

Egypt, 11, 68–69, 75, 77, 79, 88, 133, 160, 175
Elcano, Sebastian, 35, 212
Eliade, Mircea, 51
emancipation, 12, 19, 26, 56, 64–66, 68–70, 102, 105, 109, 117, 119, 122–23, 125, 127–28, 131–32, 136–39, 148, 167, 203, 205
empire: German, 23; Ottoman, 11; 89,; Roman, 24, 134; Spanish, 122
end of the earth (*finis terrae*), 33
end of the world, 68, 93, 103, 106, 109–10, 114, 162, 191
enlightenment (*Aufklärung*), 19–20, 25, 35, 56, 76, 140, 151, 183, 185, 203, 209
equator, 29, 80
Ericson, Leif, 28
estates (*haciendas*), 39, 120
Eurocentrism, 10, 19, 25–26, 32, 34–35, 56, 66, 74–75, 87, 90, 93, 101, 130–32, 135–40, 145–46, 148–49, 154, 156–58, 166, 174, 179, 182
Europe: barbarian, 35, 134; Christian, 23, 72; Eastern, 11, 88, 152, 163; Germanic, 88, 135; Latin, 17, 32–33, 57, 93, 134; modern, 10, 32, 140; Western, 23, 88, 90, 93
European Common Market, 57, 123, 129, 203
exploitation, 9, 12, 38, 47, 51, 69, 74, 90, 111, 117, 120, 128, 130–31, 154, 157, 163, 174, 207–8
Fanon, Fritz, 9
Ferdinand of Aragon, King, 17
firearms, 42, 107, 166

fishermen, 39
Florida, 84
flower-and-song (art of rhetoric),
    97–99, 112, 205
Foucault, Michel, 50
foundation (*Grund*), 50, 99, 162, 172,
    176, 183–84, 187, 189, 198, 211
Frankfurt School, 12, 132, 158
French Revolution, 10, 24–25
Fuentes, Carlos, 47, 124
Gandhi, 131
Gante, Pedro de, 68
Germany, 10, 23–24, 47, 79, 108,
    116, 129, 147–48, 150–53, 187,
    192, 203, 208
God, Christian, 13, 20, 22, 40, 43–44,
    46–48, 50–53, 67–68, 95–96,
    98–105, 107, 110, 113–14, 116–17,
    122, 125, 129, 148, 159–61, 163,
    165–66, 170–71, 176, 183–84,
    187–88, 196, 200, 204
    See also Catholicism; Christianity
gods, non-Christian, 40–41, 43,
    50–51, 55, 74, 77, 93, 95, 97,
    100–7, 113–14, 126–27, 183–84,
    187, 192, 195, 197, 200, 212
gold, 13, 28, 32, 37–38, 40, 42, 47,
    53, 102, 107, 115–16, 122–23,
    147, 155, 160, 163, 200
Golden Chersonesus, 30–31, 154–55
González, Felipe, 57, 206
Granada, city in Spain, 13, 17, 28, 31,
    42, 105, 127, 134, 153–55, 211
Greco-Roman imagery, 53
Greeks, 33, 37, 40, 47, 54, 79, 90,
    108, 110, 112, 116, 133–34, 173,
    175, 177, 181, 183, 187, 192, 200

Guadalupe, island of, 47, 123, 126,
    177, 191, 195, 197, 204–5
Guadalupe-Tonantzin, 125–26
Guaracuya, 108
Guaraní, 73, 85–88, 95, 109–11,
    180–82, 184, 186, 189, 197
Guexozingo, 52
Gulf War, 64, 162
Guyana, 124
Habermas, Jürgen, 10, 25–26, 33, 35,
    87, 129–30, 132, 135, 145, 151,
    160, 163, 209
Haiti, 123, 129, 205
Hammer, Heinrich, 28
Hassan, Ihab, 9
Hayek, F., 105
Hegel, Georg Wilhelm Friedrich, 12,
    19–26, 35–36, 50, 67, 74–75, 90,
    93, 98, 130, 134–35, 148–51, 156,
    158, 161–62, 167, 169, 171, 177,
    183, 188–89, 194, 208
Heidegger, Martin, 28, 85, 152, 158,
    166, 173, 182, 191
Helluland, 28
hermeneutics, 12, 29, 59, 93,
    100–101, 112
Hispañola, 122, 212
Historia Eclesiástica Indiana (Mendi-
    eta), 68, 106, 164–65, 187
*Historia general de las cosas de Nueva
    España* (Sahagún), 52, 70, 96, 165,
    172, 186, 189
history and philosophy, 9, 12, 19–20,
    22, 25, 27, 131, 148–50, 167, 169,
    177, 188, 208
Holland, 11, 21, 47, 102, 116, 123,
    127, 202

holocaust, 120, 122, 168, 172, 201, 203
Honduras, 31, 108
Horkheimer, Max 26, 147, 151–52, 209
horses, 39, 42, 69, 79, 105, 107, 109, 162, 194
Huehuetéutl (mother of the gods), 95
Huitzilopochtli (the sun), 48, 81, 98–99, 102, 104–5, 113, 116, 126, 192–93, 211
humanism, 64, 67, 87, 161, 171, 174, 177, 190
ideology, 9–10, 20–21, 24, 32, 51, 55–57, 75, 78, 134–36, 149, 158–59, 167, 171, 173–75, 197
idolatry, 49, 51–52, 68, 70
illegal workers (braceros), 131
imagery, 49–51, 53
immaturity (Umreife), 19–21, 65–66, 69, 72, 117, 131, 136, 209
independence, 69, 119, 128, 166, 205
India, 11, 13, 17, 24, 28–31, 33, 37, 75–76, 81, 88, 116, 141, 146, 155, 157, 166, 168, 175, 177
Indians: American, 32, 45; Caribbean, 39; compensation (desagravio), 46, 57, 147, 168, 208; economic exploitation of (repartimiento), 69; Peruvian, 116, 122; riches, 13; women, 45–47, 55, 124, 137, 158
See also Amerindians; tribal cultures
Indian Council of South America, 121
Indies, East, 29, 36, 38, 44, 74, 117, 155, 158–60, 163, 178
Indigenous Salvadoran Association (ANIS), 121
Indus valley, 75, 77, 79
Inquisition, 55

Inter caetera (papal bull), 29
interregional system, 11, 146
Invención de América, La (O'Gorman), 27
Italian Renaissance, 10, 134
Italy, 11, 23, 203
Jamaica, 31, 124, 128
Japan, 30, 54; 83, 116, 129
Jaspers, Karl, 76, 174–75, 185
"just war," presumption of, 63, 66, 72, 136, 163, 170
Katunes (epochs), 110
Kierkegaard, Søren, 22, 162
Laberinto de la soledad, El (Paz), 124, 191, 204
labor, 25, 39, 46–48, 80, 115–16, 120, 122, 129–31, 141, 147, 160, 163, 201, 207
ladino (Indian term for mestizo), 125
Lafaye, J., 100, 191, 204
land, the, 13, 21–23, 28, 30, 33, 42, 45, 47, 74, 76, 79, 100, 107, 111, 125, 128–29, 153, 158, 189, 205; land distribution, 13, 74; landlords, 128
las Casas, Bartholomé, 29, 37–38, 64, 68–72, 112, 121, 131, 153–55, 159, 170–72, 196, 213
Latin America, 11, 17, 20–22, 26, 32, 35, 45, 48, 55–57, 74–75, 93, 116, 124–25, 129, 132, 134, 147, 149–50, 156–58, 160, 163, 166–68, 174–75, 177, 195, 201, 203–4, 206–8
León Portilla, Miguel, 56, 96, 100, 167–68, 178, 183–95, 197–98, 200
Lévi-Strauss, Claude, 76, 176

liberty, 12, 19–20, 23, 43, 56, 65, 70,
 107, 117, 123, 125, 128, 132,
 138–40, 146, 158, 160, 168–70,
 174, 177, 205, 210; subjective, 19,
 65
Libro de los libros de Chilam Balam,
 El, 114
life-world (*Lebenswelt*), 28–29, 37,
 45–46, 54
Lucayos, island of, 30
Luther, Martin, 24, 38, 147, 159–60
Lyotard, 12, 26, 129
machismo, 46, 138
Machu Pichu, 109
Magellan, Fernando de, 35, 155, 212
Malinche, la, 45, 47, 55, 124–25, 164
maps, 17, 28, 34, 37, 78–79, 109,
 123, 142–43, 153–55, 157–58,
 167, 178–80, 211–12
marginal peoples, 74, 90, 128,
 130–31, 208
market: free, 71, 129–30, 150, 207;
 merchants, 28, 122; mercantilism,
 45, 47–48, 51, 116, 123, 129, 140,
 147, 150, 202, 207
Marini, Mauro, 129
Martellus, Henricus, 17, 33, 78–79,
 142– 43, 153–55, 157, 173, 179,
 211
Martinique, 123
Marx, Karl, 25, 47–48, 67, 69, 123,
 130, 138, 149, 162, 170–71, 182,
 188, 194, 200–201, 203, 206–7
Mayan culture, 39, 45, 75, 80, 84, 93,
 105, 108, 110–11, 114–15, 172,
 174, 178, 183, 187, 196, 200
Mediterranean, 13, 21, 28, 31–32, 53,

 76, 88, 122, 152, 155, 157, 175
meeting of cultures, 42–43, 52, 55–57,
 76, 121, 165, 167, 174, 213; meeting of two worlds, 42, 55, 57
Melanesia, 80
Mendieta, Gerónimo de, 64, 68–69,
 98, 106, 146, 164–65, 171, 187,
 195, 202, 213
Mendoza, Pedro de, 109
Mesoamerica, 75, 79, 84, 175
Mesopotamia, 11, 74–76, 79, 175
mestizo, 20, 45–47, 55–57, 74,
 124–28, 130, 134, 138, 157, 164,
 167, 204, 206; mestizo culture, 45,
 55, 57, 125, 164, 204
Mexico, 11, 14, 20–21, 26, 40–41,
 43–46, 50, 52, 56–57, 68, 76, 81,
 84, 90, 100–103, 105, 108, 115,
 121, 126, 128–31, 147–49, 152,
 155, 159–60, 162, 164–65,
 167–69, 171–76, 178–80, 182–88,
 190–91, 194–96, 198, 200–209,
 211–13
Mexico-Tenochtitlan, city of, 102,
 104, 131, 211–12
Micronesia, 80
Middle Ages, 10–11, 13, 24, 34, 209
military technology, 42, 106, 192
millenarists, 68
minorities, 9, 128
Mires, Fernando, 52, 166
Moctezuma, 40–41, 43–44, 51, 97,
 100–103, 106, 110, 161, 190–94,
 198
modern: Modern Age, 10, 34; modern
 ego, 25, 34–36, 39, 42–43, 46, 48,
 125; modern subjectivity, 10, 17,

25, 38; modernization, 10, 17, 33,
45, 48, 56, 64, 66, 68, 87, 117,
131, 136–37, 157, 204, 209
modernity, 9–12, 17, 19, 24–26,
32–33, 35, 42, 45, 50–51, 63–72,
74, 85, 90, 93, 97, 105, 112,
116–17, 119–20, 122–23, 125,
128–33, 135–40, 145–46, 151–52,
158, 160–61, 167, 169–70, 172,
196, 202–3, 207, 209, 212–13; discourse of, 111–12, 151–52, 209;
myth of modernity, 12, 19, 26, 50,
61, 63–67, 69, 71, 93, 97, 116–17,
122, 125, 130–32, 136–37, 167,
169, 207, 209
Mogols, the, 88
Mohammed, 90, 163
Mongols, the, 79, 90, 153
Montaigne, 12, 139, 213
Moors, the, 13, 153–54
mulattos, 127–28
Muslims, 13, 26, 28, 31–32, 34, 42,
79, 88, 90, 133–34, 152, 154, 160,
163, 171, 211
Náhuatl culture, 88, 96, 101, 108,
110, 119, 125, 172, 178, 183–95,
197–99, 204–5; language, 96-99
Nanhuatzin, hummingbird god, 104
navigators, 13, 28, 32–33, 78, 97,
152, 211
Nazism, 121, 134–35, 138, 203
New Constellation, The (Bernstein), 9,
145
nomads, 39, 84, 86–87, 95, 109, 113
North America, 11, 30, 124–25, 134,
147, 158, 163, 167, 203
North, the, 24–25, 28, 77, 80, 84, 99,

155, 183, 185, 197, 209
Nosotros y los otros (Todorov), 139
Núñez de Balboa, Vasco, 38, 155,
173, 212
Occident, 22, 28, 30, 32, 35–36, 48,
74, 133–35, 138, 146, 150, 154,
156, 174, 201, 206
O'Gorman, Edmundo, 27–28, 30, 32,
34–36, 56, 78, 134, 152, 154–58,
167–68, 173, 179, 193
Ometeótl, 95, 98–102, 104, 113,
187–89, 192, 199
open-in-flower imagery, 173
oppressed, the, 12, 39, 44, 54, 72, 74,
105, 107, 119, 125–28, 131, 137,
174, 177, 194
Orient, 22, 78, 133–35, 149
Orinoco River, 28, 31, 84, , 153–54,
212
other face (*te-ixtli*), 26, 45, 51, 74,
119, 123, 125, 128–31, 137, 146,
160–61, 185–86
Other, the, 12, 17, 26, 32, 36, 38–39,
41–46, 48, 50–51, 55, 64–65, 67,
69–70, 72, 74, 85, 87, 90–91, 93,
103, 111–12, 131–32, 137–38,
146, 158–59, 185, 194, 198–99
Ottoman Empire, 11
overpopulation, 130, 151, 209
Oviedo, Fernandez de, 36
Pachacámac (universal soul), 53, 96,
113, 184
Pacific Ocean, 35, 39, 74–75, 78–81,
84, 88, 90, 93, 123–24, 134,
154–56, 173, 175, 178–79, 185,
212
Panama, 13, 31, 38, 81, 155, 178, 196

Pánfilo Narváez, 103–4, 193, 212
Paraguay, 68–69, 85, 87, 109, 182
parousia (encounter), 93, 95, 97, 104, 106, 183, 212
passage to India, 24, 31, 33, 155
Peru, 11, 21, 76, 78, 80–81, 96, 116, 157, 160, 165, 201, 204, 212
phallic ego, 46, 164
Philip II, 52, 68–69, 72, 157, 165, 171, 213
philosophy of liberation, 12, 132, 146, 158, 160, 168, 170, 174, 177, 210
Philosophy of Right (Hegel), 130, 151, 194, 208
Pizarro, Francisco, 45
plantation, 38–39, 46, 74, 122, 147, 160
Poland, 11, 23, 163
politics: and culture, 11, 45, 48, 69, 124–25, 172; and economics, 11, 45, 48, 57, 125, 132, 139, 181; and language, 9
Polynesians, 80–81, 98, 109, 175, 178, 180
pope, 29, 50–51, 53, 121, 159, 171
populism, 125, 129, 207
Portugal, 11, 17, 26, 33, 57, 90, 127–29, 135, 158, 202, 206, 211
postmodernism, 10–12, 26, 74, 129, 132, 137–39, 170; postmodern irrationality, 26
Puerto Rico, 13, 108, 166
pyramid (ziggurat), 76, 117
Quetzalcohuatl, 40, 74, 99–102, 104, 110, 126, 173, 188–93, 204-5, 211, *quilombos* (liberated territories), 123
racism, 138, 202–3

rational thinking, 10, 12–14, 17, 20–23, 25–26, 28, 36–37, 42, 48–50, 52–55, 63, 65, 67, 70–72, 76, 85, 87, 93, 96, 98, 100–102, 111, 117, 122, 131–32, 136–39, 146, 148, 170–72, 176, 179, 181, 191, 193, 198, 200, 203; conceptual thinking, 97; ratiocination vs. mythic reasoning, 98; reason and liberation, 70, 117, 132, 138
Recopilación de las Leyes de los Reynos de las Indias, 44
Reformation, the, 10, 23–25, 35, 104, 140, 160
rhetoric, 97, 112–14, 172, 191, 198–99
rights of people, 23–25, 50, 121, 123, 151
Ringmann, Matthias, 34
Rio de la Plata, 84, 87, 109
rites and ceremonies, 36, 41, 52, 55, 100, 170, 189; ritual dance, 86; ritual song, 85, 181, 184
Rocky Mountains, 84
Romans, 17, 24, 28–29, 45, 50, 54, 111, 113, 133–35, 152, 154, 159–60, 165, 169, 179, 187, 192, 197, 203, 211; Roman Empire, 24, 133, 135, 165, 203
Rorty, Richard, 12–13, 26, 55, 87, 129, 146
Russia, 11, 23, 90, 149, 163, 183
sacrifice, 12–13, 26, 36, 47–48, 50, 64, 66–67, 93, 96–97, 100, 103–5, 110, 116–17, 119, 125, 131–32, 137, 147, 187–89, 192, 200–201, 203, 207

Sahagún, Bernardino de, 52, 70, 96, 162, 165, 171–72, 186, 189–90, 193, 197, 200

Same, the, vs. the Other, 12, 32, 34–36, 38–39, 44–45, 70, 159, 167

Santo Domingo, 38, 47, 107–8, 122, 196, 212

Sepúlveda, Ginés de, 63–70, 87, 160, 169–71

servants, 38, 40, 46, 63

servitude, 46, 64, 68, 70, 97

Sierra Madres Mountains, 84

silver, 13, 32, 47, 53, 69, 116, 122–23, 160, 163–65, 200, 202, 212

Sinus Magnus, 30–31, 33–35, 79, 154, 156, 173

slave trade, 11, 20, 29, 38–39, 45, 48, 51, 56, 69, 74, 108, 120, 122–25, 127, 130, 137, 160, 167, 169, 202–3, 211–12

Smith, Adam, 105, 129

socialism, 125, 147, 149, 182

sociology, and economics, 148–49

South America, 17, 21, 30–31, 33, 121, 125, 134, 154–55, 157–58

South, the, 10, 23, 25, 77, 80, 99, 134, 153, 155, 185, 209

southern hemisphere, 9

Spain, 11, 17, 26, 31, 38, 42, 44, 47, 55–57, 90, 107, 109, 116, 122, 127–29, 135, 147, 158–59, 162–63, 183, 204–5, 208, 212

Spirit, the (Geist), 21–23, 149, 151

spiritual conquest, 49–50, 52–54, 97, 164–65, 171, 212–13

subjectivity, 10, 17, 25–26, 38–39, 43, 74, 186

sun: fifth, 99, 101–5, 107, 109–10, 187, 193, 195, 197, 200; fourth, 113; sixth, 97, 105–7, 114, 116–17, 119, 122, 125, 129, 131, 195, 201, 213

symbol or metaphor, 45, 48, 76, 85–86, 93, 97–98, 117, 122–23, 126, 183, 185–88, 190, 194, 203

syncretism, 45, 55, 57, 124, 135, 138, 164, 167

Tao Te Ching, 78

Taylor, Charles, 9, 145

technology, 11, 39, 42, 65, 69, 106, 180, 192, 206
    See also economics

teko, tekoha, 85–87, 181–82

Tenustitlan, Mexico, 43

Teotihuacan, 76, 104, 114

Texcoco, 52, 81, 108, 175, 205

The Jewish Question (Marx), 48

Third World, 9, 84, 93, 103, 117, 138, 151, 166, 172, 191, 209

Thornton, Russell, 120, 201

Tierra del Fuego, 84, 105, 179, 183

Tlacaélel, myth of, 97, 103–5, 110, 187, 191, 194, 211

tlamatini, tlamatinime, 95–104, 111–13, 184–85, 188, 191, 193–94, 198, 200

Tlaxcala, Mexico, 46, 52, 102, 105, 108, 163

Todorov, Tzevan, 139

Toltecs, 101, 105, 114, 187, 192, 211

Tonantzin (little mother), 47, 126, 205

Toscanelli, 28, 134

Toulmin, Stephen, 9, 145

transmodernity, 12, 117, 131–32, 138–40, 170

triangle of death, in slave trade, 122
tribal cultures: the Akiris, 80; the
    Amazons, 84; the Araucanians, 80,
    99, 109; the Arawaks, 84; the
    Caribs, 84; the Chibchas, 84; the
    Chiquitanos, 68; the Cordilleras,
    84; the Eskimos, 79, 84, 99, 180;
    the Mapuches, 109; the Moxos, 68;
    the Querandís, 109; the Tupi-
    Guaraní, 84–85
    See also Aztec, Guaraní, Mayan,
    Toltecs
Trinidad, 31
Túpac Amaru, 109, 173, 195–96
Turkestan, 79, 88
Turks, 28, 32, 79, 88, 90, 134
United States, 9–10, 20, 24, 84, 93,
    116, 120, 123, 128–29, 131, 134,
    149–50, 167, 173, 196
universal history, 19–22, 35, 149, 167
utopia, 64, 68
Valladolid dispute, 64, 67, 131, 147
Vattimo, 12, 26, 129
Vega, Garcilaso de la, 52, 96, 168
Velázquez, Diego, 38–39
Vespucci, Amerigo, 33–34, 78, 104,
    156–58, 212
victim: blaming the, 19–20, 49–50,
    55, 64–67, 69, 72, 77, 119, 124,
    131, 137, 163, 165, 169–70, 182,
    204, 209; victimization, 13, 26, 45,
    47, 49–50, 55, 64, 66–67, 104–5,
    110, 116–17, 119–20, 125,
    137–38, 165, 203

Vikings, 28, 141
Villa, Francisco, 129
Viracocha, 53, 175
Vitoria, Francisco, 69, 171, 209
Wachtel, N., 100, 191
Waldseemüller, Martin, 34
warrior god, 99, 104
wealth, 13, 29, 32, 37, 39, 42, 50,
    107–8, 116, 130, 147, 155
weaving, 39
Weber, Alfred, 75, 174
Weber, Max, 10, 75, 135, 145–46,
    160, 163, 174
West, the, 19–20, 31, 35, 74–75, 88,
    99, 111, 146, 211
will-to-power, 26, 43, 74
word-soul, 85, 87; fundamental word,
    85–87
workers, 105, 128–29, 207
world history, 9–11, 20–24, 32, 35, 57,
    73–75, 78, 85, 90, 113, 117, 140,
    146, 148, 150, 168, 172, 174, 177
world vision (*Weltanschauung*), 26,
    28–29, 34, 53, 73, 78, 103, 111,
    172, 194
world-system, 9–10, 116, 145–46,
    157, 163
Yellow River valley, 75, 77, 79
Yucatán, 39–40, 45, 115
Yukon River, 79
zambos (of black and Indian parent-
    age), 127–28
Zapata, Emiliano, 129
Zempoala, Mexico, 44, 102, 131